An Introduction to Communication

Prioritizing brevity and clarity, this textbook introduces the study of communication through examples and applications in a variety of contexts.

With a unique focus on diversity and the impact of culture, each chapter opens with a case study that identifies a communication challenge which the chapter addresses throughout, and concludes with questions that respond to that challenge. A consistent, organized structure with numerous features including *Questions for Understanding and Analysis*, *Theoretical Insight* (examining a particular relevant theory), and a *Skill Set* section, easily guides you through the foundations of the study of communication. The *Connections* feature cross-references between chapters demonstrating the multidimensional nature of communication. The *Everyday Talk* sections demonstrate how each topic relates to technology, the workplace, or health issues.

Offering a wealth of diverse examples from students' personal, professional, and online lives, this book teaches skills allowing students from all academic backgrounds to understand communication.

LYNN H. TURNER received her Ph.D. from Northwestern University and is Professor in Communication Studies at Marquette University in Milwaukee, Wisconsin.

Lynn has served as President of the Central States Communication Association as well as President of the National Communication Association (NCA), the oldest and largest professional communication association in the world.

RICHARD WEST received his Ph.D. from Ohio University in Athens and is Professor in Communication Studies at Emerson College in Boston.

Rich has served as President of the Eastern Communication Association as well as President of the National Communication Association (NCA), the oldest and largest professional communication association in the world.

Together, they have co-authored five books co-edited two anthologies, *The Sage Handbook of Family Communication* and *The Family Communication Sourcebook*, the latter receiving NCA's Distinguished Book Award. They are the co-recipients of the Bernard J. Brommel Distinguished Scholarship in Family Communication Award and have served together as guest co-editors of the *Journal of Family Communication* upon three different occasions.

An Introduction to
Communication

LYNN H. TURNER
Marquette University, Milwaukee, Wisconsin

RICHARD WEST
Emerson College, Boston, Massachusetts

CAMBRIDGE
UNIVERSITY PRESS

University Printing House, Cambridge CB2 8BS, United Kingdom

One Liberty Plaza, 20th Floor, New York, NY 10006, USA

477 Williamstown Road, Port Melbourne, VIC 3207, Australia

314–321, 3rd Floor, Plot 3, Splendor Forum, Jasola District Centre, New Delhi – 110025, India

79 Anson Road, #06–04/06, Singapore 079906

Cambridge University Press is part of the University of Cambridge.

It furthers the University's mission by disseminating knowledge in the pursuit of
education, learning, and research at the highest international levels of excellence.

www.cambridge.org
Information on this title: www.cambridge.org/9781107151048
DOI: 10.1017/9781316596852

© Lynn H. Turner and Richard West 2019

First published 2019

Printed in the United States of America by Sheridan Books, Inc.

A catalogue record for this publication is available from the British Library.

Library of Congress Cataloging-in-Publication Data
Names: Turner, Lynn H., author. | West, Richard L., author.
Title: An introduction to communication / Lynn H. Turner, Richard West.
Description: Cambridge, United Kingdom ; New York, NY : Cambridge University Press, 2018. |
Includes bibliographical references and index.
Identifiers: LCCN 2018010828| ISBN 9781107151048 (alk. paper) | ISBN 9781316606919 (pbk)
Subjects: LCSH: Communication.
Classification: LCC HM1206 .T87 2018 | DDC 302.2–dc23
LC record available at https://lccn.loc.gov/2018010828

ISBN 978-1-107-15104-8 Hardback
ISBN 978-1-316-60691-9 Paperback

Brief Contents

Contents

Figures

Tables

Boxes

Preface

As we write this text, we are very aware of today's changing and challenging communication climate. From highly charged political debates to expressing complex emotional reactions in 280 characters to everyday interactions with our friends and work colleagues, communication is central to our personal and professional lives. As our choices for communication channels multiply, our communication decisions become more complex. Further, despite an ever-increasing range of communication options, many people feel misunderstood, lonely, or frustrated after communicating with others. Indeed, many people feel disconnected.

People enter a communication classroom with skills that have been acquired from observing friends, family members, and co-workers as well as from being a consumer of popular culture. These observations provide a storehouse of practical knowledge, but they fail to offer the richer understanding that comes from pairing practical knowledge with theoretical knowledge. A class in communication both allows for this pairing as well as offers a laboratory for practicing effective communication skills.

OUR GOALS FOR THIS TEXT

In writing this book, we had the following five commitments in mind.

1. **A commitment to a concise and efficient overview of the field of communication.** We approach this book with the goal of providing a succinct survey of the fundamentals of the communication field. This text provides communication majors with the building blocks for advanced courses. For non-majors we offer a complete survey that prompts them to reflect on how communication relates to their own majors. Frankly, students often get overwhelmed with the amount of material that is presented in this course. An examination of competing texts shows that most books are approximately 500–600 pages in length. Books of this length may leave students with an abundance of information that may not seem coherent. We offer the following:
   - A briefer, less expensive text comprising 10 chapters.
   - A streamlined approach to coverage, with strategic consolidation of some topics such as treating verbal and nonverbal communication in one chapter, and the fundamentals of presentational communication in only two chapters.

2. **A commitment to student learning and understanding.** We write in a manner that respects students and that offers them examples that are relevant to their lives. To actualize this commitment, we include the following:

- A consistent template for each chapter. This unique template provides a solid framework for the information presented. The four-part sequence in each chapter – Background, Fundamental Issues, Theoretical Insight, and Enhancing Your Skills – provides students with an efficient organizational framework for comprehending the material and eliminates the confusion that may characterize many large, cumbersome introductory texts.
- *Questions for Understanding* and *Questions for Analysis*. Each chapter ends by testing students both for their understanding and their ability to creatively apply the material in each chapter.

3. **A commitment to a scholarly focus.** We believe it's important to fill the gap between what people learn from experience and what scholars learn from systematic research based in theory. Research and communication theory enable us to acquire critical communication skills and behaviors and to understand our communication encounters. Too many introductory texts fail to incorporate scholarly thinking in order to avoid intimidating students. In contrast, we embrace the dynamic interplay among research, theory, and skills. In service to this commitment, we include:
   - *Theoretical Insights.* This section, which appears in each chapter, profiles a specific theory and puts it in the context of the concepts discussed in the chapter. We feature theories from the field of communication as well as from other social sciences.
   - Research supporting counterintuitive findings. With this focus, students are able to see that common sense can be misleading and factually incorrect. For instance, the pervasiveness of so-called reality TV and personal information on public sites like Facebook and Snapchat can lead students to think that disclosing everything is a hallmark of an effective communicator. Yet, research shows that more judicious self-disclosure yields more satisfying relationships. We underscore these sorts of findings throughout the text.
   - Nearly 300 scholarly citations, expressing a balance between classic research and contemporary research.

4. **A commitment to an applied and integrated approach.** Too often, introductory texts in communication fail to provide students with clear links between and among the various topics, or between theory and skills. Yet, students should continually be reminded about the useful and integrated nature of the communication field. We embrace the practicality of communication as we include the following in the text:
   - *Communication Encounter/Communication Response* case studies. Each chapter-opening (*Communication Encounter*) is bookended (*Communication Response*) at the end of the chapter. For example, in the chapter on social/mass media and

communication, we explore the romantic relationship of an intercultural couple. One person is Chinese American and the other is European American. We look at how the two of them received mediated images of each other's culture before they met, and how they use social media to keep in touch when one goes to graduate school in a distant state. At the end of each chapter, the *Communication Response* poses a series of questions prompting students to consider how the material in the chapter relates to the case.

- *Connections* boxes to tie concepts together across chapters. To assist students in making connections across the topics of the entire book, this feature asks them to notice how a particular topic, discussed in a different chapter, relates to concepts in the chapter they are reading. For instance, in the chapter on communication in small groups and organizations, we ask students to consider the importance of listening behaviors. In providing this feature, we encourage students to apply the important concepts and principles from Part I of the text throughout all of the contexts we discuss. This feature lets students know that communication is not a series of disconnected facts but, rather, an integrated field.
- *Enhancing Your Skills* discussions and applications to specific cases. These features get students to think about how to apply the skills they learn in the text to situations they might encounter at work, with friends, or in their families.
- *Everyday Talk* boxed features. These address a range of issues, including communication and technology, workplace situations, and health issues. These boxes encourage students to reflect on how the content of the chapter applies in a variety of contexts.

5. **A commitment to ethical and civic themes.** This commitment reflects our belief that all communication contains an ethical dimension. Further, we see that participating in the community is part of that ethical consideration. And finally, we acknowledge the ethical imperative to reflect diversity with an international focus. Recent Census data establish the continually increasing diversity of the United States. Further, the world is interconnected, and no country can avoid contact with others outside its borders. Even if a classroom is relatively homogenous, teachers still recognize the need to teach students about diverse communication practices to prepare them for communication in a global classroom. We undertake the following to address this commitment:

- We devote an entire chapter to how culture and communication interrelate. This chapter appears early in the text, Chapter 2, because we believe it's difficult to imagine any communication issue or decision without considering culture.
  In addition, in every chapter we provide examples from a variety of cultural communities as well as diverse family backgrounds, physical abilities,

socioeconomic classes, and so forth. We take an expansive view of diversity and cannot envision relegating this topic solely to one chapter.

- A solid foundation for ethical thinking. In Chapter 1, we introduce several ethical systems for decision making about communication choices.
- *Do the Right Thing.* This boxed feature encourages students to consider the ethical implications of the key topics in the chapter and to apply the ethical systems presented in Chapter 1.

ABOUT THE AUTHORS

Lynn Turner and **Rich West** have been best friends and writing colleagues since the mid-1980s. They met at a conference in Ohio and immediately found one another compatible and were struck by their similar senses of humor. What they didn't imagine was that they would spend so much time together writing books about the communication field and, in doing so, find a shared passion for bringing research to life for their students.

Lynn received her Ph.D. from Northwestern University, and she and her husband, Ted, recently celebrated 50 years of marriage. She is a Professor in Communication Studies at Marquette University in Milwaukee, Wisconsin.

Rich received his Ph.D. from Ohio University in Athens and is the partner of Chris, with whom he has shared his life for over 12 years. He is a Professor in Communication Studies at Emerson College in Boston.

Lynn and Rich have both served as presidents of their respective regional communication associations (Lynn, for the Central States Communication Association, and Rich, for the Eastern Communication Association). And both of them have served as President of the National Communication Association (NCA), the oldest and largest professional communication association in the world.

Together they have also co-authored five books, resulting in 18 multiple editions. In addition, they have co-edited two anthologies, *The Sage Handbook of Family Communication* and *The Family Communication Sourcebook*, the latter receiving NCA's Distinguished Book Award. They are the co-recipients of the Bernard J. Brommel Distinguished Scholarship in Family Communication Award and have served together as guest co-editors of the *Journal of Family Communication* upon several different occasions.

When Lynn is not busy writing and teaching, she enjoys discovering great restaurants, learning about new cultures through international travel, and volunteering at the art museum. She also loves spending time with her grandchildren, Sophie, Will, Ely, and Lucas who are among her greatest teachers. Rich, during his down time, loves to garden and spend time in his century-old summer home on the coast of Maine. He also keeps up with politics because he's a political science junkie.

TO THE STUDENT

Our philosophy centers on our belief that effective communication requires knowledge, skills, motivation, ethics, and patience. All of us possess communication skills that have been acquired from observing and interacting with others as well as from being a consumer of popular culture. However, personal experiences often lead us to rely too much on what we have seen and heard without understanding theoretical explanations for communication processes and outcomes, or applying a critical lens to our experiences.

Are some people "born communicators"? Perhaps. But most of us communicate poorly at one time or another, which can result in disappointment and dissatisfaction as well as limit our potential for success and growth.

We believe that while communication may be a source of division for some, careful and thoughtful communication – based in the fundamentals of the field – also serves to unify diverse people. In the process, we are introduced to issues and experiences allowing us to appreciate how we are both different and similar.

This book represents our ongoing commitment to the study and practice of effective communication. We offer students and instructors an opportunity to enter into a dialogue with each other – and with us – to explore this exciting and essential topic. We believe that as you read this text, your interest and skills in communication will increase, resulting in new skills and insights into this compelling field of study.

Acknowledgements

Like every book, this one owes much to the efforts of others in addition to our own work as authors. We wish to thank the entire Cambridge team, including Rosemary Crawley and, especially, Andrew Winnard, whose belief in us is what inspired and sustained the project. Additionally, we're indebted to the scholars whose work we drew upon to present the information within the book. Most importantly, we remain appreciative of the thousands of students who have studied with us over the past 30 years and whose questions and insights influenced our approach to the field of communication.

Lynn would like to thank her entire family, especially her husband Ted, for a lifetime of lessons in the magical intricacies of communication. And, as always, Lynn is grateful for the memory of her loving parents whose steadfast support and encouragement of her scholarship, and all her interests, sustain her in everything she undertakes.

As in every book he writes, Rich would like to acknowledge his mother for her continual focus on what matters in life: integrity and a commitment to being the best. He remains grateful for her continued positive influence. Rich would also like to thank his life partner, Chris, who knows precisely when to make things less intense and more relaxing.

Finally, both of us give special thanks to Holly Allen, a senior editor at Wiley, who was the first to believe, in 1994, that we would make a productive author team. We began writing textbooks because of Holly and with her guidance and continued friendship we have grown and matured as scholars and authors. Thanks, Holly!

PART I

Communication Foundations

1 The Communication Process

CHAPTER OUTLINE

CHAPTER GOALS

At the completion of this chapter, you will be able to:

- Define communication.
- Clarify the elements in the communication process.
- Explain and differentiate among the primary models of communication.

- Recount important turning points in the history of the communication field.
- Illustrate the destructive side of communication.
- Elucidate three ethical systems as they apply to communication.

COMMUNICATION ENCOUNTER: SOFIA CONTEDARAS

Sofia Contedaras hummed along to the music on her phone as she walked into the Federal One Bank building. She loved her job as the personal assistant to Frank Padillo, the bank's president. He was easy to work for and the bank's mission to remain in the Latinx neighborhood where Sofia had grown up was very appealing. She smiled and nodded to the security guard whom she saw every day. She turned off her music when she felt her cell vibrate. She opened a text from her husband saying he would pick up their children at the childcare center immediately after work.

As Sofia settled down at her desk, she checked her email. The first message destroyed her good mood. It was a directive from Mr. Padillo instructing her to send the following message to the head of Human Resources:

> As a result of downsizing and consolidations in the banking industry and the increase of Internet banking by many of our customers, I regret to inform you that by the end of the fiscal year, we must reduce the teller staff by half. Please see me immediately so we can strategize for this personnel change.

Sofia felt very nervous; just a month ago her niece was hired as a teller at the bank because of Sofia's recommendation. Also, several of her close friends at work were tellers. After seeing the memo, Sofia wasn't sure what to do, and she was beginning to feel a little sick. So many questions were swirling in her head. And, she couldn't help but imagine the toll that the lay-offs would take on the workers and their families.

It's not possible to go through a day without communication. From the moment we wake up to the sound of our phone alarm to the time we go to sleep listening to our favorite music, we are engaging in communication. Just think about the variety of communication activities you participate in on a daily basis. For instance, at home, television commercials tell you to buy more products, and you may get into an argument with a family member about conspicuous consumption. If you work, you receive memos and emails about the job, and you may engage in some conflict with colleagues about the best way to fulfill a boss's expectations. At school you listen to lectures and chat with friends, and you may find yourself in an internal debate about whether to study or party. At any time, you may receive texts informing you of what friends are doing, where you should meet them, and so forth. If you attend a house of worship, you'll have quiet, reflective moments with your own thoughts, and you'll also enter into conversations with others about committee work, retreat planning, or to discuss the topic of the service. What other communication activities do you encounter daily? Which ones have you engaged in today already?

In our opening vignette, Sofia hasn't said a word to anyone, but she's listened to her music, exchanged a smile and nod with the security guard, read a text from her husband, looked at her email, and thought to herself about these events. Communication surrounds Sofia (and each of us) since verbal and nonverbal communication behaviors are central to all aspects of our lives.

Even though we constantly communicate, we're not always clear about the definition of communication; sometimes we may interpret it one way and other times we'll use a different interpretation. A friend may think all behavior is communication while you believe that communication only occurs when two people understand each other. Communication is a complex process that isn't easy to define, just like most abstract concepts that are integral to human experience. When a concept is as all encompassing as communication, it may have different meanings in different situations. In this chapter, we provide a general definition for communication that allows us to use it across multiple contexts. We'll also explain the definition's critical components as well as some background and fundamental issues that affect how we understand and use communication. In doing so, we hope to develop a common interpretation of this important, yet frequently misunderstood, behavior. This interpretation forms a framework for the rest of the text.

Background

To begin our exploration of communication, we first define it, and the key terms that make up the definition. Then we discuss the concept of intentionality as it relates to defining communication. Next we examine four communication models that aid our understanding of the communication process. Finally, in this section, we briefly survey the history of the communication field.

Definition of Terms

The word communication comes from a Latin word meaning "to make common", and this sense of common or shared meaning resonates through most definitions that researchers and communicators themselves utilize. With this in mind, we offer our definition of communication: **Communication** is a transactional process using symbols to create (shared) meaning. Four critical components comprise this definition:

- process
- transaction
- symbols
- meaning

We will address each in turn.

When we state that communication is a **process**, we mean that it's an ongoing, unending activity that's always changing. Our communication encounters have no beginnings or endings. Of course, we turn our tablets on and off, we start and stop talking on the phone, and we strike up conversations and then walk out of the room when we've finished. But the processual nature of communication alerts us to the fact that these are temporary (and somewhat arbitrary) beginnings and endings. In other words, a specific communication encounter is always conditioned by what took place before it and what will take place afterwards. In the vignette at the beginning of this chapter, we see that Sofia is thinking about her relationship with the bank president she works for, the recommendation she gave that resulted in her niece's job at the bank, her friends who work as tellers, and the directive the president has just given her. She reflects on what will happen in the future based on past communication she's engaged in with a variety of people. Further, in the background of her immediate problems at work, she's also thinking about her family and how she and her husband are dividing childcare responsibilities.

Our focus on process also suggests that individuals change, and the cultures in which they live also change. For instance, contemporary US society is significantly different than US society in the 1950s. The climate of the United States in the 1950s was characterized by postwar euphoria and colored by fears about communism. The feminist movement of the 1970s and the #MeToo movement of 2017 both had yet to occur, and for many white middle-class families, gender roles were traditional. Women's roles consisted of caretaking for children and nurturing others, whereas men's roles were predominantly those of financial providers. These roles influenced decision making in various families (Turner & West, 2018). Further, women's roles in the workplace were generally subordinate to men's, and the term "sexual harassment" wasn't in the vocabulary. However, today, roles in the family are less rigid, and workplaces are focusing on eliminating gender inequities. This cultural shift underscores a process view; changing times indicate that we cannot completely understand US communication in the twenty-first century using models from the twentieth century. The same is true of other cultures, of course. In 2006, Hugh Cortazzi wrote in the *Japan Times* that over time Japanese culture has undergone multiple changes resulting in alterations in class, economic, and family structure, as well as employment practices. All of these shifts affect communication in Japan (Cortazzi, 2006).

Change is easy to understand when examining something like gender roles over time in the US or comparing the cultural climate in Japan in the 1900s to contemporary Japan. But, it's important to remember that calling communication a process also includes subtle changes. These changes occur daily (or hourly) and we often don't notice them at the time. You aren't the same person today as you were yesterday because all today's experiences have influenced you and caused changes – you learned something new, a friend surprised you, or you spent time with an old friend who reminded you of things you hadn't thought about for a while. Sometimes large changes occur in a day – you graduate, get a job, break up with a partner, lose a parent – and it's very obvious that change has occurred, and likely changed you. But, large or small, change is always occurring. Saying that communication is a process highlights the fact that we can't hold it still; it's too dynamic.

The second component of our definition states that the communication process is a **transactional** one. This means that communication involves simultaneous messages between or among communicators. Although people usually don't speak at the same time, they send nonverbal messages while another speaks. In addition, a transactional approach argues that communicators essentially create one another through communication. Think about a professor whose classes you enjoy. You think this professor is bright, funny, student-centered, and approachable. You are shocked to learn that your friend thinks the professor is arrogant, biased, and self-centered. You and your friend had different transactions with the professor and these transactions "created" different personas.

The third component of our definition is symbols. **Symbols** are arbitrary labels or representations for phenomena. Words are symbols for ideas and objects – for instance, in the English language *hate* stands for the concept of extreme dislike and the word *desk* represents the thing we sit at to do work. As you see from this example, symbols can be **abstract** (symbols that represent a concept or idea like *hate*) or **concrete** (symbols that represent a specific event or object like *desk*). To expand, the concrete symbol "car" depicts a vehicle. The abstract symbol of "democracy," however, doesn't refer to a specific thing. Although the word "car" can represent a lot of different types of cars (e.g., Mercedes, Toyota), all the objects represented are tangible. Democracy, in contrast, is not a material or physical concept and has no one specific referent.

Symbols (especially abstract symbols) may be ambiguous. For example, Beth asks "How do you like my haircut?" And Angie replies "It's *unique*." The word "unique" is ambiguous because Beth is free to choose whether Angie liked, disliked, or wasn't sure about the haircut. If the response was, "It looks great!" there would be less ambiguity. Finally, symbols are agreed upon by a group of people. The group can be large, such as an entire country (e.g., Germany, Iran), or small, such as a family. People who are outside of the group may not understand the symbols used within a particular group. The immediate members of a specific family will understand the in-joke "only Grandma knows the recipe" while those who are outside of the family may not completely understand its meaning, even though they can define the words. One way that people are socialized into a group is by learning its jargon or unique language (Becker-Ho, 2015). In Chapter 4, we discuss this issue further.

Meaning is the fourth component of our definition and it's especially important to understand because **meaning** is what people make out of a message, and shared meaning is usually considered the goal of communication. As you will learn in Chapter 4, words or symbols alone have no meaning; people attribute meaning to them. For example, if you spoke in English asking a French speaker for directions to the post office, you will have provided a message, but someone who speaks only French won't be able to make any meaning out of the message. One of the complexities in defining communication has to do with whether to include messages that don't create shared meaning as part of communication. Do you think misunderstandings, and failed explanations, equal communication?

Meaning can also be understood as existing on two levels: *content* and *relationship* (Segrin, 2015; Watzlawick, Beavin, & Jackson, 1967). The content level refers to the literal meaning of a message. If you ask your professor where the final exam will be held, the literal level of that message is a request for information about the exam's location. The relationship level has to do with the relationship that exists between the communicators. If you ask the question of your professor in a deferential tone while smiling, the relationship that is being communicated is one of power difference and, possibly, respect. If you snap the question out and frown at your professor while asking, the relationship-level meaning being communicated is one of dislike and disrespect. The content level remains the same but the relationship level changes in this example.

Our definition of communication stresses that it is a transactional process dependent on symbols that make meaning between people. Although the goal is shared meaning, misunderstandings happen so frequently that we do include them as communication, albeit poor communication. One element that is not mentioned in our definition, however, is **intentionality**, or whether a communicator means to send a particular message. Scholars debate about whether messages that are sent unintentionally actually qualify as communication.

Communication and Intentionality

An ongoing question related to the definition of communication relates to intentionality. The question, "Is all behavior communication?" is at the heart of this debate in the communication field. Suppose during a job interview with Ms. Thomas, Anthony Wells avoided eye contact with her and his voice quivered a bit. He twisted his hands in his lap and tapped his foot repeatedly. Can Anthony's shifting eye contact, vocal nervousness, and other distracting nonverbals be considered communication? Or, are Anthony's behaviors simply manifestations of his nervousness that he was unaware of and did not intend Ms. Thomas to notice?

Gerald Miller and Mark Steinberg (1975) comment that communication only exists when it's intentional. They define the communication process this way:

We have chosen to restrict our discussion of communication to intentional symbolic transactions: those in which at least one of the parties transmits a message to another with the intent of modifying the other's behavior.... by our definition, intent to communicate and intent to influence are synonymous. If there is no intent, there is no message. (p. 15)

However, other scholars argue that this interpretation is too limited and narrows the definition of communication too much.

In the 1950s, a group of researchers and theorists from different disciplines including communication, anthropology, and psychiatry, got together to study communication. They met in Palo Alto, California (home of Stanford University) and are known as the Palo Alto group. They worked to establish a common understanding about the communication process. One central (and provocative) outcome from their theoretical discussions is the phrase: "One cannot not communicate" (Watzlawick, Beavin, & Jackson, 1967). What they meant is we are continually communicating; even if we aren't saying a word or intending to convey a message. Anthony's shifting eye contact in our previous example would be communication according to the Palo Alto group.

You may be thinking that there are inherent challenges pertaining to the view espoused by the Palo Alto group. First, if *everything* is considered to be communication – all verbal and nonverbal behaviors – then studying communication in a thoughtful and organized way seems impossible. If everything is defined as communication, it's hard to consider communication a field of study. One of the first things scholars do to carve out a field of study is to define their object of study. They accomplish this by disentangling their focus of study from all other related things so they can discuss it clearly. An important question for us as communication scholars is: how does communication behavior differ from all other behavior?

One of the early pioneers associated with the Palo Alto group later clarified their initial claim. Janet Beavin-Bavelas (1990) stated that "all behavior is not communicative, although it may be informative" (p. 599). Our position is in this tradition. All behavior has communicative potential, but communication exists in a more intentional format. To establish and share meaning, some intention is required although unintended behaviors (i.e. smiling nervously) may affect the process of establishing and sharing meaning.

Four Communication Models

As you have seen, defining communication is a complicated task. We continue our efforts to interpret communication by drawing upon what theorists call **models of communication** (McQuail & Windahl, 1993). Models allow us to understand the complex process of communication by creating a visual representation of it. A model freezes the process (it's a little bit like understanding swimming by looking at a photograph of a swimmer) so it's incomplete, but it helps us get a handle on some of the important aspects of communication encounters. We present three traditional models of communication (linear, interactional, transactional) and then provide a fourth model (holistic) we've created using components from other researchers. This fourth model maps more of the complexity of communication than do the earlier three by including more components of the process. This fourth model provides the approach we use throughout this book. We begin our discussion with the oldest model as it represents early thinking about communication.

Linear Model

More than 50 years ago, two men, one a Bell Telephone scientist and the other a Sloan Cancer Research Foundation consultant, looked at how information passed through various channels (Shannon & Weaver, 1949). They viewed communication as information transmission that transpired in a linear fashion. This approach essentially frames communication as unidirectional: transmitting a message to a destination (think of someone throwing a ball to another person). Shannon and Weaver's research resulted in the creation of the **linear model of communication** (see Figure 1.1).

The linear model is based on five components:

- sender
- message
- channel
- receiver
- noise

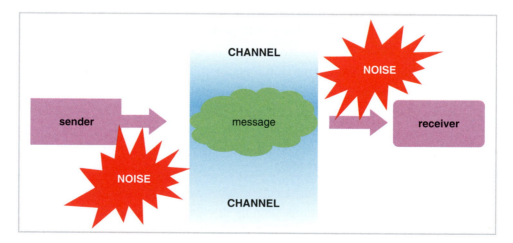

Figure 1.1 Linear Model of Communication

The first component is the **sender**, or source of an idea or thought. As the label suggests, senders begin the process by creating a **message** that encodes their thoughts. The sender uses a pathway for their message (the phone, face-to-face, a text, etc.) which is the **channel**. The message goes to the **receiver**, or the intended target of the message. You might choose to send a note to a friend on her birthday or to call, text, send an e-card, or take her out to brunch and have a face-to-face interaction. In all cases the message is "Happy Birthday," but the channels are different. Some people argue that changing the channel also changes the message. Would you respond differently to the message "Happy Birthday" if it were texted, emailed, or delivered face-to-face?

Communication also involves **noise**, or anything that interferes with the message. Four types of noise can interrupt a message. **Physiological noise** refers to biological influences (such as hearing loss or illness) on message reception. **Physical noise** (also called "external noise") involves outside stimuli that make the message difficult to hear. For example, it would be difficult to hear a message from your friend if you were talking near a highway with a lot of large trucks speeding past you. **Psychological noise** (or "internal noise") refers to a communicator's biases, prejudices, and feelings toward a person or message. If a speaker uses a derogatory term for an ethnic group you might be so bothered by the term that you're unable to attend to anything else the speaker says. Finally, **semantic noise** pertains to the language used to construct the message. Semantic noise may be jargon, technical language, or unfamiliar words and phrases. Consider, for example, a senior citizen reading a text from you. It's possible that some abbreviations (e.g. IMHO, bae, etc.) will provide semantic noise.

Although the linear model commanded high regard when it was first conceptualized, it's subsequently been criticized for its presumption that communication has a definable beginning and ending and that it moves in a one-way direction (Anderson & Ross, 2002). The simplified perspective provided by the linear model doesn't seem to capture everything going on during communication. We know that the communication process can be messy. Sometimes we jump into the middle of a message before the message is completed. Further, messages don't always flow smoothly from one person to another; there can be interruptions and feedback in the form of questions and so forth. These criticisms prompted researchers to rethink what happens during communication, leading to a new model: the interactional model.

Interactional Model

To emphasize the two-way nature of communication between people, Wilbur Schramm (1954) conceptualized the **interactional model of communication**. Schramm believed that communication flowed both from sender to receiver and from receiver back to sender

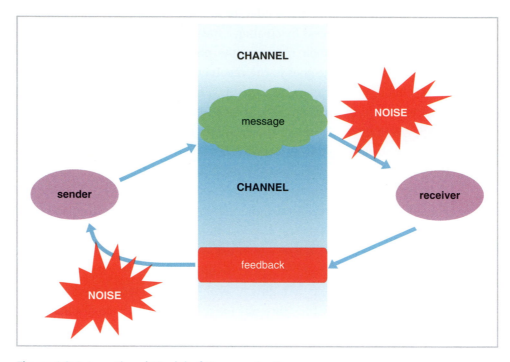

Figure 1.2 Interactional Model of Communication

(think of two people playing catch). This view of communication shows that individuals are both senders and receivers, although not simultaneously (see Figure 1.2).

The interactional approach maintained all the elements of the linear model, but added the concept of **feedback**, which can be defined as responses to a sender's message. Feedback may be either verbal (the receiver asks for clarification), nonverbal (the receiver laughs), or both (the receiver says "I agree" and smiles). Feedback may also be internal or external. **Internal feedback** occurs when you think of an assessment of your own communication ("I should never have said that. I sounded stupid"). **External feedback** is the feedback you receive from other people ("Why in the world did you say that?").

Like the linear model, the interactional model has been criticized primarily for its view of senders and receivers: only one person sending a message at a time. The model doesn't seem to take into consideration what happens when nonverbal messages are sent. For example, if a teacher is lecturing to her students, and she sees that some look sleepy, others are looking at their laptops, while still others are gazing out of the window, she may tell a joke or ask a question or have the students do a group exercise instead of finishing the lecture. She responds to their nonverbal feedback. The interactional model doesn't seem able to map this type of activity. Is the teacher the sender or are the students? Who's the receiver? It was this dilemma that led to the development of a third model of communication: the transactional model.

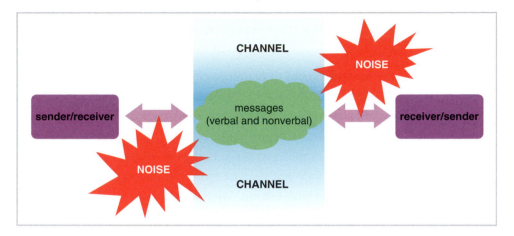

Figure 1.3 Transactional Model of Communication

Transactional Model

Whereas the linear model of communication assumes that communication moves from sender to receiver, and the interactional model allows for the presence of feedback, the **transactional model of communication** (Barnlund, 1970; Watzlawick, Beavin, & Jackson, 1967) is characterized by the reciprocal giving and receiving of messages (picture jugglers throwing balls to one another simultaneously). In a transactional encounter, people are active agents who create meaning together.

Because the transactional model relies upon recognizing that messages build upon each other, it illustrates that communicators negotiate meaning in their transaction. This is a unique feature of the transactional model. Further, both verbal and nonverbal behaviors are necessarily part of the transactional process. For instance when Justin tells his co-worker Aileen that he feels like he's going crazy, Aileen's concerned expression signals Justin that she's taking him seriously. Aileen's look prompts Justin to say "I'm only kidding." Aileen's nonverbal response to Justin prompted him to clarify his original message. As we see from this example, the nonverbal message works in tandem with the verbal message and the transactional process requires ongoing negotiation of meaning (see Figure 1.3).

The linear and interactional models paved the way for researchers to conceptualize the transactional model of communication, although all three present somewhat different views of the communication process. The linear model depicted senders and receivers with separate roles and functions. The interactional approach expanded that thinking and suggested less linearity and more involvement between communicators. The transactional model added the importance of co-created meaning and also demonstrated that messages are simultaneously sent and received. The holistic model, which we describe next, builds on the transactional approach and provides additional components further explaining the communication process.

Holistic Model

We offer the **holistic model of communication** to illustrate the complexity of communication. This model identifies some of the important elements affecting the communication process that are not explicit in the other models. The holistic model retains the transactional approach and begins with the same foundation. In this model, we try to capture what we see as the essential elements of a communication encounter, but the holistic model is certainly not the last word. Perhaps you can think of other parts of communication that we have left out. What would those elements be? We have added the following five components to the basic transactional model: (1) cultural context, (2) historical context, (3) situational context, (4) fields of experience, and (5) effect (see Figure 1.4).

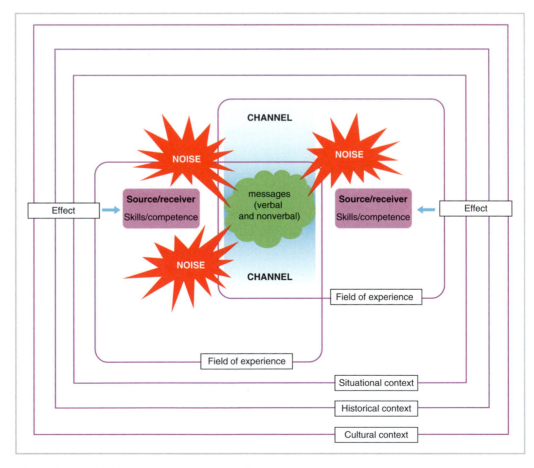

Figure 1.4 Holistic Process of Communication

First, we believe that all communication takes place in a **context**, or the environment in which a message is sent. Context is multidimensional and can be cultural, historical, and situational. The **cultural context** refers to the rules, roles, norms, and patterns of communication unique to the particular culture where the communication takes place. Imagine, for instance, talking to a classmate at your school in Iowa compared to talking to the same classmate during a semester abroad in Italy. In the first conversation perhaps you two decide that you don't like each other all that much, and don't wish to interact further. In the second case, you might find that you want to talk to the other person more because they remind you of home and they have more in common with you than other students there who don't know anything about Iowa. Culture always influences the communication that takes place between and among people. We return to a more comprehensive discussion of the impact of culture on communication in Chapter 2. For now, it's simply important to note that the cultural context influences people's communication.

In the **historical context**, messages are understood in relationship to the historical period in which they are exchanged, reflecting the processual nature of communication that we discussed earlier. A message about online class work, for instance, might have seemed like science fiction, or at least visionary, in the 1940s. Today, such a message is commonplace. Communicating about unemployment takes on different meanings if the conversation takes place during a time of high unemployment rates or relatively full employment in a country.

The **situational context** is the tangible environment in which communication occurs – the car on the way to your vacation, the dinner table, and inside a synagogue are examples of situational contexts. Environmental conditions such as temperature, lighting, and the size of the surroundings are also part of this context. The social and emotional climate is also associated with this context. For example, are the communicators friendly or unfriendly, supportive or unsupportive? Or, do they fall somewhere between these extremes? Imagine listening to a speech about climate change in an audience which mainly believes climate change is a serious problem compared to being at the same speech in an audience who is hostile to the idea.

When you examine Figure 1.4, you will note that the holistic model shows each communicator encased in a field of experience. The **field of experience** refers to a person's culture, past experiences, personal history, and heredity. Field of experience also contains two additional parts: competency and skills. **Competency** indicates how much a person knows about the subject of a communication encounter. **Skills** pertain to a person's communicative abilities. For example, you have probably had professors who you believed were experts in their subject matter but had poor lecturing abilities. Or you might have had a class with a professor who was extremely entertaining and well spoken, but who seemed to have a superficial knowledge of the subject.

Additionally, the holistic model shows a common field of experience between the two communicators. This overlap between fields of experience is where messages are exchanged. Thus, the model indicates that communication only takes place when communicators find common ground. Fields of experience change over time, and common experiences can create overlap, so it's possible to communicate with people who at first seem very different from you. For instance, writing in the *Christian Science Monitor*, John and Susan Marks (2005) explained how their organization, *Search for Common Ground*, helped conservatives and progressives find overlap in their fields of experience on the topic of poverty.

Marks and Marks observe:

> *It was important to avoid recreating the debate as it was being framed in the media and Congress: a food fight over whether more funds should be given to faith-based groups and whether they violated separation of church and state . . . They [the participants] came to see that they could work together on the basis of shared compassion. The framing question for liberals and conservatives to cooperate became: What could they do together to help poor Americans? (para. 8–9)*

Similar successes have been reported with groups consisting of anti-abortion and pro-choice members who focused on a shared goal of reducing unwanted pregnancies.

Additionally, common ground is built as communicators interact together and create shared experiences. For example, imagine Marc and Ned who met while taking a business course together at the university. Marc is a married African American man with three children who recently returned to school part-time, while maintaining full-time work. Ned is a single 18-year-old white student who came directly to college after high school graduation. Before this class, they'd never taken a course together, and there's an 18-year age difference between them. Their fields of experience, then, would appear to be limited to being male students at the same university enrolled in the same course. Yet, if the two interact in and out of their classroom, they'll develop common experiences, which, in turn, will affect the overlap of their two fields of experience in the future.

Finally, the holistic model shows that all communication generates some type of **effect** or a result coming from the communication encounter. For instance, if you hear a persuasive commercial about the virtues of a particular smart phone, you may start shopping for it. If you and your partner have a serious argument, you might feel unsure about your feelings for this partner. If you are a member of a task group at work and you have a really productive meeting, you may feel more confident about finishing the job. Effects range in their magnitude; some are large (you and a friend stop speaking to one another) while others are more minor (you feel better about the choice of car you recently purchased), but they always exist in any communication encounter (see Figure 1.5).

Figure 1.5 Communication Surrounds us all Daily in Myraid and Complex Ways

Historical Foundations of the Field

Thus far, we have established a working definition of *communication* as a transactional process using symbols to create (shared) meaning. Further, we discussed four models of communication. We elaborated upon the holistic model that illustrates several components of the process, and how each interact to allow meaning. Now, we'll briefly investigate the history of the field of communication, giving you a sense of its breadth and depth. Of course, this is only a cursory presentation; other writers have discussed this topic in much more detail (e.g. Gehrke & Keith, 2015).

Since the beginning of recorded history, communication has been on the minds of philosophers, teachers, scholars, practitioners, poets, and people of all backgrounds. According to Sherry Morreale and Matt Vogl (1998) "systematic comment on communication goes back at least as far as *The Precepts of Kagemni and Ptah-Hopte* (3200–2800 B.C.)" (p. 4). The field of communication has evolved over thousands of years and the academic discipline of communication has reached literally billions of people during its long history.

There are a few caveats to keep in mind as you read the following history, however. First, it's of necessity a brief history and we leave out a great deal of detail and just provide highlights. Second, it's a *general* history and we don't distinguish among nations (for instance, we talk about the Renaissance as a whole, rather than the Renaissance in Italy or England specifically). Finally, it's a *Western* history and we include no information about Asia or Africa, for example. We invite you to do further research filling in these gaps. We've divided our history into four chronological sections:

- Classical Origins
- The Post-Classical Period
- The Modern Period
- The Contemporary Period

Classical Origins (466 BC–AD 400)

In the ancient Greek world, oral communication skills were revered, and speaking well was viewed as a practical and necessary skill. This reverence for oral communication was enhanced in 466 BC during the revolution in Sicily, in ancient Greece. The people of Sicily overthrew Gelon, the dictator, and established a constitutional democracy. This event coincided with the spread of democracy throughout the ancient Greek world. The ideals of democracy placed a premium on effective communication and understanding the nature of persuasion. Indeed, citizens (that is to say, men, because women were not considered citizens in ancient Greece) needed to plead their own cases in court, argue their political ideas publicly while running for public office, and secure their own civil rights through persuasive speaking. Further, common citizens were asked to take part in society by doing such things as serving as jurors and overseeing city boundaries (Golden, Berquist, Coleman, & Sproule, 2011).

All these sorts of public speaking activities required knowledge of persuasion. Persuasion was also known as **rhetoric**, or using all available means to convince others, and rhetoric would become the central cornerstone of democracy in ancient Greece. Rhetoric was so important during this period that it was known as the "queen of disciplines". Plato and his student, Aristotle, were primary figures during this era. While Plato believed that searching for *the* truth should be a goal of every citizen, Aristotle argued that there were many truths. We return to the rhetorical tradition in Chapters 9 and 10.

In addition to Plato and Aristotle, Cicero was an important scholar of the classical period. He was a Roman politician and was considered to be the finest speaker of his day. One of his contributions to rhetoric was the elaboration of a model dividing communication into five parts or the **five canons of rhetoric** (http://rhetoric.byu.edu/Canons/Canons.htm). The five canons included: invention, style, arrangement, memory, and delivery. **Invention** referred to discovering evidence about a topic and deciding what to say about it. **Style** concerned wording, and deciding what language would be most effective in persuading the audience. The third canon, **arrangement**, had to do with organizing the ideas in the most effective manner for persuasion. In the next canon of rhetoric, **memory**, speakers concentrated on how to remember their material. This was extremely important because ancient society was oral, and speeches had to be memorized, not read. Finally, rhetoric consisted of **delivery**, or the ability to use a pleasing voice and significant gestures. Delivery was considered the least important of the canons, but still necessary for effective speaking. It's interesting to note that public speaking is still taught today using this same approach.

The Post-Classical Period (AD 400–1600)

What we are calling the post-Classical period comprises two major epochs of Western history: the Middle Ages and the Renaissance. However, neither of these historical periods had much impact on the development of rhetoric, especially when compared to the Classical period. In fact, the importance of oral communication actually declined during this time. During the Classical period rhetoric's importance and theories of rhetoric virtually exploded; perhaps it was inevitable that after all that energy was expended, there would be a resting period.

During the Middle Ages or the Medieval period, which lasted from approximately 400 to 1400, Christianity became vitally important. As religion became dominant, there was a decline in practices seen as irreligious or pagan, and this included rhetoric. Medieval thought held that Plato and Aristotle's goals for rhetoric, about seeking truth, were problematic for religion. Religious leaders reasoned that Christianity already taught the will of God and that was all the truth people needed. Oral communication was only needed for good preaching to reveal the will of God.

During the Renaissance (1400–1600), people moved away from a strict emphasis on religion, and turned again to an interest in the Classical roots of rhetoric. The Renaissance provided a focus on the individual, in place of the group or institutional focus that was fostered in the Middle Ages, and on art. Rhetoric was seen as an art. Despite this more hospitable climate for rhetorical thought, the Renaissance was a relatively quiet time in the development of rhetoric.

The Modern Period (1600–1942)

In the early part of the Modern period, the world became more secular, and religion was less influential than it had been previously (Golden et al., 2011). This opened the door for science to become a discipline separate from religion. Interest in science led to the rise in the empirical method that paved the way for seeing communication as a social science. But not all those who studied communication in this period were interested in the same things.

Some modern thinkers followed classical scholars like Aristotle and sought to apply Aristotelian rhetoric to modern situations. Other modern thinkers applied scientific approaches to the study of communication and focused on communication as a social science. Still others in the Modern period were mainly interested in style and presentation. The early nineteenth century saw the rise of what is called the **elocution movement**. This movement also harked back to the Classical period, but its emphasis was strictly on elevating the canon of delivery. Those in the elocution movement were most interested in the nonverbal aspects of oral communication. They were quite precise in their prescriptions for effective gestures and vocal behaviors (such as pitch, volume, and speaking rate). This movement was not helpful for the stature of rhetoric, however. Prior to the elocution movement, Harvard University had established a position in rhetoric. After the movement took hold, Harvard gave the position to the literature department. Harvard argued that rhetoric was not a fit subject for university study because the emphasis on elocution reduced rhetoric to a rote memorization of a series of behaviors (Haiman, 1982).

During the mid-to-later nineteenth century, major state universities were founded. Most of these schools, and those that followed, placed the study of rhetoric in departments of English to honor the rhetorical roots of the discipline. Emerson College in Boston, MA, and Northwestern University in Evanston, Illinois, were two exceptions. They both established schools of oratory (speech communication). Although not every university and college separated speech or communication from English during this period, this division was beginning. The first Ph.D. in speech was awarded in 1937 (Haiman, 1982).

The Contemporary Period (1942–Present)

Today the communication field is quite diverse, and part of the reason for the wide range of topics that comprise communication studies has to do with the evolution outlined above. In addition to its classical roots in the study of rhetoric, the contemporary field of communication also owes debts to studies in the areas of elocution, English, philosophy, and psychology, especially social psychology. During and after World War II, the small group dynamics movement arose, and it was folded into the burgeoning speech field. The study of small groups originated in psychology departments, and was often sponsored by the US government's Department of Defense (DoD). The DoD was interested in learning how propaganda could be used to persuade the US public to do various things for the war effort, such as participate in food and gas rationing and buy war bonds. This government research was particularly interesting to communication scholars because persuasion is the touchstone of our rhetorical heritage, and is a communicative activity.

The United States government is still interested in persuading its citizens to engage in behaviors that are beneficial to both the country and individual citizens. The *New York Times* (Porter, 2016) reported that the Obama administration hired consultants to figure out how to get people to save for retirement and do other productive things that will keep them from needing government assistance. The consultants came up with some communication solutions that have been implemented with good results. They found that low-income high school graduates were more likely to enroll in college when they received text messages about college requirements. In addition, well-written emails sent to military service members increased their participation in the federal employees savings' plan, and their enrollment in health insurance plans. Do you think you'd be persuaded to save money if you got a persuasive text from someone?

What we think of as communication studies today came from at least three sources in the past:

- English or rhetoric departments teaching public speaking
- The elocution movement which founded the performance area of the field
- Psychology departments teaching about group dynamics, which focused on a social scientific approach to communication (http://www.natcom.org/history/)

This diversity may be confusing as it allows for so many sub-specialties; however, some agreement exists centering the contemporary communication field within eight fundamental areas. In fact, many communication departments, and communication textbooks, like this one, are built around some or all of the following areas:

- intrapersonal communication
- interpersonal communication
- intercultural communication
- communication in groups and teams
- organizational communication
- public and rhetorical communication
- mass or mediated communication
- performance studies

This diversity suggests that the communication discipline has permeable, dynamic boundaries. Communication studies, too, is a field that responds to cultural and technological changes. Thus, researchers in the contemporary era study intercultural communication, reflecting the rise of international business and travel. We also study communication and technology given the explosion in technological advances and social media. What facet or subspeciality of communication interests you? You might think about how you wish to apply your knowledge of communication processes. Are you most interested in people building friendships through communication, how doctors and patients communicate, how people negotiate across cultural differences, or some other aspect of communication studies?

Given this brief history, we turn now to an examination of two fundamental issues in communication: the mistaken idea that all communication is positive and capable of solving all our problems; and three ethical systems for judging right and wrong in communication decisions.

Fundamental Issues

There are myriad issues we could address in this section; we have chosen two of the most discussed issues relating to communication. The first acts as a corrective to the belief that communication is always a good thing. Communication can be destructive as well as constructive, and we discuss that here. In addition, and relatedly, communication is always intertwined with ethical choices, so we review some commonly applied ethical systems for judging the rightness or wrongness of communication choices.

The Destructive Side of Communication

Popular self-help books make millions of dollars selling the idea that communication is the magic cure for all of life's ailments. We can scroll through Amazon book titles, for instance, and find many books promising to solve relational and job-related problems through effective communication. Think about how many times you've seen books promising that communication can solve your problems. Television and radio talk shows as well as advice blogs suggest "talking problems out", and communicating with another to solve the problems between you. And it is true, that often communication is a good thing, promoting better understanding among people and even better mental and physical health for individuals. Yet, there are times when communication results in less-than-satisfying experiences. A research area in communication studies focuses on the destructive aspects of communication (e.g., Cupach & Spitzburg, 2014; Gilchrist-Petty & Long, 2016; Spitzberg & Cupach, 2009; West & Turner, 2017). The **destructive side of communication** generally refers to negative communication exchanged between people or negative effects that result from communication encounters.

Brian Spitzberg and William Cupach, as well as other researchers, challenge us to think about problems that result from communicating with others. These researchers remind us that people can communicate in manipulative, deceitful, exploitive, homophobic, racist, sexist, and emotionally abusive ways. In other words, at times communication can be downright nasty. Thankfully not all people engage in this sort of communication, but we should be aware that at times, people do. And, we need to remember that there may be a destructive side when communication is aided by technology, especially as we consider issues such as pornography on the internet, cyber-bullying, lack of accountability for the material published on blogs, violence and sexual exploitation in the media, among other areas.

During the 2016 US presidential campaign, for instance, commentators discussed the negativity shown in Republican primary debates, as well as the negativity evidenced in the debates between the eventual nominees: Hillary Clinton and Donald Trump. When actual physical violence erupted at rallies for Donald Trump, some suggested that the heated rhetoric of the campaign had nowhere to go except toward violent acts (Barbaro, Parker, & Gabriel, 2016). In 2017, the deadly protests in Charlottesville, VA, concerning Confederate monuments in the USA, as well as terrorist attacks in Barcelona and the seaside resort of Cambrils, Spain, again turned international attention toward the relationship between speech and violence.

Everyday Talk: Cyberbullying

In 2014, Neil Tippit, Fran Thompson, and Peter Smith wrote on the website www .education.com (https://www.education.com/reference/article/cyberbullying-research/) that while cyberbullying is a relatively new phenomenon, it has grown exponentially over the past few years. They articulate several different types of cyberbullying, including those involving email, chat rooms, websites, and game sites, among others. The team also notes that cyberbullying is different from other types of bullying in several ways:

- Victims of cyberbullying are unable to hide, and they can be targeted at any time and in any place.
- Cyberbullying usually involves a relatively wide audience because of the reach of the internet.
- Those who cyberbully others do so in relative anonymity which can safeguard them from punishment or retaliation.
- Those who cyberbully do not usually see the response of their victim(s), which allows them to be relatively immune to the harm they cause, but also may deny them the satisfaction bullies often receive from their behaviors.

There is no doubt, Tippit, Thompson, and Smith argue, that the internet has provided a new channel for bullying behavior, with terrifying repercussions. The authors assert that today, parents and educators are working together to try to fight this growing problem and yet, so much work still needs to be undertaken.

1. Have you had personal experience with cyberbullying?
2. Do you know anyone else who has?
3. How can you apply any of the material in this chapter to cyberbullying?

In interpersonal communication, the destructive side of communication also may be evidenced, perhaps more benignly, through excessive talking. Some individuals, known as talkaholics, can actually inhibit communication. Jim McCroskey and Virginia Richmond (1995) point out that compulsive communicators may talk more than they should and talk when they know they should be quiet. Further, McCroskey and Richmond contend that talkaholics are aware that their talking is seen as excessive but they don't change their behaviors. We suggest that these people are engaging in destructive discourse, because they choose to talk compulsively and ignore others' needs. In this way they demonstrate scant understanding of the value of listening (a topic we discuss in Chapter 5).

As you read the material in this book, keep in mind that communication is a tool, and people can use it for both productive and destructive ends. We need to understand those moments when communication is employed improperly or inappropriately. Further, it's also the case that a single communication encounter can incorporate both positive and negative aspects. For example, when Zoe helps an international student, Dylan, learn English, she is expressing support, which is a positive use of communication. But in their conversations, Zoe may also be trying to manipulate Dylan so that he will dislike the same people she does, and she'll have an ally in her conflicts.

Our discussion of the destructive side of communication points to the need for ethical guidelines for communication encounters. We now turn our attention toward three ethical systems that guide us toward making constructive communication choices. If you can recognize what is ethical and what is not, you are well on your way to using communication appropriately, effectively, and thoughtfully.

Ethical Systems of Communication

According to communication ethicist Richard Johannesen (2000) "ethical issues may arise in human behavior whenever that behavior could have a significant impact on other persons, when the behavior involves conscious choice of means and ends, and when the behavior can be judged by standards of right and wrong" (p. 1). In almost every communication encounter, ethical questions arise. It's not an overstatement to conclude that a consideration of ethics is critical to all communication. Thinking back to Sofia's situation from the beginning of this chapter it's clear that the email instructing her to write to HR puts her in an ethical quandary. What are some communication encounters in your own life that have had ethical implications?

Ethics can be defined as the perceived rightness or wrongness of an action or behavior, and it involves moral decision making (Pfeiffer & Forsberg, 2005). As Raymond Pfeiffer and Ralph Forsberg concluded: "To act ethically is, at the very least, to strive to act in ways that do not hurt other people, that respect their dignity, individuality, and unique moral value, and that treat others as equally important to oneself" (p. 7). You can see how acting ethically is fundamental to being a competent communicator, and you can probably also see that it's not always easy to make ethical communication decisions.

When confronted with ethical decisions, we are acting in a cultural context, and what's perceived as right in one culture may not be universally accepted by all cultures. As Pfeiffer and Forsberg (2005) observe, ethics are woven into "our society's cultural, religious, literary, and moral traditions. Our values have emerged from and are deeply enmeshed in these traditions" (p. 8). Making sense of the world and of our communication encounters requires us to understand cultural values. When communication scholars discuss ethics in this way, they concentrate on the rightness or wrongness of specific communication decisions or practices. This approach is different from how philosophers study theories of ethics.

There are many ways to make value judgments in communication encounters. Scholars and researchers have discussed a number of different ethical systems (e.g., Andersen, 1996; Englehardt, 2001; Jensen, 1997). We will briefly overview three of them here:

- the categorical imperative
- utilitarianism
- the ethic of care

Each of these systems attempts to provide us with a road map for ethical communication.

Categorical Imperative

The **categorical imperative** is based on the work of eighteenth-century philosopher Immanuel Kant (Kuehn, 2001) and advances that acting ethically refers to following moral absolutes. According to this system, the key question to ask when you are confronted with an ethical decision is: What is the ethical principle governing this situation? Your answer will guide you in making your decision. Further, Kant believed that the consequences of actions are not important; what matters is the logical soundness of the rule or ethical principle people use to guide their actions. In this system, rationality, not consequences, drives moral goodness.

For example, let's say that Rick confides to his co-worker, Sasha, that he might want to get another job. Occasionally he has called in sick so he can go to interviews at other companies. Rick asks Sasha not to mention anything to anyone at work because he isn't 100 percent sure that he is going to leave the company. Lenora, the supervisor, asks Sasha if she knows what's happening with Rick because he has missed several days of work. The categorical imperative dictates that Sasha tell her boss the truth, despite the fact that she's promised Rick she wouldn't tell anyone. If Sasha tells Lenora about Rick she might be affecting Rick's job, his future with the company, and the relationship she has with him. But the categorical imperative requires us to tell the truth because Kant believed that truth telling is a rational approach, and upholding rationality is more important than the possible negative short-term consequences that might arise from telling the truth.

Utilitarianism

Utilitarianism, a theory of ethics developed by the nineteenth-century philosopher John Stuart Mill (Capaldi, 2004), states that ethics are governed by what will bring the greatest good for the greatest number of people. Mill differed from Kant (in the categorical imperative) because he believed the consequences of actions were more important than the moral principle motivating the actions. For example, think again about Sasha's dilemma. In this case, using utilitarianism as a guide, Sasha might not tell Lenora about Rick's job search reasoning that she, Rick, and the members of Rick's large extended family, who all depend on his salary, might be harmed if she tells the truth. Using utilitarianism, Sasha could reason that because Rick might not even take another job, it's difficult to see who is directly being harmed at the moment.

Making a decision based on utilitarianism, or what is best for the greater good, means you have to weigh the harms and benefits to the many people who might be touched by your decision. In this approach, principles are not important because they are rational, but rather because they produce the most good or happiness in a given situation.

Ethic of Care

Developing an **ethic of care**, means making ethical decisions based on connection or relationships. In the twentieth century Carol Gilligan (1982) first conceptualized the ethic of care by examining women's ways of making ethical decisions. Gilligan observed that women tend to make moral choices based on relational considerations. For instance, using the ethic of care might guide Sasha to remain silent because of her concern for her relationship with Rick. However, Gilligan also found that people implementing an ethic of care often reconstructed the moral dilemma so they didn't have to make an either-or decision. If she were using an ethic of care, perhaps Sasha would tell Rick that Lenora is asking about his absences and suggest that Rick tell Lenora himself.

Although most of Gilligan's work showed that women employed the ethic of care, she did note that an ethic of care isn't exclusive to women, nor is it the case that all women employ it as an ethical system (Gilligan, 2011). Some men adopt the ethic of care, and some women do not. Like utilitarianism, and in contrast to the categorical imperative, the ethic of care is concerned with consequences of decisions, specifically those consequences that affect a relationship with others.

Communication encounters offer many opportunities for us to practice ethical decision-making practices. How do you talk to a former friend or former partner in future encounters? Is it ever okay to lie to protect a friend? Is it right to make a commercial for a product you don't believe to be worthwhile? How far should you go to persuade someone to do something that you think is good? Is it okay to use unattributed sources in a public speech? These kinds of questions challenge us to bring some type of ethical standards to our communication encounters.

In this chapter, we presented a comprehensive look at the communication process.

We articulated a definition of communication and examined its central elements: process, transaction, symbols, and (shared) meaning. We also examined the debate pertaining to intentionality. We introduced the linear, interactional, transactional, and holistic models of communication. We briefly reviewed the history of the field of communication to gain an understanding of how its diverse origins in rhetoric, psychology, and elocution support the diversity we find in the field today. Because not all communication is positive, the ways in which communication can be destructive were noted. Finally, because of these destructive results, communication can never be discussed without an examination of ethics and consequently, three ethical systems, the categorical imperative, utilitarianism, and the ethic of care, were provided as guidelines for determining the "right" course of action when we're deciding how to communicate. As you read the rest of this text, we hope you'll keep these foundational elements in mind to aid you in understanding what happens in communication encounters.

Communication Response: Sofia Contedaras

In our Communication Encounter, Sofia came to her job interacting with many communication technologies. She was happily anticipating her day until she read the memo from the President of Federal One Bank, Mr. Padillo, indicating that Human Resources should begin laying off 50% of the window tellers because of increased on-line banking activity. Further, the difficulty of this action took on a personal tone as Sofia realized that her niece and some close friends would inevitably be on the list for termination. Based on your reading of the chapter and understanding of the material, answer the following questions:

1. How does the holistic model of communication help explain Sofia's morning?
2. What should Sofia do about her boss's directive?
   (a) Should Sofia let her niece know about the impending notice?
   (b) Should Sofia talk to Mr. Padillo and ask him for some special accommodation for her niece?
   (c) Should Sofia talk to her sister and let her deal with the situation concerning her niece?
   (d) Is there another alternative you can think of to suggest to Sofia?
3. How might any of Sofia's potential actions activate the destructive side of communication? Use examples to expand and justify your views.

Questions for Understanding

1. List some of the underlying differences about the nature of the communication process that are inherent in the four models presented in the chapter.
2. List the primary thinkers who influenced the direction of the communication field.
3. Identify examples of the destructive side of communication in a variety of situations such as at your job, in your family, or with your friends.
4. Explain the basic tenets of the three models of communication ethics.

Questions for Analysis

1. Provide an argument for and against including unintentional behaviors in the definition of communication. Take your own position and defend it.
2. Develop your own model of communication and explain what assumptions about the process it reflects.
3. Apply one of the ethical systems to a communication dilemma you have confronted in the past.
4. Give an example of a communication encounter that has both a positive and negative side. How did you decide what you labeled positive and negative?

Suggestions for Further Reading

Arnett, R. C., Fritz, J. H., & Bell, L. M. (2009). *Communication ethics literacy: Dialogue and difference.* Thousand Oaks, CA: Sage.

Dennis, E. E., & Wartella, E. (eds.) (2009). *American communication research: The remembered history.* New York: Routledge.

Gehrke, P. J., & Keith, W. M. (eds.) (2015). *A century of communication studies: The unfinished conversation.* New York: Routledge.

http://www.forbes.com/sites/gregsatell/2015/02/06/why-communication-is-todays-most-important-skill/#7c31dd1d3638

2 Culture and Communication

CHAPTER OUTLINE

CHAPTER GOALS

At the completion of this chapter, you will be able to:

- Delineate the definition of culture.
- Recognize how cultural diversity has increased substantially around the globe.

- Discuss various imperatives related to culture and communication.
- Identify various dimensions related to national culture.
- Summarize various barriers to intercultural communication.

- Explain co-cultural theory and its relationship to marginalized populations.

- Demonstrate skills for intercultural communication.

COMMUNICATION ENCOUNTER: DORA ELLISON AND AUGUSTINA RIVERTON

As a suburbanite for almost two decades, Dora Ellison was used to commuting into the city to her job at an investment firm. Over the years, she pretty much experienced everything – from trains breaking down to a man singing Broadway musical songs on a late afternoon train. But, Dora did not seem prepared for Augustina Riverton, an African missionary from Nigeria who sat next to her on the 30-minute commute to the city. Although Dora rarely chatted with anyone on her commute, she was intrigued by the accent, demeanor, and colorful outfit of her seat companion. As the two began to banter about the weather and their children, Dora was feeling pretty much at ease, even though she hadn't had any interactions with African missionaries in the past. The two talked about several things, including women's rights and gay children (Dora was parenting a 16-year old gay son). After about 10 minutes, Augustina told Dora: "You do realize that God is loving and forgiving and even your son can find forgiveness if he accepts God." Dora was a bit annoyed since she didn't really want to hear proselytizing so early in the morning, and definitely didn't want to hear it about her son, whom she accepts and adores. Soon, Dora found herself biting her lip as Augustina told her: "You see, God doesn't really approve of homosexuals and you ... " "Wait! Wait. Just. One. Minute.," Dora interrupted, loudly punctuating a rather quiet train car. She continued: "You don't know one thing about my son or my life. I don't need someone telling me – someone from another continent – telling me whether or not my son is going to hell or whatever you're saying. You are visiting this country and I suggest you learn about our values. Mothers don't hate their sons here." Augustina sat motionless and didn't know whether to apologize or to explain herself better. She only knew that she had angered Dora and she wanted to make the situation calmer. Finally, Augustina said: "I'm sorry if I offended you, but my 'parent' is God and he is ... " Dora never let her finish. She got up, picked up her shoulder bag and moved to another seat in the crowded train car. As she worked her way through the train, Dora couldn't help but think about how odd, rude, and inappropriate Augustina was.

Most people are aware of and informed about the people surrounding them. When we go through the "conversation motions" – saying hello to our colleague, waving goodbye to our physician, explaining directions to a tourist, or even sitting next to a missionary on a commuter train – we can gain insight into our desire and ability to communicate with different people from various backgrounds. But Dora Ellison's experience on her commute represents the challenges people may have with others who look, think, and sound different from them. What was it that bothered Dora and caused her to move her seat? Was it Augustina's spiritual and religious values? Her "differentness"? Or, was it that Augustina didn't understand the cultural norms in the USA about commuter travel? Did Augustina comprehend the implications of talking about a member of the LGBT community to a parent of a gay son? Clearly, a host of issues coalesced to bring about this provocative encounter between the two women.

Although the United States has been called a **melting pot**, or a place where different cultures blend into one national culture, this sort of metaphor is especially limiting, particularly at this time in US history. Calling the USA a "melting pot" may have been appropriate in 1908, when the term was coined (Zangwill, 1908), but today the desire to assimilate distinctive and unique cultures into one nation (or pot) is sometimes met with confusion, curiosity, or in Dora's experience, frustration and anger. The fusion of personalities, cultures, and nationalities is often not a harmonious ("melting") experience, as we see with the two commuters. Further, today, retaining the unique features of a native culture is important, even when people join a new culture. Rather than a melting pot, we're now encouraged to see the USA as an orchestra where different cultures retain their individuality (like the separate instruments), but work together to create a unified whole (like the performance). All of this is done with different rhythms and at times there is harmony. At other times, discord takes place.

In Chapter 1, we introduced you to the communication process, and we now turn our attention to one profound influence on communication: culture. We present this information early in the book because all communication is framed by culture. Being able to understand the influence of culture on the communication process is an important skill. Among many other benefits (which we address throughout this chapter), being culturally aware will assist you in appreciating and understanding the differences (and similarities) between and among people with whom you communicate.

Background

Functioning in a society that's as culturally diverse as the USA enhances opportunities for communicating with diverse people, including work colleagues, classmates, friends, roommates, and family members, among others. We now address four issues forming the background to our discussion of culture and communication. Specifically, we discuss the notion of US diversity, a few definitions and fundamental assumptions about culture, and several urgencies related to studying this very relevant and compelling topic in our personal and professional lives.

Cultural Diversity in the USA

With over 320 million people in the United States, and nearly 40% of them belonging to one of a variety of racial groups (e.g., African American, Hispanic or Latinx, American Indian) it's nearly impossible to communicate in the USA without having an intercultural experience. We find this diversity in an assortment of institutions, including workplaces, schools, houses of worship, and the media. In other words, cultural diversity forms the US mosaic. We believe that celebrating and embracing the heterogeneity around us helps to move us toward effective communication.

Beyond the USA, perhaps nowhere is worldwide cultural diversity more evident than in recent patterns of immigration. Some countries welcome immigrants with emotional support, resources, and employment while others wish to build walls, deny drivers' licenses, and begin mass deportations. Demetrios Papademetriou and Natalian Banulescu-Bogdan (2016) of the Trans-Atlantic Council on Migration explained that this anxiety is related to "a variety of other concerns, including those about economic security, changing cultural norms, crime, terrorism and the ability of the government to effectively manage these challenges" (p. 2). Regardless of where you stand on this topic, one significant conclusion remains: The movement of people around the globe continually alters the world's landscape. Figure 2.1 shows how immigration is impacting the US map.

Figure 2.1 The Influence of Immigration in the USA

Defining and Interpreting Culture

The multidimensionality, complexity, and abstraction surrounding the meaning of culture makes it difficult to define. For our purposes, we look at **culture** as a learned system of life experiences of a group who have a common set of values, beliefs, norms, and traditions. Culture is a framework we use in understanding the world around us, making sense of it, and participating in it. Culture relates to communication because it serves as an impetus for processing information. We interpret interactions through the prism of cultural values and norms.

When we say culture is learned, we're referencing the Latin phrase, *tabula rasa*, meaning that individuals are born as "blank slates." We're not born with any knowledge of the ongoing practices of our culture. We learn about culture both directly and indirectly. Learning directly about culture, for instance, can include a Cherokee mother telling her daughter about wedding rituals like the Wedding Prayer, Sacred Fire Ceremony, or Stomp Dance (Duvall & Jacob, 2011). Learning indirectly about culture includes the lessons we absorb without direct instruction. When we attend weddings in our culture, or read about them or see them performed in the media, we observe how the traditions and rituals of our culture are enacted without having anyone specifically instruct us. As we learn a culture's practices and values, we engage in **enculturation**, which is the process of identifying with a particular culture and its various customs, values, and patterns of interaction.

One implication of the previous definition is that culture is not static. Cultures are fluid, unpredictable, dynamic, and they change over time. Think about how the US culture has changed from 1950 to the present, for instance. What traditions have you heard about from the past in your own culture that are no longer practiced today?

In this book, we adopt an expansive view in our definition and understanding of culture. We embrace the breadth and depth of culture by including the following components:

   *Gender (e.g., feminine, androgynous)
   *Sex (e.g., male, female)
   *Generation (e.g., Millennials, Baby Boomers)
   *Race/Ethnicity (e.g., Asian American, Navajo, German)
   *Social Class (e.g., homeless, lower middle)
   *Sexual identity (e.g., gay, lesbian)
   *Ability (e.g., physical challenges)
   *Spiritual and/or Religious identity (e.g., Catholic, Jewish)
   *Geographic region (e.g., Midwesterner in the USA, Greater London in the UK)

*Family type (e.g., stepfamily, single parent family)
*Nationality (e.g. US, Iranian)

Although other cultural nuances may exist, these comprise the majority of the cultural mix. Culture can be a springboard for conversation or a force impeding conversation. Consider, for instance, the perceptions and reactions of Dora in our opening story. What influence does culture have upon her dialogue with Augustina?

Assumptions about Culture

The preceding information provides a preliminary foundation to discuss culture, but to further unpack it, we present three assumptions that will help as you consider your own background and the backgrounds of others. We discuss each of these next.

Culture is Complex

The intricacies and complexities of culture cannot be overstated. By now, you already know that we live in diverse times and as we write this, cultures across the globe – including your own – continue to evolve. Although it's difficult to avoid cultural generalizations in this chapter, we caution tentativeness as well. After all, cultural beliefs are not monolithic. The idea that you're "rich" in one family, for instance, is quite different than being "rich" in another family. For one person, "rich" is defined in economic terms; for another person, being "rich" is viewed as having great health and having family around. You can see, then, that the complicated nature of culture needs to be understood, appreciated, and ultimately embraced if we are to avoid over-generalizing about an individual's beliefs based on their culture's beliefs.

Culture Creates both Divisions and Community

Because culture relies on a common set of values, beliefs, norms, and traditions, culture, by definition, typically brings people together in community. Cultural practices revolving around food, celebrations, spirituality, and so forth draw people together. When 19-year-old Marla goes to church with her mom, she feels a sense of belonging and community. She is inspired by the words of the service and enjoys the rituals of her church. However, at times, **culture clashes**, or disagreements and conflicts over cultural expectations, take place. Marla may take a college class on feminism and religion and begin to question how her church treats women, resulting in some conflicts with her family. The clash may resolve itself in that Marla may simply accept the church's teachings/practices. Or, the clash may escalate if she decides to leave the church because its teachings/practices ultimately conflict with her principles.

Culture and Communication are Intertwined

Over 50 years ago, anthropologist Edward T. Hall (1959) stated that "culture is communication and communication is culture" (p. 169). Hall suggests that to discuss one without the other is similar to talking about an Oreo cookie without milk! Even decades ago, Hall understood the value of the relationship between these two terms. We cannot communicate with another without knowing that our communication is, in part, based upon our cultural background. Whether or not we achieve shared (transactional) meaning in a conversation is related to the cultural backgrounds of both communicators. For example, think about Dora and Augustina in our opening. It seems that both need to understand the influence that culture is playing in their interpersonal conflict. Perhaps some of their tension could be alleviated if they tried to understand each other's cultural background.

Thus far, we have introduced you to important definitions and assumptions concerning culture and communication. We next discuss some specific reasons for studying this area.

Imperatives for Studying Culture and Communication

Why is it important to learn about intercultural communication? We advance three answers to that question taken from the system of "imperatives" of Judith Martin and Tom Nakayama (2017). We explore three imperatives below: self-awareness, demographic, and peace.

Self-Awareness Imperative

If you've ever visited another country, you probably became aware of your presence rather quickly. Maybe you felt that your clothing was different than that of those living in the host culture. Or, perhaps you immediately noticed that others' physical appearance (skin color, height, or weight) differed from yours. You may have noted greeting rituals being different from what you're accustomed to. Or, your use of eye contact or body movement may be different from others in the new country. Each of these differences relates to the importance of recognizing your sense of self and your own cultural identity.

Understanding how and where you "fit" within a culture is important for two reasons. First, self-awareness allows us to interrogate our own beliefs, and become more deliberate and inclusive in our thinking and behaviors. You may feel that a culture is "backward" if its citizens weren't wearing designer clothes, speaking English, or looking at us while speaking, we may be prone to this sort of self-centered cultural thinking, a topic we return to later in the chapter. Spending less time judging another culture by an arbitrary standard allows us to appreciate the uniqueness of a particular culture. Second, self-awareness allows you to become better able to perceive your own culture and your own sense of self. We've already mentioned that the USA, for example, has become much more diverse. It's important to understand that intercultural contact will necessarily affect awareness of our perceptions and our self (a topic discussed in Chapter 3).

Demographic Imperative

The USA (and the world) continues to grow increasingly diverse and an educated and engaged citizen cannot and should not ignore this cultural dynamic. Increased racial/ethnic diversity is already evident. For instance, Sandra Colby and Jennifer Ortman (2015) of the US Census, report that people who identify themselves as being a member of at least two races is projected to increase 226 percent over the next 50 years, from 8 million to 26 million. Further, the two demographers also note that in the United States alone:

*between 2014 and 2060, the population will grow from 319 million to 417 million;
*by 2030, one in five people living will be 65 years old and over;
*by 2044, more than half of all people living will belong to a minority group;
*by 2060, nearly one in five will be foreign-born.

These statistics show that the US population will not only explode to about 100 million more, but grow more diverse.

Demographic signs also point to significant changes in spiritual (religious) diversity both in the USA and around the globe. Years ago, it was fair to say that the USA was a rather Christian-centered country. Today, however, the numbers have changed radically. Gabe Bullard (2016) found that those who are unaffiliated with a religion or "the nones" have surpassed Catholics, Protestants, and adherents to non-Christian faiths. Globally, the religions of the world are far more diverse than those in the USA.

All of the preceding changes, coupled with technology, provide demographic opportunities to communicate with heterogeneity in mind. A heterogeneous population offers opportunities to understand the differences that exist among people, ultimately resulting in enhanced conversational meaning.

Peace Imperative

Writer Joichi Ito stated: "We have a long way to go before we are able to hear the voices of everyone on earth, but I believe that providing voices and building bridges is essential for the World Peace we all wish for." This sentiment may sound impossible, even old-fashioned, to some of you. But Judith Martin and Tom Nakayama (2017) contend that much of the world's conflict and violence occurs because of economic disparities, racial and ethnic intolerance, and religious or spiritual differences. Efforts to reconcile these enormous challenges will likely become the pathway to peace, as Ito suggests.

Everyday Talk: Life Experience, Culture, and Technology

Fifty-six-year-old Dan Lyons presents a first-person narrative of his experiences working in the "youth-obsessive" tech companies in Boston, MA. Because Boston is home to nearly 200,000 college students, Lyons suggests that this youthful population has failed to both understand and appreciate the work ethic and life experiences of older workers (www.bostonmagazine.com/news/article/2016/07/24/ageism-tech-industry/). Lyons notes that "again and again I hear the story of the gray-haired job applicant who makes it through a phone-screening process based on his or her qualifications, then shows up for the in-person interview and sees the lights go out in the eyes of the twenty-something manager who is doing the hiring." He further notes that the definition of "old" keeps getting younger and that these "youth-full" companies would do well if they paid more attention to the workers who can contribute "know-how" that millennial workers simply don't possess. Lyons notes that he has received scores of letters from readers with similar experiences. In particular, Lyons writes about a 32-year old who expressed frustration about being in the youth-oriented tech industry. With many tech companies resembling "frat houses," Lyons laments that the future does not look optimistic for older workers, despite the skills they may possess.

1. Do you believe that most companies overlook age as a cultural concern? Why or why not?
2. If you had the ability to establish your own start-up, how would you incorporate a diversity of age groups into your personnel?
3. Should there be company policies in place that require hiring people of various ages? Why or why not?

Think, for instance, about the Middle East and the fact that the Israeli–Palestinian conflict has been going on for decades. Over the years, we have seen millions of refugees flee their homelands, only to be confronted with hate, hunger, fear, and violence (Bokore, 2016). Pilfering country resources and stomping out competing ideologies pervade so many societies and scores of residents risk their lives fleeing this oppression. This **diaspora**, or the movement of a group of people from their native country, continues today. Yet, any vision of "freedom" is soon undercut by a reality that is fraught with uncertainty. Refugees face so many struggles that thousands risked their lives crossing the Mediterranean alone in 2016.

These sorts of data and human loss are difficult for most of us to imagine or grasp. Yet, learning about these crucial events is an important part of intercultural communication.

While an ideal goal may be *establishing* peace, a more reasonable goal seems to be *working toward* peace. Global understanding can only be achieved if we understand the people around the globe. Some may view war as an inevitable cost of living among diverse

Figure 2.2 People Around the Globe Have Began to Recognize the Value of Intercultural Communication

populations. In fact, the Institute for Economics and Peace provides some sobering statistics that reveal only 11 countries as low in conflict: Switzerland, Japan, Qatar, Mauritius, Uruguay, Chile, Botswana, Costa Rica, Vietnam, Panama, and Brazil. More engagement in understanding diversity and effective intercultural communication may help move this number higher.

Fundamental Issues

A host of various issues makes cultural understanding an extremely important behavior across the globe (see Figure 2.2). In this section, we first articulate several dimensions of culture. We then explore a number of obstacles that inhibit intercultural understanding.

Dimensions of National Culture

The scholar most recognized as a pioneer in understanding the dimensionality of culture is Dutch anthropologist Geert Hofstede. Prior to becoming a professor, Hofstede worked at IBM as a trainer and manager of personnel where he oversaw the use of 100,000 opinion surveys at various IBM locations across the globe. After leaving IBM, Hofstede (1980, 1984, 1991, 2001, 2003) published many articles focused on the various cultures he studied. He identified five dimensions that varied among cultures: individualism-collectivism, uncertainty avoidance, distribution of power, masculinity-femininity, long- and short-term orientation. We discuss each of these below.

Individualism-Collectivism

This dimension refers to the extent to which a culture values connections to others, including friends, families, and the culture at large (Kadoya, 2016). When a culture values **individualism**, it prefers the individual over the group. The individualistic culture values competition over cooperation and the private over the public. The use of "I" functions prominently in individualistic cultures and individual responsibility is emphasized. Individualistic cultures such as Italy, Canada, the United States, and Australia tend to embrace the philosophy of "pick yourself up" when things go wrong.

Collectivism places the group's norms, values, and beliefs over the individual's. Whereas individualistic cultures prefer people to "pick themselves up", collectivistic cultures such as Pakistan, Peru, Colombia, and Chile believe that the community can, should, and will provide help. In particular, collectivist communities typically believe that family members should assist each other in times of need. What are some of the ways you see individualism and collectivism within the US culture?

Uncertainty Avoidance

The extent to which individuals wish to avoid ambiguity and avoidance is what Hofstede called the **uncertainty avoidance** dimension. How tolerant are you of uncertainty? How willing are you to avoid certain communication encounters? Do you resist change when it is thrust upon you? All of these areas are part of this dimension.

If you are a person who doesn't like change and gets rather anxious when change happens, you have a high degree of uncertainty avoidance. Cultures that reflect this value – Japan, France, Greece, and Portugal, for instance – tolerate little uncertainty (Craig, 2013). People in these countries usually want to have everything clearly delineated so there is little misunderstanding. You can imagine, then, why some people will actively avoid risky decisions in these sorts of countries. If a culture has a low degree of uncertainty avoidance, it is relatively unthreatened by change. Countries including Sweden, Denmark, and Ireland are those cultures that typically have little problem with change and uncertainty.

Do the Right Thing: The Challenge of Diversity

You have always prided yourself as someone who is culturally compassionate and as someone who is proud to have gay friends, friends of color, and friends who disagree with your political beliefs. But, at a recent training workshop, you were called out as being naïve. Glen, the seminar leader, was discussing the importance of working with diverse customers. He advocated for employees to understand various cultural differences with clients and to educate themselves to avoid embarrassment and loss of business. At one point in the workshop, you stated: "I think it's important to understand our clients, because diversity is one of the most important issues in sales." It was a rather innocent-sounding comment, but one of the workshop participants – Nashota – yelled out: "What do you know about diversity? Try living in a poor community. Try having a job and losing it because you're not the right skin color. Try even for one minute to imagine what it's like to speak a language where people make fun of you!". What do you do?

What do you say, if anything, in response?

1. If you used the categorical imperative as your ethical system, how would you proceed?
2. If you used utilitarianism as your ethical system, how would you proceed?
3. If you used the ethic of care as your ethical system, how would you proceed?
4. Specifically, if you had to write out a script for your conversation with Nashota, what would you say to her?

Distribution of Power

Power distribution relates to **power distance**, or the degree to which the less powerful expect and accept that power is distributed unequally. Those citizens from countries such as Malaysia, Panama, Mexico, and Singapore tend to possess a large degree of power distance. What this means is that, in these countries, there is a tendency to revere and respect those in power. People tend to accept the clear dichotomy between the powerful and the powerless and deference is paid to those, for instance, who have higher income and advanced education. Let's look at one country in particular to give you a better understanding of power distance: India.

India has a rich history rooted in what is called the caste system. Stephen Knapp (2016) explains four **castes**, or classifications of social standing: Brahmanas (priests and intellectuals), Kshatriyas (military and governmental administrators), Vaishyas (bankers and farmers), and the Shudras (laborers and musicians). Knapp contends that this caste system does nothing but oppress those of lower social standing and renders it "useless" (p.7), despite some scholars who believe that the system is beginning to change significantly over the past few years (Farek, Jalki, Pathan, & Shah, 2017).

Those cultures that believe that power distribution should be done equitably regardless of age, sex, or status, for instance, are those that are low in power distance. The United

States, Israel, Denmark, and Austria are countries that advocate the 1970s John Lennon song, "Power to the People". Many of these cultures also believe that one can attain power, regardless of background. For instance, there are several cases of powerful people who are products of economically challenging backgrounds, including Oprah Winfrey, Ralph Lauren, Jim Carrey, and Jennifer Lopez.

Masculinity-Femininity

The extent to which a culture represents masculine or feminine traits is the **masculinity-femininity dimension**, the fourth component of Hofstede's system. Countries such as Italy, Venezuela, and Japan are considered masculine because they tend to value aggressiveness, competition, achievement, and materialism, all masculine traits. Further, the notion of success is prominent in **masculine cultures** and success is usually defined as "the best" or "the winner." In masculine cultures, the division of labor is generally sex-based, meaning women and men are assigned various tasks based on their sex and not their qualities.

The countries Thailand, the Netherlands, and Finland are all viewed as **feminine cultures** because they emphasize equality and caring for others. Unlike masculine societies, those feminine cultures define success as "the quality of one's life." Standing out in the crowd is not embraced. In cultures that are higher in femininity, you would find both women and men as cooperative.

Before we close our discussion of this dimension, an important caveat is needed. The feminine-masculine dimension may be the least applicable to Western cultures. Millennials, in particular, are now identified as the "gender-fluid generation" (Marsh, 2016), prompting social media sites such as Facebook to offer customized gender identities.

Long- and Short-Term Orientation

To understand this fifth and final dimension of national culture – long-term orientation (LTO) and short-term orientation (STO) – think about how societies tend to view the future. Some are more disposed to focusing on the future, enthusiastic about the possibility of change. These are considered **long-term orientation cultures**. LTO countries such as Poland, Canada, and Germany support change and persistence and the social relationships in these countries tend to be organized by status. Hofstede believes that people from LTO cultures usually make quick money judgments, such as decisions related to purchasing luxury items or investing in the stock market. Personal adaptability is very important in LTO societies.

Those counties that emphasize the present and the past and still support tradition are termed **short-term orientation cultures**. Asian countries, in particular (e.g., China, Taiwan, Japan, and South Korea), are viewed as STO societies. Greetings and favors are reciprocated by STO cultures and typically, these countries view societal change with resistance. In addition, leisure time is important in these cultures as is the protection of one's "face" to avoid embarrassment or shame (see Table 2.1).

TABLE 2.1 Hofstede's Dimensions of Cultures

Dimension	Example
Uncertainty Avoidance	High Uncertainty: Avoidance cultures like Japan desire predictability. Low Uncertainty: Avoidance cultures like England have no problem with change.
Distribution of Power	High Power Distance: Cultures like India show respect for status and allow only a few to have power. Low Power Distance: Cultures like the USA believe that power should be equally distributed among citizens.
Femininity-Masculinity	Cultures high in Femininity like Denmark value nurturing care, quality of life, and cooperation. Cultures high in Masculinity like Italy value material success, aggressiveness, and competition.
Individualism-Collectivism	Cultures that value Individualism like Australia value the individual's accomplishments and place individual goals above group goals. Cultures that value Collectivism like Chile value the group over the individual.
Long-term-Short-term Orientation	Cultures with a Long-term Orientation like Canada are those that focus on the future. Cultures with a Short-term Orientation like South Korea focus on the past and tradition.

These five dimensions may seem rather narrow or limiting to you as you consider the diversity that pervades most cultures today. Still, this system is an important foundation to consider as we try to understand the cultural variability that exists across the globe.

Challenges and Barriers to Intercultural Communication

Handling difference with people who are similar to you can be tough; it can be even more challenging with people who look, speak, or behave differently from you. It's important for us to realize not all of our cultural encounters result in effective communication. In fact, because of the various fields of experiences (such as those of Dora and Augustina in our opening), intercultural *mis*understanding is likely to occur.

Building bridges between and among diverse individuals is essential to meaning. To avoid an uncomfortable or conflictual cultural encounter, take some time to understand the challenges and barriers to cultural understanding and communication. In this section, we identify five of the most common: ethnocentrism, stereotyping, anxiety and uncertainty, the assumption of similarity, and prejudice.

Connections: Culture and the Listening Process

Culture is an area that affects and influences every topic in communication. That's why we discuss it early in the book, and revisit the topic quite frequently throughout. Consider, then, the interplay between culture and the listening process. We already know culture can affect how we listen. Now think about the following situation in which Caroline and Gabe find themselves:

As a newcomer to the USA, 21-year-old Gabe Gutierrez was accustomed to being misunderstood. English is not his primary language and other than those who had Spanish fluency, very few people understood his pronunciation or took the time to . . . except for Caroline. While Gabe was in line asking the sales clerk at a convenience store for lottery tickets, Caroline could not help but note how rude the clerk was: "You should know English if you're going to be in this country!" the 50-something-year-old worker shouted to Gabe. Gabe clearly was having a hard time coming up with the right wording until Caroline interrupted. Caroline proceeded to tell the salesman to have more patience, and to remember that at one time in history, his family probably did not know English when they immigrated to the USA. She turned to Gabe and asked him to slowly pronounce what he wanted, including the number of tickets and the type. She repeated back his words so not to misunderstand. She was quite patient. Even though a line was forming behind them, Caroline ignored their presence. Taking time to understand the message so she could relate it to the clerk was more important.

Discuss how the listening process and culture are illustrated in this story. Identify the essence of the communication problem and explain how culture either helped or hindered. Does it make a difference what Caroline's cultural background is? Why or why not? In the future, how might Gabe approach the convenience store clerk? Should the onus of clarity fall upon Gabe? The clerk? A passerby? All of them? Should immigrants to the USA only speak English because that's the main language of the country?

Ethnocentrism

Over a century ago, sociologist William Sumner (1906) proposed that group members tend to put themselves above others in the group. Although his conclusion was soon rejected by other scholars, his original thinking remains central to intercultural communication. When we place our own beliefs above others, when we believe that the cultural group to which we belong is somehow superior to others, and/or if we view ourselves as morally above others, then we are engaged in **ethnocentrism**. Ethnocentrism derives from the Greek words *ethnos* (nation) and *kentron* (center). When we combine these terms, "nation at the center" becomes the newly formed combination. When we are ethnocentric, we fail to think about the views and life experiences of others and we are not open to their ideas or customs.

Ethnocentrism can have lasting and sometimes devastating results on relationships and upon meaning-making in our conversations. It's probably clear to many of you that ethnocentric tendencies can occur if, for example, you traveled to another country and openly criticized that country for not being similar to your own country ("Hey, guys don't hold hands," or "Bowing to someone seems weird to me," or "Why doesn't this country have food like we do?"). These sorts of claims suggest that in some way that particular culture does not measure up to the level that an ethnocentric individual may find appropriate.

Let's think about a central issue that you may not have considered before. It's a common practice around the USA and the globe to refer to those living in the United States as *Americans*. And yet, the term can be considered ethnocentric in that the USA is just one part of the Americas – there is also *South* America and *Central* America, not to mention the other North American countries of Mexico and Canada. While this issue may appear harmless, not everyone agrees. For instance, Karena Martinez-Carter (2013) contends that when the term *American* is used to describe those living in the USA, it reinforces an "imperialistic tendency" (p. 15). In her travels to such countries as Argentina, Martinez-Carter concludes that using the term is not only ethnocentric, but also problematic as expecting people to speak English around the world. As far back as the late 1940s, writers (Mencken, 1947) have been lamenting about the arrogance of calling those from the US *Americans* and ignoring the global implication of the term. So, although we don't expect everyone to stop using the word *American*, as an informed communicator you should be aware that its usage can be troubling to some. And, we do not employ the term in our text.

Being ethnocentric can affect perceptions of your credibility and impact your job effectiveness. Think about Theo Forrester, a 25-year-old sales expert who just joined Innov8Now. During a business trip to Beijing, China, Theo was invited to dinner with several of his colleagues living in China. During the dinner, Theo spoke to his Chinese work colleagues about some creative ways to save Innov8Now a lot of money. At one point, Theo said: "I've spent almost two days explaining this to you all, but I haven't heard anything about whether or not you're ready to go with my ideas. It's like I wasn't even explaining things." If Theo had investigated the nuances of doing business with his Chinese counterparts, he would have learned that US businesspeople are results-driven. In addition, they prefer action to talk. Yet, in China, mulling over the ideas and discussing them with others is important. Clearly, Theo was operating with an ethno-graphic lens because he was inappropriately applying US conversational norms to another culture.

Stereotyping

Walter Lippman (1946) coined the word *stereotype*, which he called a "picture in our head" (p. 3). Today, **stereotyping** is, in a broad sense, the process of conjuring up a fixed mental image of a particular group of people and communicating with a single person as representative of that group. Although some stereotypes may be viewed as positive (e.g. all Asians are high academic achievers), they inhibit communication because they stop us from interacting with our conversational partner as a unique individual.

Stereotypes are usually problematic because they are often untrue. For instance, if you believe that older citizens are inept, then think about a conversation with 86-year-old Warren Buffet, who served as the CEO of Berkshire Hathaway, the company that owns Geico and Dairy Queen. Further, imagine someone who believes that women cannot be effective leaders. Then, imagine introducing that person to Facebook's COO, Sheryl Sandberg. The 2016 Orlando, Florida nightclub massacre prompted a vocal outcry about Middle Eastern men. Although he was a US citizen, the shooting by a man named Omar provoked numerous assumptions that he had to be Middle Eastern and a terrorist. Such erroneous stereotypes are common following such terrible tragedies (Goren & Neter, 2016).

Stereotypes are found in nearly all professions, including entertainment ("They all get Botox!"), politics ("They're all dishonest!"), journalism ("The Media are too liberal!"), law ("Crooked and money-hungry lawyers!"), sports ("Another dumb jock!"), medicine ("Doctors don't listen to their patients!"), among many others. While many of these claims can be applied to some, they cannot and should not be applied to everyone. There are, for instance, smart sports heroes, honest politicians, and physicians who spend a great deal of time listening to their patients. It becomes problematic in our relationships with others if we communicate with people as if they are members of a group, rather than as if they are individuals.

Anxiety and Uncertainty

A third obstacle preventing cultural understanding relates to our own abilities. At times, our anxiety and uncertainty surrounding intercultural interactions may restrict our effec-tiveness. Imagine, for example, Lana, a 35-year-old suburban mom, who has only had close relationships with white people throughout her lifetime. Do you believe that she would be anxious and uncertain if she walked into work one day and found out that her new boss was Latinx? Would her supervisor's cultural identity make a difference? Should it? Would Lana rely upon a stereotype to communicate with her new boss? What role, if any, would her past play in her current situation? These and many other questions influence the extent to which Lana will be effective on the job.

Lana's challenge is not unique. Because there are few formal cultural rules in place for communicating with people with different backgrounds, many people rely upon stereotypes or simply behave awkwardly. If we are members of an in-group (a group to which a person feels he or she belongs), we may be more comfortable with another; if we are members of an out-group (a group to which a person feels he or she does not belong), then we feel anxious and uncertain as Lana does.

Our affiliation with a cultural group is related to the connections we feel we have to that group. Let's say that Jamal and Will, a couple in their 40s who were recently married, decided to invite their friend, Cara, a devout Christian, to their holiday party. Although Cara, Jamal's longtime friend, believes that the Bible does not sanction same-sex marriage, she is Jamal's friend and feels in-group affiliation. Now, suppose that Jamal and Will were introduced to Cara's husband, Kenny, who believes that the marriage between the men is not only immoral, but also against the Bible's tenets. Kenny would likely view the couple as an out-group because, unlike his wife, he doesn't have a long-term friendship that helps him feel a sense of belonging and connection to the couple. Being a member of either an in-group or out-group can influence our comfort with communicating with diverse people.

The Assumption of Similarity

Many of you may be thinking that one sure way to secure intercultural understanding is by homing in on the similarities between people. After all, you might think, when we focus on what we have in common, we can achieve meaning in a much more efficient way. Overall, this thinking *sounds* fine in theory, but in practice, assuming similarity may also result in rejecting difference. Indeed, a lesbian mom from Texas may be quite dissimilar from a lesbian mom living in Boston. And, it's true that a lesbian mom living in Dallas may be quite dissimilar from a lesbian mom living in Houston!

Assuming similarity across cultures is also problematic as you consider how others view the USA. Reddit, an entertainment and news social media platform, asked the following question to those living outside of the United States: "What aspect of the (US) culture strikes you as the strangest?" The answers below may be surprising to you if you're from the USA:

> **"Obsessed with being the 'best' country in the world"
>
> **"Cheerleaders – getting young women to dress up in short skirts to dance around and cheer on young men strikes me as odd."
>
> **"Being able to buy anything you want at Walmart – you [can] buy 24 rolls of toilet paper and a 12-gauge shot gun in the same store."

Again, while those born in the USA may take these things for granted and accept them as part of what it means to live in the USA, it's useful to realize that those from other cultures find them strange. While we can work toward common ground and develop some similarities, it's best not to assume that we're all just alike at the outset of interpersonal exchanges.

Prejudice

At the heart of **prejudice** is a loathing or vitriol toward a particular group. In a very real sense, prejudice exists in nearly all aspects of all societies (Croucher, 2017). In fact, prejudice – the fifth obstacle to intercultural understanding – can be traced all the way back to Babylonia and Egypt where hatred of Jewish people was commonplace. Stephen Eric Bronner (2014) points out that prejudice did not stop during early Greek and Roman times. It continues today. He identifies the seemingly "decent people" (p. 13) who had little or no problem accepting segregated armed forces, baseball leagues, and public establishments.

The word "prejudice" comes from the Latin roots *prae* (in advance) and *judicium* (judgment); therefore, when we are prejudiced, we are making judgments of people in advance of meeting them. In many cases, those who are not in the dominant cultural group (e.g., white, male, educated) are the targets of prejudice. Many people believe that they are not prejudiced, but their words and behaviors suggest otherwise. For example, think about Howie when he said, "I'm not racist, but … " Many wonder what could possibly justify completing the rest of that claim. Or, what about Charlotte who says "I don't have a racist bone in my body," but then goes ahead and says that she thinks that people should "speak English if they're in America." One unfortunate irony of the last claim is that people like Charlotte cannot speak a language other than English while traveling abroad. As we noted earlier, prejudicial communication can come in different forms, including those based on sexual identity, race, and age. Today, especially, because of the ongoing refugee migration in and out of nations across the globe, **xenophobia**, or the fear of those from other lands, continues to be a significant challenge for societies everywhere (see Table 2.2).

Each of the five preceding barriers is clearly an obstacle to having meaningful cultural encounters, both via face-to-face and also over social media. In fact, Facebook, Twitter, and Instagram have all seen account holders targeted with hateful messages. In addition, video game culture is fast becoming yet another opportunity for prejudicial messages to be delivered (Gonzalez, 2014).

Theoretical Insight: Co-Cultural Theory (Orbe)

This chapter is written with the understanding that culture is an essential component in human communication. In addition, we wanted to make clear that unless you try to

TABLE 2.2 Challenges to Effective Intercultural Communication

Challenge	Example
Ethnocentrism	"The US is the best! No other culture can touch us."
Stereotyping	"There's no point in talking to a police officer. All they want to do is rob us of our civil rights."
Anxiety/Uncertainty	"I better just keep quiet at this function. There's too many people from other cultures here and I'm scared I'll say something wrong."
Assumption of Similarity	"C'mon. I'm going to Italy, not Mars! People are the same. We're all human."
Prejudice	"My religion teaches me that if someone doesn't believe in Jesus, they're not saved. I can't stand people who don't accept Jesus as their savior."

understand your role in a diverse culture, meaning making is virtually unattainable. By now, you know that cultural understanding can make you a more effective communicator and enhance your sensitivity to others. But, you may not know how you function in that understanding. One theory – Co-cultural Theory – helps us to unravel the extraordinariness of diverse cultural experiences. We address the primary concepts and themes of this theory next.

Years ago, it was very common to use words like "subculture" to describe those people who had views or experiences different than those in the dominant class of people. Today, however, intercultural scholars and practitioners agree that the word no longer has relevancy and is being replaced with the word "co-culture". Let's interrogate this a bit more.

Theorist Mark Orbe (1998) advanced that words like *subculture* and *minority* are laden with negative inferences. Instead of assuming and expecting that one dominant voice exists in diverse and complex societies such as the USA, communication researchers like Orbe advocate that we "co-exist as co-cultures." At its core, Co-cultural Theory suggests that societies are hierarchical and that those at the top of the hierarchy are afforded power, privilege, and position. In most Western cultures, the rich are given opportunities that other social classes can only imagine! Co-cultural theorists propose that co-cultures – often referred to as marginalized or disenfranchised cultures – struggle to get their voices heard.

In a real sense, co-cultural communication is what takes place between the unrepresented people and those individuals in the dominant group.

Orbe believes that it's important to uncover the commonalities among these marginalized groups (e.g., African Americans, the disabled, women, gay men and lesbians, etc.) as they communicate in a dominant society. Yet, he also contends that we need to understand that each group has uniqueness and this diversity needs to be acknowledged rather than assuming that each co-culture thinks and acts alike with common visions (think back to our discussion about assuming similarity).

Moreover, Co-cultural Theory suggests that non-dominant groups usually experience mutedness, and they try to get their voices heard "to reinforce, manage, alter, and overcome a societal position that renders them outside the center of power" (Orbe, 2005, p. 65). What this means is that the marginalized "aren't gonna take it" and that they will engage in both assertive and aggressive communication so that they are not rendered silent. In fact, co-cultural theorists have borrowed from other theories such as Standpoint Theory to advance the notion that people's **standpoints** – or positions that influence their perspectives and experiences – are necessarily affected by their communication with dominant populations. Still, Melinda Weathers and Mark Hopson (2015) discovered that it's very difficult for co-cultural group members to establish close networks with those in the dominant structures.

Let's provide an example so that you can better understand this ground-breaking theory. Consider the challenges that are ahead for Aafa, a 14-year-old Muslim girl who was adopted by a family in the Midwest. The girl – an orphan at the age of 10 – spent many years in a run-down home in Syria and the bombings pretty much decimated her town and her family; Aafa is the only surviving member of her family. After a non-profit organization found a home for her in the USA, Aafa thought she would be able to start a new life in a caring community.

She was wrong. First, Aafa's English is not good; her US family helps her, but she is having a hard time grasping the basics, even with a tutor. Second, she is not used to going to school because her school was bombed when she was nine. Her mother tried to teach her at home, but the chaos and killings surrounding them simply made that impossible. So, having a school routine is something new to Aafa. Third, imagine Aafa's anxiety when she is confronted by many of her peers as she struggles to hide her Muslim background. Teenagers can be unforgiving of difference, and some verbally harass her at school. Further, think about the cultural challenges of not being able to practice her faith openly because her adoptive family prefers that she attend church with them. Clearly, Aafa's transition to the USA is not only culturally challenging, but also emotionally, physically, and psychologically difficult as well.

If co-cultural theorists tried to apply their principles to Aafa's experiences, they would explain the enormous struggles she has because of the complexities of her six standpoints: a teenager, a girl, a Muslim, a Syrian refugee, an orphan, and a non-English speaking person. In addition, co-cultural theorists would be interested in studying how the dominant group (e.g., her teen peers, the English-speaking world she is in, adoptive parents, etc.) treats her. Then, those scholars like Mark Orbe would find it important to analyze whether or not Aafa would use any assertive communication to get her voice heard. What would you recommend to Aafa as you try to understand her situation?

Enhancing Your Skills

Trying to improve your intercultural communication can be a messy process. After all, people with different fields of experiences are coming together and trying to create meaning together. Yet, it's important that we try to achieve intercultural sensitivity and there are four skills we explain below that will accomplish that. Researchers have found that those who practice these skills will have enhanced intercultural relationships (Bowe, Martin, & Manns, 2014):

- **allowing the unknown**
- **working toward commonality**
- **establishing cultural equity**
- **educating yourself**

We will also apply one skill – working toward commonality – to the workplace and in the family.

Allowing the unknown is more than tolerating someone who has a different cultural background than you. It means that you work hard toward being comfortable with having ambiguity in your interactions. Let's face it: Nearly everyone desires valuable and satisfying dialogues with others. Regardless of cultural background, most of us wish for our words to be heard and respected. Although we may be uncomfortable with various cultural practices of, say, co-workers, craftspeople, or others, allowing for cultural unknowns may be a good time to ask questions and to avoid judgments. Seeing a Romanian man kiss another man on the cheek, listening to a Christian espouse the belief that Jesus is the son of God, or reading about some Greek children who toss their discarded baby teeth on the roof of the house for good luck may all appear to be odd and perplexing. But, such diverse beliefs and practices – like, perhaps, some of you who celebrate the death of a family member by eating a big meal after a funeral – have a rich history. Understanding that these practices are all justified by cultural sanctions will go a long way toward cultural competency.

Earlier we noted that ethnocentrism is a belief that one culture is superior over another. And, we advocated abandoning this tendency, even though it may be difficult. One skill to help rid us of ethnocentric beliefs is working toward commonality within an intercultural encounter. When we seek common ground with those who are different, we not only begin cultural sensitivity, but, in turn, we may help avoid unnecessary conflicts. Think about, for instance, the possible challenges that Eric and Doc will encounter unless both work toward commonality. As a junior social work major doing an internship in a senior center, Eric was assigned different tasks, including reading the Sunday *New York Times* headlines to Doc – a 77-year-old Vietnam War veteran. As a devoted anti-war protester and founder of a progressive student club, Eric simply didn't acknowledge Doc's past nor did he ask him questions about what it was like to be on the front lines in the war. Doc had lost his best friend in the war and while he was drafted and never wanted to go, defending the country was important to him. Doc despised anti-war protests and felt that the younger generation should respect those who sacrificed.

Eric and Doc have some real opportunities to understand their very different fields of experience. They could, among other things, engage in **cultural empathy**, which is a process of learning about the cultural experiences of another and conveying that understanding responsively (Ting-Toomey & Chung, 2005). Each could question whether or not they've ever regretted anything they've said about "the other side," or openly discuss what they both think of the current wars going on around the world, or undertake a game of sorts and find articles in the paper that reflect both Eric's and Doc's points of view. The goal in establishing commonality is to avoid focusing on difference and work toward focusing on similarity. Of course, no one really expects Eric and Doc to become best friends – although these kinds of relationships have flourished. Rather, the goal is for each of them to be appreciative of the worldviews of the other. This mutual respect will likely result in less conflict and increased consideration of their cultural backgrounds as they relate to war, protest, and love of country.

A third skill recommendation for improving intercultural understanding pertains to establishing cultural equity. When we establish this sort of equity, we are not prioritizing one culture over another. Any perception of cultural priority should be avoided and instead, both intercultural communicators need to work toward the adage: "We're all in this together."

Related to cultural equity is *cultural appropriation*. Individuals who culturally appropriate use a culture's values and practices and use them in ways that are incongruent with or unintended by the original culture. Appropriation can be undertaken without others noticing or without consequence. For instance, singer Katy Perry frequently dresses in Geisha costume, seemingly unaware that such dress is akin to mocking a centuries-old Japanese form of entertainment by women. Perry also found herself the target of further criticism as she donned "black hairstyles and dance moves" in a song with backup by the rap group, Migos. As Daisy Murray (2017) ponders: "Is her dancing racially insensitive or just bad?" (p. 53).

On a less grand level, cultural appropriation takes place in many ways. Mia Mercado (2017) notes that "borrowing" from another culture is not bad. What becomes problematic is when this sort of "appreciation" becomes rooted in stereotyping or a fetishizing of another culture. Think about the everyday appropriations, including the view that one can understand a culture based upon eating a particular type of food (tacos – Mexicans), (spaghetti – Italians), and (grits – Southerners in the USA). Mercado put it succinctly when she noted that one should not cherry pick cultural elements without understanding the consequence of such ignorant behaviors.

Our final suggestion for cultural understanding is something you do each week: study. Don't be shy and commit to educating yourself about other cultures and cultural practices. Taking this course is a beginning but it is only a brief foray into an exciting and life-changing area. Nearly every job you encounter will require you to be culturally aware, and becoming informed about culture and diversity should be a lifelong practice. How can this be done? Several opportunities exist. Listen to community lectures and discussions about cultural groups. When possible, make it a point to talk with people with various cultural backgrounds. Visit Internet sites dedicated to cultural issues. Yet, like everything else online, don't believe everything written about a cultural group. Be a reflective and critical consumer of this information.

With this backdrop, we now discuss one of these skills, working toward commonality, and illustrate how it can assist you in intercultural understanding.

Applying *Working Toward Commonality* at Work

The trouble began for Jean when she came to the office and put a picture on the desk in her cubicle. It was a photograph of Jean and her bride-to-be, Julia, at Disney World and both were standing between Goofy, smiling with thumbs up! Although Jean had only been on the job for two months, she didn't give a second thought to bringing in this picture of her own family – after all, everyone else had photos on their desks. But, her co-worker, Nick, saw the photo as a potential workplace problem. He politely talked to Jean and told her that because she was new to the office, she probably didn't know that many colleagues found her impending marriage (and photo) pretty difficult to accept. Nick also told her that while he has a gay brother and had no personal prejudice, removing the photo would probably be in Jean's best interest.

Jean and Nick may have a turbulent encounter brewing, yet there are avenues to explore in order to avoid conflict. Both of them can focus on what they have in common. Jean, for instance, can remind Nick that "love is love" and that finding a life companion is important to nearly everyone. Or, she could ask Nick what it was like when he met his wife and then tell him what she felt when she met Julia. Nick, too, could practice commonality by suggesting that he has a gay brother who is dating and display a picture of his brother and his boyfriend for everyone to see.

Applying *Working Toward Commonality* in the Family

Isa's fear in bringing home Jay, her Jamaican partner of three years, was palpable. The two had met while she was waiting tables in a resort and after he asked her out, they both knew that it would be anything but fleeting. Isa, however, is white and while her mother was raised in the 1940s, she was usually pretty progressive on cultural issues. Isa warned Jay about possible communication problems, but he wasn't worried. This time, though, the cultural issue literally came home. Upon meeting Jay at the door, Isa's mom welcomed him into the house this way: "Well, we weren't expecting this to happen to our daughter, but we have no choice now, do we?" Isa became both embarrassed and enraged. She and her mother always had a good relationship but this time, she just couldn't imagine staying for dinner, let alone staying the night. No, this time Isa and her mother were about to experience a cultural clash like no other they've seen in their lives.

To avoid clashing of any kind, Isa should first sit down with Jay and her mom and talk to her mom about whether or not she ever had a friend who was not white. If so, then Isa should continue to make the point that first and foremost, Jay is a friend who happens to be Jamaican. She could also remind her mom that she fought against racial segregation as a young woman in the 1960s and that the way she's acting with Jay is not consistent with those ideals. Isa's mom, too, has a responsibility to avoid bias and talk to Jay about his feelings toward Isa. Her mom will likely find out that Jay and she both share a love, concern, and deep respect for the same person: Isa.

Communication Response: Dora Ellison and Augustina Riverton

Our opening scenario of Dora Ellison and Augustina Riverton depicted a cultural conflict that was both unexpected and challenging. After many commuter trips alone, Dora found herself speaking to someone who spoke, looked, and acted differently than nearly every other commuter on the train: Augustina. And, Augustina found a person to talk to who was very different from herself. Clearly, the two struggled in establishing intercultural understanding. After thinking about the material in the chapter, answer the following questions:

1. What barrier(s) to intercultural communication were present in the dialogue between Dora and Augustina?
2. Explain what, if any, cultural dimensions exist in their dialogue.
3. Discuss how *working toward commonality* might function in the relationship between Dora and Augustina.
4. If the two were to start over again in their conversation, what would an ideal intercultural dialogue look like?

Questions for Understanding

1. Provide the prevailing assumptions guiding the interpretation of *culture*.
2. Identify three cultural imperatives and provide an example of each.
3. What are the primary dimensions of culture?
4. List and explain the various barriers to intercultural communication.

Questions for Analysis

1. Today, many believe that characteristics such as masculinity and femininity are outdated. What is your view on this claim?
2. In several US states, hate speech is legislated and its use can result in being prosecuted. Do you believe that someone can have a deep commitment to First Amendment rights and also support the elimination of hate speech? Explain with examples.
3. Suppose you had a chance to sit and have coffee with a researcher interested in white supremacy and its pervasiveness in Western cultures. What direction would you take in the conversation? What topics, if any, would you avoid?

Suggestions for Further Reading

Mateev, A. (2017). *Intercultural competence in organizations*. New York: Springer.

Orbe, M. (1998). *Constructing co-cultural theory: explication of culture, power, and communication*. Thousand Oaks, CA: Sage.

Sandel, T. (2017). Editor's statement: Ten years of JIIC, looking back, looking ahead. *Journal of International and Intercultural Communication, 10*, 1–3.

The Intercultural Communication Institute: www.intercultural.org

3 Perception, the Self, and Communication

CHAPTER OUTLINE

CHAPTER GOALS

At the completion of this chapter, you will be able to:

- Explain the perception process and its relationship to communication.

- Discuss how culture affects the perception process.

- Recognize common biases in perception.

- Define the self and its various components.

- Explicate Attribution Theory and illustrate its utility in understanding perception.

- Demonstrate skills for effective perception.

COMMUNICATION ENCOUNTER: GRETA BRIGHAM AND JACKSON WILMONT

Greta Brigham and Jackson Wilmont found themselves laughing – once again – after math class. The two had the same goofy sense of humor. They were happy they'd met each other right at the beginning of college. They'd been inseparable ever since they were in the same group at orientation. They'd cracked up when the group leader told them about some of the famous people who'd attended their college. They noticed no one else found it funny, but they kept giggling.

Today their laughter was interrupted by Greta's cell. As she talked, Jackson saw tears streaming down her cheeks. She motioned to Jackson that she was ducking into a doorway to finish her conversation. Jackson stood on the sidewalk, wondering what was upsetting Greta so much.

When Greta returned she told Jackson that her father had had a heart attack, and she needed to get on the next plane and go home. Jackson asked if he could help in any way. Greta said she needed him to make phone calls explaining her absence to teachers, and a couple of friends she was supposed to meet over the next day or two. They sat on the curb and made the calls. Twenty minutes later, their calls were finished and they looked at each other wordlessly.

They walked quickly to Greta's apartment so she could pack. Putting her clothes in a suitcase proved too much for Greta; she broke down on the bed and sobbed. Although Jackson tried to comfort her, it was obvious that no hug was going to diminish the fear and sadness Greta was experiencing. He felt he had to say or do something but couldn't figure out what would help. Jackson sat on the bed next to Greta, patting her back and telling her he hoped things would be okay.

Among all the activities surrounding communication, perception is one of the most critical. Perception cuts across all the communication areas we mentioned in Chapter 1: intrapersonal, interpersonal, intercultural, group and team, organizational, public and rhetorical, mass or mediated, and performance studies. Because communication is the process of meaning making, it's relevant to ask: "How do we use perceptions to attach meaning to our own and others' behaviors?"

Our focus in this chapter is on perception in interpersonal interactions, although perception functions in many of the other areas of communication as well – think about how you form opinions about political leaders, bosses, or anonymous commenters on the internet. Or consider how you perceive information (and entertainment) you receive from media. Perceiving a performer, like Taylor Swift for example, as petty and self-centered affects your reception of her messages. Alternatively, perceiving Swift as brave and talented provides a different reception.

In encounters with others, we have impressions of them, the situation, and our self-impressions. We might check these perceptions against the opinions of others. For instance, think about what you'd do if you wanted to challenge your boss about a poor performance evaluation you just received:

- Would you note the boss's eye contact and body language, your own behaviors (e.g., vocal nervousness, fidgeting, etc.), or your overall gut feeling upon entering the boss's office?
- Would you ask other employees about their experiences with the boss and challenges they might have made?
- Would you mentally rehearse your comments before going into the office?
- Would you reflect on your prior interactions with the boss?

Doing any or all of these things engages your perceptual processes. Yet, perceiving involves more than simply hearing or seeing. Perception is an active and challenging process.

Background

It's important to understand perception because of its impact on communication behaviors. To begin, we provide definitions for several critical terms. Next, we examine some cultural influences on the perceptual process.

The Process of Perception

We define **perception** as a social process using the five senses – visual, auditory, tactile, gustatory, and olfactory – to assign meaning and respond to stimuli in our environment. The perception process happens in four stages:

- selecting and attending
- organizing
- interpreting
- retrieving.

Selecting and Attending

On an average day, we are bombarded with stimuli. Stop for a minute and think about your surroundings and what you're seeing and hearing right now. You may be in your room reading this chapter for tomorrow's class. There may be the whine of a siren outside or the sound of car horns in the distance; you might hear your roommate talking on the phone, and there may be music playing in the room. Or, you may be reading in a coffee shop, where people are milling around you, chatting or yelling and giving their coffee orders to the clerk. You may choose to ignore most of these stimuli, while you concentrate on reading. This is known as **selective attention**, or attending to some things while ignoring others.

Selective attention involves stimuli passing through a filtering system consisting of our moods, environment, and needs. Some stimuli are filtered out, and others are let in for you to focus on. Consider, for instance, what happens when you take notes in class. You may be in a large classroom, with books and laptops opening and closing, classmates whispering, doors banging, your own thoughts about another issue intruding, and lights buzzing above. Yet, you manage to attend selectively to the lecture. You do this, in part, because you attend to things that fulfill your needs. Knowing the subject matter and getting an "A" may be quite important to you, and you came to college expecting to work hard in your classes. These goals allow you to *select* the lecture as the most important stimulus of all those occurring in the classroom.

In our opening Communication Encounter, Greta undoubtedly screened out all other stimuli while she spoke on her cell and simply attended to what she was hearing about her father. When Jackson sat in Greta's room, he probably didn't notice the décor because he was concentrating on Greta. During the selection stage, we choose which details we'll focus on and which to ignore.

To get a more concrete understanding of how selective attention affects our communication with others, suppose that Henry, a technology assistant (TA), was asked to see his boss, Sherry. In her office, Henry hears Sherry talk about the need for the company to reduce costs. Immediately, he thinks he's going to be laid off. As Sherry talks about the daily costs of having TAs in the company, Henry listens for information regarding his employment. He watches Sherry's eye contact and listens to the tone of her voice. As a result, he ignores other information, such as Sherry's discussion of the costs of running the company and the aggregate salary for the TAs. He chooses to ignore many other stimuli in the conversation – the phone ringing, the details about the company's finances, and so on. He's focusing only on anything Sherry does that will tell him whether or not he is about to lose his job.

Organizing

Once we've selected the stimuli to attend to, we need to organize them in some way. The second stage of the perception process, **organizing**, refers to placing potentially confusing pieces of stimuli into an understandable, accessible, and orderly pattern. For example, imagine you're having dinner at a restaurant, and you glance over at the table next to yours and see an older woman and man with a younger woman. Your perceptional processes kick in and you organize the group as a mother, father, and their daughter. You may be incorrect in this assumption, they might be three unrelated people who are attending a conference together, but organizing is an important shortcut we take when we perceive stimuli.

When we organize, we may use a **schema**, or a mental framework or memory structure that people rely on to understand their experiences (Batanova & Loukas, 2014). Schemata come into play during the perception process insofar as they allow us to recognize consistencies. It would be too effortful to communicate with each person we meet in completely unique and individual ways. So, we seek out familiar classifications: college students, children, families, and so forth, to save on cognitive effort and make the communication process move faster.

Schemata are helpful in allowing us to see similarities within groups, but not so useful in focusing on differences. For example, the category "college students" is diverse: there are college students who study hard and those who slack off, some who are younger than average and others who are older, and some who pay for their own education and others who rely on relatives to pay their tuition. Using the general category "college students" doesn't allow us to see all this diversity. What do you think changes when you're talking to a student who's juggling three jobs to pay for tuition compared to conversing with a student whose parents are paying the tuition?

Organizing is critical for facilitating the perception process. However, we need to avoid automatically lumping people into easily recognizable categories, such as police, plumbers, young people, and then imposing the qualities we've assigned to the category to all those we've placed within it. As we discussed in Chapter 2, when we have a fixed mental impression or assessment of a group, we are stereotyping. Although not all stereotypes are negative (e.g. "students are motivated to learn"), stereotyping is problematic. We must be aware of the dilemma inherent to organizing our perceptions: it's necessary to the perception process, but it can promote problems like over-generalizing and lead us to erroneous perceptions.

Interpreting

After we have selected and organized stimuli, we then engage in the third stage of the process: interpreting. When we're **interpreting**, we assign meaning to our perceptions. Once we have organized a group of people as a family, for instance, we use interpretation to decide that the family seems to be happy and well adjusted. We need to have interpretation to achieve meaning, which is the goal of the perception process. Yet, it's not always easy to decide what a particular communication encounter means. How do you respond, for instance, to a partner who tells you how much your relationship means to them, but seems to spend all their time at work? Or, what about a politician who speaks about compassion for all, but votes to cut back on social programs that benefit those below the poverty line? How do you interpret their behaviors relative to their words?

A particular type of schema, called a **relational schema** (Batanova & Loukas, 2014), influences interpretation. Relational schemata provide us with frames that guide our expectations and understanding of relationships. So, we classify relationships into categories such as BFFs, acquaintances, romances, or friends. These schemata help us to know what type of communication to use in a specific relationship and help us to interpret the communication of others in the relationship (Schrodt, 2016). Thus, your relational schemata help you to decide how to interpret the interactions of a partner who says "I love you," but never finds time to be with you.

Finally, the process of interpreting relies on our relational history with another person. Relational history pertains to past relationship experiences you've had with another person. There's a difference, for instance, between communicating with someone who has been your co-worker for 15 years and with someone who just got hired. It's likely that the 15-year relationship has included both good and bad times and this shared history has given the two of you the ability to communicate in unique ways. For instance, sometimes co-workers may use abbreviated language after working together for some time (Langan-Fox, Code, Gray, & Lanfield-Smith, 2002). If a long-time co-worker tells you "the boss looks like she did after the Baker contract," you know your colleague may be warning you to stay out of the boss's way for a while. If a new co-worker heard this comment, they wouldn't know exactly how to interpret it.

Retrieving

The final stage in the perception process is called retrieving. When we're **retrieving**, we recall information stored in our memories. Retrieving may seem rather simple, but the process is anything but easy. We may have **selective retrieval**, which means remembering information that agrees with our perceptions and selectively "forgetting" information that does not. Erin may recall, for instance, her conversation with her painter, Curt, about how much painting her dining room will cost. She may have selectively forgotten, however, the fact that the quote was only for one coat of paint. When it turns out that the job requires two coats, Erin becomes angry and believes that Curt's taking advantage of her.

Because recalling is not an easy undertaking, we need to remind ourselves of the various influences on our ability to retrieve, including age, physical ability, and mental preparedness. John Gunstad and his colleagues (2006) suggest that as we get older, our ability to remember things may gradually decrease. Similarly, very young people may not have honed their recalling abilities yet, and they may not recall information accurately. As a result, age can be influential in the retrieval process. In addition to age, we may not be physically prepared to recall information. That is, we have some physical reason that prevents thorough and accurate recall. Whether it's a migraine headache, hunger pangs, or something more serious such as a head injury, our physical condition can affect the extent to which we are able to recall.

Further, retrieving is also influenced by our mental preparedness. Are we distracted at the time of retrieval? Do we have biases or prejudices that influence our ability to remember information? If Emily believes that only college graduates have credibility on the job, will she be able to retrieve information that she heard from a co-worker who has only a high school diploma?

Everyday Talk: Perceptions of Health

In 2012, the website psychologicalscience.org reported on research by Keith Petrie and John Weinman (www.psychologicalscience.org/index.php/news/releases/mind-over-matter-patients-perceptions-of-illness-make-a-difference.html) who found that when people are ill, how they perceive their illness has a direct relationship to many important health outcomes. The researchers recount how people perceive illness could be more important to health outcomes than the actual severity of the disease. This is probably the case, note the authors, because if people don't think that a prescription is making them better, they'll probably discontinue using it even if a doctor tells them not to. Petrie is quoted on the site as saying that if a doctor doesn't take a patient's perceptions into account then treatment is likely to fail. The article concludes by arguing that doctors should talk to their patients about how they view their illness. Once physicians understand patients' illness perceptions, they can have a productive conversation that may result in better health outcomes.

1. How do you perceive your health?
2. Many people rely on doctors to assess their health and well-being. Do you believe that physicians know best? Why or why not?
3. How do you think patients and doctors can learn to have this type of conversation about patients' illness perceptions?

As we mentioned earlier, we're discussing the perception process primarily with reference to everyday encounters with others, although there are perceptual issues going on while we watch a public speaker, enjoy a movie, or chat or text online. Becoming aware and understanding the complexity of the perception process – as outlined above – will help you in your relationships with others and in understanding yourself. See Figure 3.1 for an illustration of the perception process.

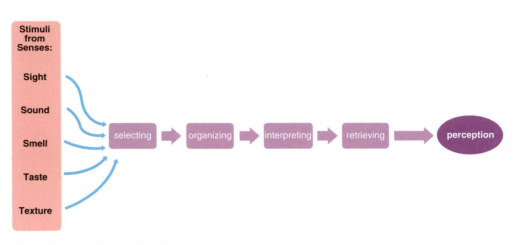

Figure 3.1 The Perception Process

Influences on Perception

Throughout this chapter we're emphasizing how important perceptions are to the communication process. One reason we have difficulties communicating with others results from differences among people – that is, we all perceive from our own particular vantage points. Individual differences create differing perceptions of the world and social situations. Of course, that is what makes things interesting; we certainly wouldn't like to have everyone be alike and perceive things in exactly the same ways. Yet, individual differences may stand in the way of achieving co-created meaning and thus impede communication. We want to be able to understand each other even when we do not necessarily agree with one another.

As we discuss the ways culture, especially sex and gender, affect perception, we need to remember that not all members of a given culture (or sex) behave or see the world in the same way. There can be vast differences within groups (all men don't love football and all women don't feel at home in the kitchen, for instance). Yet, some similarities do exist within groups, and we'll focus on how these similarities impact perceptions.

Culture is a complicated term; as we stated in Chapter 2, it refers to a learned system of life experiences of a group who have a common set of values, beliefs, norms, and traditions. Culture is transmitted through language, food, rituals, art, and other activities that are passed from one generation to the next. As you can tell from this general definition, culture is multi-leveled – national (we can refer to US or Chinese culture, for example), local (culture may differ by region so that "the South" in the USA has its own cultural norms, for instance), family (a particular family has its own way of doing things, and it can be said to develop a specific family culture), and so forth. Further, cultures may be created around a variety of things people hold in common that are highlighted in their society: age, sex/gender, spirituality, and so forth. Finally, culture is inherently related to communication. As Michael Hecht, Mary Jane Collier, and Sidney Ribeau (1993) state, "all communication exists in a cultural context and all culture is communicated" (p. 1). In particular, with regard to perception, culture provides meanings for behaviors and gives us instruction in how to organize stimuli.

For instance, in the USA, time is an important concept and we're conditioned to be on time for meetings and classes. How long do you sit in a classroom to wait for a professor who's late? What do you think of another student who's consistently late for the group meetings? What's your perception of a person who is late for a job interview? In the USA, we have a negative impression of these people and we tend to believe this is the "natural" way to think about time. However, there are some countries, such as Italy, Spain, and the Middle East, where time and being "on time" have other meanings. In these cultures the passing of clock time is secondary to human interaction. If completing an interesting conversation with someone means that you linger and are "late" to another appointment, then so be it.

In 2015, a successful cosmetic dentist from the USA, Dr. Michael Apa, opened an office in Dubai. He observed that he had to get used to cultural differences concerning time. Dr. Apa explained that the Arabic word *"inshallah,"* meaning "God willing," is used a great deal in Dubai. This affects time because patients will say they have an 11:00 AM appointment, *inshallah.* This means that they might arrive for the appointment at 3:00 PM. Dr. Apa has learned this is not disrespectful, it's simply a cultural difference. It does require that he recalibrate his own inclinations about time, however, as people in Dubai are more flexible when it comes to schedules, appointments, and even payments than he has learned to be in the United States (Sile, 2016).

Further, cultures also vary in terms of how many things should be done at one time. The United States is considered a **monochronic culture**, which means that value is placed on time commitments and doing one thing at a time. Despite the concept of multi-tasking, most people in the USA would find it distracting if they were called into the boss's office and found the boss talking on the phone and doing paperwork at the same time they were supposed to be meeting together. Polychronic cultures are the opposite. Latin America, the Arab world, and sub-Saharan Africa tend to have **polychronic cultures**, where many things are expected to take place at once. In polychronic cultures, things like family time and work time are not separated the way they are in monochronic cultures.

These cultural distinctions are generalizations, of course, and are a matter of degree. When people of different cultures communicate, however, these differences in priorities and differing perceptions can cause misunderstandings and a lack of shared meanings. It's difficult to imagine that someone doesn't perceive time, for instance, in the same way you do.

As we've mentioned, sex and gender are components of culture, so we turn to a discussion of how they affect perception next. First, however, it's necessary to differentiate between sex and gender. Historically, researchers have conceptualized sex as a biological category with two levels (male and female). Gender was defined as the behaviors that a given society prescribed for females and males (femininity and masculinity). Thus, sex was believed to be an enduring aspect of a person, whereas gender was learned and more fluid (i.e. a person could be biologically male, but be nurturing and empathic). Transgender individuals challenge the enduring nature of biology and the "fit" between how one feels and the biological category assigned, as well as the utility of constructing only two dichotomous categories for sex and gender.

Language such as **cisgender**, meaning being consistent among sex, gender, and sexual/affectional identity (i.e. a biological male who's masculine and heterosexual) reflects the idea that this alignment is *only one* way to organize sex, gender, and sexual/affectional preferences. However, it's still true that gender refers to learned, socially sanctioned behaviors. It's important to realize that these gendered behaviors are subject to change, so what we see as masculinity in contemporary society is different than what people believed a generation earlier, for example.

Some research we'll review examines the effects of sex, as a biological category, on perception. Other studies focus on how gendered expectations affect perceptions. In the future, we should expect to see studies linking perceptions to being transgender, for instance. This will be an exciting new area of research.

One study focused on sex interrogated college students' perceptions of rape (Vandiver & Dupalo, 2013). The researchers found that male students were more likely than female students to perceive there was no rape when the scenario presented to them was ambiguous. A study examining gendered expectations (Franzoi & Klaiber, 2007) shows college-aged women are more likely to compare themselves with professional models in terms of physical appearance than are college-aged men. You can imagine that such comparisons have an impact on self-perceptions. As a way to counteract the potential for negative self-perceptions, some celebrities have posted Instagram or Twitter pictures of themselves without cosmetics or styling. There is a YouTube video (www.youtube.com/watch?v = VwkWu9ftKWM) showing 50 celebrities ranging from Oprah to Kendall Jenner to Lady Gaga. Pictures of them without any make up are shown next to pictures of them completely made up with styled hair. The video is titled "The Power of Make-Up."

One study examined the overlap between sex and gender. Raina Brands, Jochon Menges, and Martin Kilduff (2015) found that in teams where the leader role had the most authority in the group, women were perceived as less charismatic leaders than men. However, when the team adopted a shared leadership structure, women leaders were judged as more charismatic than men leaders.

The relationship between culture and perception is a complex one, but it is safe to say that all aspects of culture have an impact on how individuals see others as well as themselves. Further, people's culture provides some evidence that others use to guide their observations about them.

> ### Connections: Perception, Nonverbal Communication, and Culture
>
> When thinking about perception, it is important to remember that it's a process related to all the other concepts discussed in this text. Reflect on how nonverbal communication and cultural practices make an impact on perceptions in the following scenario:
>
> *Brad works in a company that has recently hired a manager, who is now Brad's supervisor. The new manager is from Thailand, and was hired because Brad's company is interested in increasing its reach in the Asian market. Brad hasn't really gotten to know Mr. Aromdee too well, but he was concerned when he attended a meeting shortly before the holidays and Mr. Aromdee mentioned he wanted to send New Year's gifts to all the customers. He went on to list individual gifts he'd selected specifically for each of their 20 biggest clients. Brad knew that the company had a policy against giving individualized gifts; if they gave gifts at all, they would buy something in bulk and everyone would get the same thing. In Thailand, however, this type of individualized gift giving was seen as a gesture of respect and was expected. How is Brad to respond? How should these differing nonverbal cultural practices be balanced? Should the manager conform to US business practices? Should Brad explain how the company usually does this? Should the company change and embrace Thai practices? Is there some type of middle ground?*
>
> How does this scenario illustrate the connections among nonverbal communication, perception, and cultural practices?

Fundamental Issues

Researchers have discussed several issues impacting perception and communication. Here we discuss two: biases and the self.

Biases Affecting Perception

It would be nice if our perceptions were always accurate and always resulted in more meaningful communication experiences. Of course, we know this isn't the case and if it were, there would be no reason for this chapter! Most of us encounter obstacles that bias the perception process. Here, we identify four biases, and explain how our perceptual practices are affected by each. We also offer suggestions for managing these biases.

Homogeneity Bias

No matter how hard we try not to, we often assume that people are similar to us. This bias, called **homogeneity**, stretches from assuming that others talk as we do to assuming they hold values similar to ours. When you assume homogeneity, you forfeit the uniqueness of the communication encounter. Assuming homogeneity may also prompt some uncomfortable moments with others. For instance, imagine you were asked to give a toast at your friend's wedding. As a member of the wedding party and a friend of both the bride and groom, you may have thought some good-natured ribbing would make them laugh. But, assuming that everyone shares your sense of humor may be problematic in front of wedding guests. In fact, your jokes and personal anecdotes may cause the wedding guests to feel awkward and uncomfortable, and the wedding couple may, in turn, be embarrassed.

Or suppose that Franklin was designated by his co-workers to go to their supervisor and ask for a day each week when the employees can dress casually during the summer months. Dressing less formally, they felt, would make them more comfortable, thereby increasing their productivity. The group wanted Franklin to be their spokesperson because he had the most seniority on the job. Franklin's demeanor with the boss, however, proved problematic. He communicated with his supervisor with the same style he maintained with his work colleagues. Franklin was blunt and sarcastic. The boss found Franklin's communication immature and lacking deference. Consequently, Franklin's request was rejected.

Believing in homogeneity may not always result in embarrassment or a failure to gain job privileges. But, it does raise the issue that when we believe that others have similar views, similar communication styles, similar feelings, and similar values to our own, problems can ensue. Avoiding the assumption of homogeneity and discovering the uniqueness of another is not that difficult. Reflect on your "audience." Are you speaking to someone you know well? Hardly know? Is there a possibility that what you say can be misunderstood? Can you check your perceptions with another? Remember to use caution in your word choices (especially when using humor) and think through the consequences of what you say before you say it. Certainly, there are times when others are similar to us, and telling "inside" jokes or sharing personal stories is appropriate, and increases satisfaction with the relationship. Yet, many times, assuming similarity prevents you from being effective in your conversations with others.

Negativity Bias

Research shows that we tend to give more credence to bad information than to good (Rosin & Royzman, 2001). This is called the **negativity bias**. Imagine you are in a class where the grade is determined by ten different small assignments. Perhaps you have received positive feedback on all of them. In particular, the professor praised your original thinking, your creative use of the sources, and your ability to organize the papers well. Yet, the professor also mentioned on one of the assignments that you'd misinterpreted a source and the ideas you were attributing to that source were incorrect. The negativity bias suggests that as you reflect on the professor's comments, you'll focus on the one negative statement and push all the praise you've received to the background. It may not make a difference to you what positive characteristics or qualities the professor noted; chances are, you'll attend most to the one negative comment, and feel badly about your performance in the class.

Why we believe negative perceptions over positive perceptions is an intriguing question. The media may play a role in this perceptual error. After all, most of the news stories we read, see, and hear are negative (e.g., terrorism, murder, kidnappings, etc.). Further, exposure to such negative mediated images may have resulted in a more cynical population. Many people have grown tired of societal institutions, including politics, entertainment, business, and even religion. This lack of trust has found its way into our everyday conversations and relationships. How many times, for instance, have you heard "all politicians are crooked", "the media report fake news!", or "all big corporations want to do is make money at our expense!"? Some people attributed the success of Donald Trump and Bernie Sanders in the US primaries of 2016, and Trump's eventual election as president of the United States, to this cynicism and distrust of traditional social institutions. It's difficult for our interactions to remain inoculated from these negative perceptions and for us to "think positive."

Trying to rid yourself of negativity requires you to see the proverbial "silver lining." We surely should not ignore our own or others' negative qualities, but we need to place those in context. We cannot and should not solely focus on the negative. We need to engage in positive self-talk emphasizing the relative nature of the bad compared to the good in our self-evaluations and our evaluations of others.

Simplicity Bias

The fact that people communicate all the time is not news, but it does surprise communication professionals that many people think communication is both simple and easy, which is known as the **simplicity bias**. We live in a society that views communication as the panacea for all our challenges. Yet, we also live in a society that spends little time – other than in communication classes – teaching us how to communicate effectively. Being an effective communicator is not simple or easy. Believing that people can express themselves thoughtfully and listen effectively without education in these practices is naïve, and can result in erroneous perceptions.

Even the most skillful and visible celebrities and philanthropists experience communication challenges. For instance, Oprah Winfrey has articulated her vision to increase literacy via her online Book Club. However, she soon found that while celebrity endorsements increase book sales, they don't increase people's reading behaviors. This is probably the case because celebrity book clubs don't show their members *how* to read (Fay, 2012). Winfrey learned from her first experience and created online Book Club 2.0, making an effort to be more interactive. While this is helpful, Winfrey will still be struggling with the problem for a long time (Fay). The Bill and Melinda Gates Foundation has many causes, one of which is to eradicate polio. Their website notes (www.gatesfoundation.org) that it is critical "to tailor communications to particular social, cultural, and political contexts ... " Thus, they acknowledge the communication principles that the same message won't work with different populations and persuasion requires skill, flexibility, and sensitivity.

We can avoid the simplicity bias by understanding that communication is not something natural like breathing; the process is complex and needs to be practiced and refined. We therefore should take into consideration that all people need to work at communication skills, and even skilled communicators are not successful at all times. Recognizing the work that goes into effective communication will make a difference in how you view others' words and actions, as well as how you develop your own.

Self-Serving Bias

Somewhat contrary to the negativity bias, we may also have a bias that leads us to believe others are responsible for problems, and we're responsible for what goes right. When we view information in a way that places us in a favorable light, we are engaging in the **self-serving bias** (MacDonald & Standing, 2002). This bias leads us to be more inclined to take credit for successes and deny involvement in failures relating to our activities and interactions with others. The self-serving bias interferes with message accuracy. If we think we are immune from responsibility for problems, or we evaluate ourselves more favorably than others in an interaction we may trigger defense mechanisms in those with whom we interact.

Suppose that Avery has been asked to lead a small group at work whose task is to establish a new company logo and different branding. After several meetings Avery notices that a group member named Anna is uncooperative and challenges everything Avery says. Anna believes that Avery's communication is vague and that she's not providing adequate leadership. After a meeting they have the following conversation:

AVERY: So, Anna .... I'm not sure what the problem is here, but we're not working well together.

ANNA: I don't get it. You were asked to take charge of this group and you can't seem to get us beyond basic stuff.

AVERY: Well, you may be one reason for that.

ANNA: What does that mean? You're in charge, not me!

AVERY: Yeah, but a leader is only as good as her group members. And, all you do is complain about what's happening. You don't listen, and there are obviously some problems with you being clear about your ideas.

ANNA: We're not going to meet the deadline. At. All.

AVERY: Listen, I've done everything I can to get this group moving. If we don't meet the deadline, that's not my fault. I've been sensitive to your childcare issues and meeting conflicts. And, it hasn't been easy. And whatever we've accomplished, it's really because I've pushed us to that point. I don't get a lot of support from you though.

ANNA: Oh yeah, like I've been just sitting around doing nothing since we started! Look! We go nowhere because you can't lead the group.

In this interaction, both Avery and Anna use the self-serving bias. Avery communicates to Anna that the real reason why the group hasn't been productive is because of group members and their "issues" (e.g. child care and meeting conflicts). Avery promotes her own self-worth by suggesting that *she* is the reason why the group has accomplished any work at all. Anna counters that Avery is a poor leader and that's why the group's not accomplishing much. The self-serving bias has prompted both to be defensive. They put all the blame for the group's lack of productivity on the other without recognizing their own role in the problem.

In sum, Avery and Anna's distorted perceptions prevent each of them from accepting any responsibility for the group's lack of progress. To control for such a self-serving bias, they both should be more receptive to their own faults and embrace accountability as part of the group. They need to listen carefully to the other's points. Both should think about ways to improve their own behaviors, rather than focusing only on how the other person should change.

These four perceptual biases suggest that we need to be cautious about our perceptions. We must be cognizant of the ways that biases distort them. Being an effective communicator requires us to test our thinking and check our perceptions so that we can reduce the negative effects of bias. We return to this idea at the end of the chapter.

The Self and Impression Management

As we've discussed the perception process so far, you've probably noticed that it's difficult to separate our sense of self from perception. Underlying most of what we've been discussing relative to perception is the notion of **self-concept**, or the relatively stable set of perceptions we hold about ourselves. A person's self-concept reflects their core beliefs about their abilities, intellect, and other characteristics. Although the self-concept is fairly stable, as we grow and age certain aspects do change. When Marty became established in his career, his confidence in his ability to manage personnel grew, for instance. When Wes was 25 years old, he thought of himself as able to meet any athletic challenge that came his way. When he was 45, Wes tore his Achilles tendon playing basketball, and he began to revise his estimation of his athletic abilities.

Our self-concept can be broken down into two parts: self-image and self-esteem. **Self-image** is composed of the roles that we play in life. When James thinks about himself he sees that he's a son, a husband, a father, a part-time student, an employee in a real estate firm, and a friend to many. James's **self-esteem** consists of how he evaluates his performance in those roles. He may think he's a helpful son, a neglectful husband, a loving father, an average student, an adequate employee, and a loyal friend. James's self-esteem is shaped by his intrinsic self-judgments as well as by the feedback he receives from others. When James's wife berates him for putting his parents, job, and friends before her, James begins to evaluate himself as a neglectful husband. Self-esteem is flexible, however, and if James and his wife manage their time better, go to counseling, or set aside one night a week for "date night", James will probably change his evaluation. How do you reflect on your own self-image and self-esteem? Do you see those as distinct parts of your self-concept?

Some research focuses on how technology affects a person's sense of self. Jill Walker Rettberg (2014) writes "self-representation with digital technologies [such as blogs, selfies, digital counters] is also self-documentation. We think not only about how to present ourselves to others, but also log or record moments for ourselves to remember them in the future" (p. 11). Rettberg notes that digital technologies enable us to communicate with others while simultaneously reflecting on ourselves, in a more systematic way than earlier communication media, such as self-portraits or diaries, allowed. Think about how you present yourself on social media. Are there differences in the way you do this across different platforms? For instance, LinkedIn is a professional network so if you're on that, you probably present yourself differently than you do on the less formal platform of Instagram.

When people post a lot on Facebook, Instagram, Twitter, Snapchat and have many followers they become what Alice Marwick (2013) calls "micro-celebrities". But, as Marwick notes, this can be problematic for regular people who do not have PR consultants or agents to protect them from negative press that could damage their self-concepts. Katie Rogers (2016) writes about this problem in the *New York Times* when she addresses the debate about the nude selfie Kim Kardashian West posted on Twitter with the caption "When you're like I have nothing to wear LOL". In her article, Rogers speculates about whether controlling your image online (i.e. you are the one who poses yourself and chooses to post) is liberating or exploitative. She concludes that for Kardashian West,

Figure 3.2 How are these Young Women Managing the Impressions they're Recording in this Selfie?

posting on social media is working, and she has managed to become very wealthy doing so. But Rogers argues that's not the case for girls growing up in small towns where everyone who sees their picture knows them personally, and may write or talk about them in negative ways after seeing it.

At the core of this discussion about the self is the idea of impression or identity management (Imahori & Cupach, 2005). **Impression management** is a term we've borrowed from social psychology referring to the attempts we make, consciously or unconsciously, to influence others' perceptions of us. It is often thought to be synonymous with the term self-presentation. The sociologist Erving Goffman (1959) wrote about impression management using a theatre metaphor in his famous book, *The Presentation of Self in Everyday Life.* Goffman asserted that we're all playing characters in a performance for others, and we wish to make certain impressions on the "audiences" as we perform our roles (see Figure 3.2).

Some researchers (e.g., Brown & Levinson, 1987) refer to this as **face**, or the public self that we present to others. Maintaining our public self is something that we cannot do ourselves; others must cooperate with us to do this. This transactional task of maintaining our public self is called **facework** (Samp, 2015), and requires us to act in cooperation with others to preserve two types of face: positive and negative. When we wish another to like us, and they express that they do, the two of us are maintaining **positive face**, or our ability to think highly of our competence in the social encounter. If we approached a friend and that friend ignored us, that act would threaten positive face.

Negative face is not about feeling badly about our competence, but rather about feeling free to act as we wish. Negative face is threatened by a friend who continually imposes, and pressures you to do things that you don't want to do. Usually people cooperate to "save" each others' faces in conversation, as in the following dialogues illustrating first, maintaining positive face (thinking positively about our social competence) and second, maintaining negative face (feeling free to act as we wish):

Positive Facework

Roxie: I am pretty sure I embarrassed myself with Jon last night. I know I had too many and I don't think he knew what to make of me. I think I kept saying that 'I need an album' when I meant an aspirin.

Nan: Don't worry about it, Rox, I was there and you were fine. Yeah, I heard you say that about the album, but Alissa told Jon that was a private joke, and everyone still had fun.

Roxie: That's a relief.

Negative Facework

Bethany: Jessica, you really need to clean up our apartment. You've made a mess, and it's gotta get cleaned up.

Jessica: Yeah, I'm pretty busy now. I'll have to get to it tomorrow.

Bethany: O.K. I guess it can wait till then. I know you're busy.

The use of social media has prompted researchers to examine how people maintain face when conversations are not conducted face-to-face. Gina Chen (2015) found that Facebook users retaliated aggressively when they felt their face was threatened. People sent "virtual ticking bombs" to others who had excluded them from a group or who had criticized them when they were in the group. In addition, others have examined self-presentation online and found people are rather deliberate in the way they present themselves online from their choice of screen names (Bechar-Israeli, 1996) to the construction of personal home pages (Campbell, 2014). Further, Catalina Toma and Mina Choi (2015) found that the ways people presented themselves on Facebook relative to a relational partner (for instance, listing themselves as "in a relationship," or posting pictures of themselves and their partner together, and writing privately on the partner's wall), correlated with increased commitment toward the relationship and the likelihood of staying together over time.

Do the Right Thing: Deception Online

Your friend, Ashley, has just told you that she's created a profile for herself on Match.com and she's excited to see what kinds of responses she gets. You know that Ashley's been unhappy since she broke up with her long-term boyfriend, Matt, and she hasn't been able to find anyone else, so you're happy your friend is being proactive. Then Ashley emails you the profile she just posted. You want to be supportive, but you're quite surprised to discover that Ashley has shaved about 20 pounds off what you know she weighs, and has made herself a bit taller and younger than she is. You also notice that she says she loves to hike and be outdoors, when you know she hates outdoor activities. She's listed a few books that she claims to have read recently, and you're pretty sure she's never read any of them. You hope that Ashley can find someone she'll be happy with, but you can't see how that'll happen when she's being so deceptive in her profile. In addition, you are concerned that Ashley's sense of self is such that she feels she has to lie to attract someone. You didn't say anything after reading the profile, but you're going to see Ashley next week. What do you do?

1. If you used the categorical imperative as your ethical system, how would you proceed?
2. If you used utilitarianism as your ethical system, how would you proceed?
3. If you used the ethic of care as your ethical system, how would you proceed?
4. Specifically, if you had to write out a script for your conversation with Ashley, what would you say to her?

Theoretical Insight: Attribution Theory (Kelley)

Many theories address how the self and communication interact. Here we review one specific theory: Harold Kelley's (1967) Attribution Theory. In the beginning of this chapter we noted that the perception process underlies all our communication with others, and as we communicate, we're often asking ourselves about the meaning of our own and others' behaviors ("OMG, why did I just say that?" "What's wrong with her? She keeps interrupting me!"). Attribution Theory addresses the question of how we use perception to answer these questions and make meaning. Kelley's version of Attribution Theory drew on some themes developed by Fritz Heider (1958). Heider talked about three important areas that inform Kelley's work: naïve psychologists, internal attributions, and external attributions.

   Heider used the term **naïve psychologist** to express his belief that people try to make sense of their social interactions, sort of like researchers search for explanations for the questions they pose in their studies. People also search for explanations and use their observations to form them. Clearly, this is a simplified version of the social scientific process, and not as rigorous as what researchers undertake. It's simpler because naïve psychologists are usually satisfied with the first explanation that makes sense to them without doing extensive testing like researchers would ("O.K, I guess she interrupts so much because she's self-centered"). Deciding that a friend is self-centered as an explanation for their behaviors illustrates making an **internal attribution**, or an explanation rooted in personality traits. Heider said we're likely to attribute the causes of others' behaviors in this way. On the other hand, an explanation such as "I probably just said that because I'm feeling so pressured right now" exemplifies an **external attribution**, or a cause for behavior that's outside a person's control. Heider argued the **fundamental attribution error** occurs when we attribute the cause for our behaviors to external factors and the cause for others' behaviors to internal traits. This fits in with the self-serving bias we described previously.

Many theorists expanded on Heider's ideas, but we're focusing on the most popular theory: Harold Kelley's (1967) **Covariation Model of Attribution**. Kelley called his model the "covariation model" because he believed when a person has information from many sources at different times and in varied situations ("I've seen Hannah interrupt me at work, she interrupted Todd at the game, and she interrupted Olivia when we all went for drinks after work"), then they can observe the ways that the information covaries, or works together.

Kelley agreed with Heider that in trying to discover causes for behavior, people act like scientists. More specifically they take into account three kinds of evidence: **consensus**, or the degree to which other people behave in the same way in similar situations (maybe everyone interrupts at a football game because they're excited and all yelling at once); **distinctiveness**, or whether the individual behaves the same way across situations (maybe Hannah interrupts all the time); and **consistency**, or how likely it is that an individual does the same thing across time (maybe Hannah only interrupts every time the Packers play).

Kelley believed that each of these types of evidence (consensus, distinctiveness, and consistency) can be measured as either high or low. For instance, if everyone interrupts at a football game, Hannah's interrupting behavior is high in consensus, but if only Hannah is interrupting then her behavior is low in consensus. If Hannah always interrupts when she's at a football game, her behavior is low in distinctiveness. Finally, if Hannah always interrupts when the Packers play but not when other teams do, then her behavior is high in consistency. The model predicts when consensus, distinctiveness, and consistency are all high we'll make an external attribution. So, in the example above if everyone else is interrupting, Hannah only interrupted when the Packers play, and she does that consistently, we'd make the attribution that she interrupts because of something external (like the excitement of the game and the skill of the Packers football team). If that's not the case, and there's low consensus and distinctiveness, but high consistency: i.e. no one else is interrupting, Hannah interrupts at all games, all the time, we'd make an internal

TABLE 3.1 Attribution Theory

Consensus: How do other people behave?	Consistency: How likely is X to behave this way across time?	Distinctiveness: How unique is X's behavior to this situation?
HIGH: Most people behave like this.	HIGH: X nearly always behaves like this.	HIGH: X only behaves this way in this situation.
LOW: Few people behave like this.	LOW: X seldom behaves like this.	LOW: X behaves like this in most situations.

High Consensus, High Consistency, and High Distinctiveness = External Attribution
Low Consensus, High Consistency, and Low Distinctiveness = Internal Attribution

attribution (she interrupts because she's rude or socially inept). Table 3.1 illustrates Kelley's approach.

Kelley was pointing out that people attribute causality on the basis of correlation. That is to say, we see two things occurring together, and we therefore assume that one causes the other. However, we may not have enough information to make that kind of judgment. For example, if we don't know Hannah that well we wouldn't necessarily have the information to know if her behavior is consistent over time. So what do we do then? According to Kelley, we'll look for one of two things: multiple necessary causes or multiple sufficient causes. **Multiple necessary causes** occur when we can come up with a lot of reasons for the behavior (e.g. the game was really close, we were talking about something very exciting, and so forth). With multiple necessary causes, all of these things must be present for us to make an attribution. **Multiple sufficient causes** are when we observe a behavior and can think of one satisfying explanation, and that's all we need to make the attribution (e.g., "I know Hannah hasn't talked to anyone about this topic, and she's just bursting to give her opinion").

Enhancing Your Skills

Throughout this chapter we have emphasized the importance of perception to the communication process. We've also noted that while we perceive without much effort, it does take effort to improve our perceptual abilities so that we're effective in our communication encounters. Now, we offer five suggestions for developing a strong skill set in perception and then provide some specific examples for how one of these skills works in two different contexts: the workplace and with friends.

Let's first briefly explain the following five skills for enhancing perception:

- **distinguish between facts and inferences**
- **surround yourself with positive people**
- **understand your own vantage point**
- **realize the incompleteness of perception**
- **check your perceptions**

When you practice the skill of distinguishing between facts and inferences, you understand that saying a friend has crossed her arms and taken a step back from you as you talk is an observation of facts. If you conclude that your friend's nonverbals mean she is angry with you, you're making an inference. Inferring, or making meaning, is a critical part of the perception process but you should be careful not to confuse facts with the inferences you draw from them. Secondly, surrounding yourself with positive people is a good way to help your self-perceptions. People who are positive, and who provide a positive atmosphere when you're around them, help you to feel positive too. Positive people are supportive of you and give you honest, clear feedback when you ask for it. They have your best interests at heart. Communicating with positive people offers good role models for your own communication. Positive people make you feel better about yourself, and provide constructive support aimed toward your self-improvement.

The third skill involves understanding the vantage point from which you make perceptions. When you understand your own vantage point, you acknowledge that your perceptions are influenced by all the things that make you you. When you realize that you "see" a directive from the boss differently than your friend Peter does because you've had a bad experience with the boss in the past and Peter hasn't, you acknowledge your vantage point. Acknowledging your vantage point means that you understand that perceptions are not universal, and it's possible for two people to perceive the same event or person differently.

Related to that is the fourth skill: realizing the incompleteness of perception. This occurs when you know that the selection process we discussed in this chapter means you don't pay attention to everything, but rather pick and choose what's important, based, again, on your vantage point. This realization leads you to the last skill, checking your perceptions. Perception checking occurs when you ask others, did you see what I saw and do you interpret it the same way I do? Did the boss seem unusually upset to you? I thought Vanessa seemed really tired, was I wrong about that? You sound angry, Mom, are you?

Next, we'll illustrate how the last skill, perception checking, can help your communication in two different contexts.

Applying *Perception Checking* at Work

Leslie is a landscape architect who owns her own small company. She employs four others, and they usually all get along well. Right now, the company is doing a big job for a firm downtown that wants to turn their courtyard into a relaxing environment where their employees can have lunch and take brief breaks during the workday. Leslie has just returned from a frustrating meeting with her contact person at the job site, Don. Don and Leslie disagreed about a critical part of the design and Leslie isn't sure what her next step should be. Of course, Don is her client and in the end she will have to do what he wants, but the conversation left her feeling uneasy, and nervous that her company could lose the contract.

It might be helpful for Leslie to call a meeting of her employees and explain the conversation she had with Don. One or more of them might hear something in her account that can help her decide what to do next. If her employees tell Leslie that it sounded like she came on too strong with Don, she might consider calling him to clarify her position and the fact that she knows he has the final word on the design. Or she might set another meeting with Don to make that clear. Alternatively, Leslie might want an employee from her company to attend another meeting between her and Don, so she can further check her perceptions of their interactions.

Applying *Perception Checking* with Friends

Jack and Austin have been friends for 10 years, since they were in high school. They have seen each other through a lot of ups and downs. Jack was the first person Austin called when his mom passed away, and he's also the first person Austin wants to talk to about good news. Lately, Austin has been thinking that he may want to move to another part of the country to get a change. It turns out that there's an opportunity at work to make the move. When he tells Jack, Jack doesn't seem all that happy for him; he's curt in his responses and he's frowning.

Austin could ask Jack immediately what's wrong, telling him what he's observing. If Jack confirms Austin's perceptions, Austin could put himself in Jack's place and talk about how much he'll miss the two of them hanging out together. Austin could explain to Jack some of the reasons he feels he needs a move, while being mindful of Jack's feelings of loss and sharing that it will be a loss for him too. But, Austin needs to be open to hearing Jack say that his frown was unconscious, and he didn't mean to sound curt. In other words, Austin may have misperceived Jack's responses.

Communication Response: Greta Brigham and Jackson Wilmont

In the Communication Encounter, Greta Brigham and Jackson Wilmont were joking around when they were interrupted by a phone call. Greta's father had had a heart attack and she wanted to get home immediately. Jackson helped Greta get ready to leave town and as he watched his good friend crying, he wondered what he could say or do to console

Greta: Should he leave her alone, help her gather her belongings, sit and just follow her lead, hug her and tell her everything would be okay? All of this? None of it? After reading this chapter on perception and the self, answer the following questions:

1. How does the perception process function in this story?
2. How are Jackson and Greta's perceptions different?
3. How do sex and/or gender factor into this situation?
4. What would you advise Jackson to do?

Questions for Understanding

1. Define perception and the stages of the perception process, providing a brief example for each stage.
2. What is selective attention? Provide an example in your response.
3. Explain attribution theory and apply it to a situation you've experienced.
4. Give an example of how impression management works online. Explain a few strategies people employ to provide others with a positive impression of themselves.

Questions for Analysis

1. How is the perception process affected by your emotions and moods?
2. What are the consequences of paying more attention to negative attributes than to positive attributes (i.e. the negativity bias)? Provide a specific example.
3. How does impression management influence relationship development?

Suggestions for Further Reading

Broadbent, D. E. (1966). *Perception and communication*. Oxford, England: Pergamon Press.

McGauran, D. (2016). Jumping to conclusions: Six ways perception affects our lives. http://www .activebeat.com/your-health/jumping-to-conclusions-6-ways-perception-affects-our-lives/? x-class-type = Class-A

Solomon, J. F., Solomon, A., Joseph, N. L., & Norton, S. D. (2013). Impression management, myth creation and fabrication in private social and environmental reporting: Insights from Erving Goffman. *Accounting, Organizations and Society*, *38* (3), 195–213.

Weiner, B. (2012). An attribution theory of motivation. In P. A. M. Van Lange, A. W. Kruglanski, & E. T. Higgins (eds.) *Handbook of theories of social psychology*. London: SAGE.

4 Verbal and Nonverbal Communication

CHAPTER OUTLINE

CHAPTER GOALS

At the completion of this chapter, you will be able to:

- Provide definitions of verbal and nonverbal communication.
- Explain the relationship between verbal and nonverbal communication.
- Identify the primary characteristics of verbal communication.
- Identify the primary types of nonverbal communication.
- Exemplify the influences on verbal and nonverbal communication.

- Acknowledge problematic aspects of verbal communication.
- Illustrate the utility of Linguistic Relativity Theory and Expectancy Violations Theory in understanding verbal and nonverbal communication.
- Apply a variety of strategies to improve skills in verbal and nonverbal communication.

COMMUNICATION ENCOUNTER: NADINE HELLMAN AND RANDY MITCHELL

Nadine Hellman and Randy Mitchell meet regularly to study at the Student Union. Today, they're preparing for their first test in Introduction to Communication. They liked studying at the Union, even though it was noisy, because Nadine uses a wheelchair and the Union had a parking lot with handicapped spaces. The library was difficult for Nadine because there was no convenient parking. When Nadine arrived she mentioned to Randy, as she often did, that their campus was totally inaccessible. But she said it with a resigned smile and a shrug. Although it bothered her a lot, she'd pretty much given up on anything changing. She commented for the umpteenth time that, "Most places weren't meant for people in wheelchairs!" Randy pointed out that the curbs on the campus had cuts, and that should make life easier for her. Nadine admitted that those helped, but her voice tightened as she tried opening Randy's eyes to the many obstacles she found on campus. She was stumbling over her words and almost sputtering as she tried to explain her situation. It wasn't easy describing to Randy how hard it was for her, and she really didn't want to spend all their time together whining about how tough she had it. Randy was a good, sensitive friend, and Nadine didn't want to stress their relationship. So, she smiled at Randy and said: "We better start studying or we'll flunk this test tomorrow!" Randy smiled back, and they opened their books.

Verbal and nonverbal codes connect us to others and allow us to make our thoughts and feelings known (Hall & Xing, 2015). Think about your friendships, work, school, and family relationships or think about listening to a politician's speech. What do you recall? If you're like most people, you'll think about what your friends, family members, or the politician said and did. Even when thinking about casual encounters, like picking up your dry cleaning, you'll often remember things that were said and done during the interaction. When Nadine, in our Communication Encounter, thinks about Randy, she's likely to recall how Randy listens patiently when she struggles to talk about getting around campus. She also may think about how she failed to fully explain her feelings to him. In this way, she's thinking about verbal and nonverbal communication.

Although verbal and nonverbal communication systems are critically important, they're imprecise, ambiguous, and can sometimes lead to misunderstandings, misinterpretations, and hurt feelings. Of course, communication also helps us feel understood and supported, and allows us to accomplish goals. We get both positive and negative effects using verbal and nonverbal communication. In this chapter, we discuss verbal and nonverbal communication's unique attributes, and suggest skills for maximizing positive outcomes and minimizing negative ones. We separate our presentation of verbal and nonverbal communication here, but in practice they're intertwined, and we often draw meaning from the interaction between them.

Background

We begin by offering definitions of verbal and nonverbal communication. After providing these interpretations, we discuss important ways that the two interact with each other.

Interpreting Verbal Communication

Verbal communication occurs when people exchange **verbal codes**, or the vocabulary comprising a language. Verbal codes are governed by **grammar**, or a set of rules dictating how words should be combined to make a meaningful message. If Randy told Nadine: "Cut curbs they put," she wouldn't understand the sentence completely, though she'd probably make some meaning out of it (like thinking Randy was joking around or losing his mind). The words in that sentence are all recognizable parts of the English vocabulary, but their arrangement doesn't follow the rules for English sentences. **Verbal communication** occurs when communicators exchange mutually understood verbal codes, following the rules of grammar governing the use of those codes.

Interpreting Nonverbal Communication

Nonverbal communication, which may occur simultaneously with verbal communication as well as independently, involves the exchange of nonverbal codes between people to make meaning. **Nonverbal codes** encompass all behaviors – other than spoken words – that communicate messages. Thus, we define **nonverbal communication** as the process of exchanging non-linguistic cues. When you smile, wave your arms, stammer, or whisper you're contributing to the meaning a listener interprets even though none of those behaviors are words.

The Relationship between Verbal and Nonverbal Communication

Some researchers (e.g., Malandro & Barker, 1983) suggest five ways that verbal and non-verbal communication interact with each other: repetition (saying "I've tried this three times" while holding up three fingers); emphasis (saying "I've never been so angry before!" in a loud tone with inflection on the words "so angry"); reinforcement (saying "I'm glad to see you" while smiling); contradiction (saying "I'm glad to see you" while frowning); and substitution (waving hello without saying anything). See Table 4.1.

TABLE 4.1 The Relationship between Verbal and Nonverbal Communication

Function	Verbal Communication	Nonverbal Communication
Repetition	"I've tried this three times*	Holding up three fingers
Emphasis	"I'm so angry"	Loud tone of voice
Reinforcement	"Glad to see you"	Smiling warmly
Contradiction	"Glad to see you"	Frowning, eye roll
Substitution	Silence	Waving hello without speaking

Furthermore, nonverbal communication *regulates* verbal interactions. For instance, when you're talking with someone, how do you know when it's your turn to speak? Turn taking in conversation is usually managed through nonverbal communication. When someone is ready to yield the floor to another, they'll usually stop talking, make eye contact, and perhaps make a hand gesture indicating that it's okay for the other person to speak. If you don't want to yield the floor to a conversational partner, you might hold up your hand, palm facing your partner, and shake your head "no" when you see them getting ready to open their mouth and interrupt you.

Finally, nonverbals are considered more *believable* than verbals. For instance, if you ask a friend how they're feeling and they reply "fine" in a low tone while frowning, which do you believe – what your friend said or what they did? When Nadine tells Randy she's frustrated trying to get around campus, but she smiles and shrugs while saying it, Randy probably assumes her frustration isn't that big a deal. People may grant greater credibility to nonverbal communication because nonverbal behaviors are more difficult to control than verbal behaviors. Deception researchers (e.g. Burgoon & Dunbar, 2016) talk about *leakage*, which refers to nonverbal behaviors that are exhibited without conscious knowledge (like smiling nervously when trying to make a good impression). However, we can be misled by our faith in the accuracy of nonverbals. Someone crossing their arms tightly in front of them may be cold rather than angry. Both verbal and nonverbal codes mean many things, and effective communication requires accurately choosing among various interpretations.

Connections: Verbal, Nonverbal, and Audience Analysis and Speech Delivery

When using verbal and nonverbal symbols, it's important to remember that doing so relates to all the other concepts we discuss in this text. Reflect on how verbal and nonverbal communication relate to presentational communication. Think about the following scenario:

Raj has been assigned to make a presentation about new sales techniques to the sales force in his company. He knows the material he needs to present very well, but he's not accustomed to public speaking. He thinks he does well when he's explaining something one-on-one at work, but he's nervous now that he has to talk to over 50 people at once. When he just speaks to one person, he can tell by their facial expressions if they understand the concepts he's discussing, and sometimes they interrupt to ask a question so he can be sure he's getting his points across clearly. But with such a large group in a formal setting he's unsure how he'll be able to tell if they understand him. And, if he's honest, he's afraid he might look stupid to the audience. When the day comes for the presentation, Raj is well prepared and has dressed nicely in his best business suit. During the entire speech, Raj remains behind the podium and he unconsciously grips its edges till his knuckles turn white. His nervousness prevents him from smiling much, and he seems to have a frown on his face as he knits his eyebrows together. As he warms to his subject, however, he begins to relax. But, the audience is perplexed because Raj is using very technical vocabulary that most of them fail to comprehend. Because Raj is nervous, he's looking over the heads of the audience members – he doesn't want to make direct eye contact because he's afraid that will cause him to lose his place in his notes. As he looks over the audience's heads to the back of the room, he's unable to see the looks of confusion on their faces.

How does this scenario illustrate verbal and nonverbal communication in the context of audience analysis and speech delivery? How does it help you understand the ways verbal and nonverbal communication interact with one another? What are some of the nonverbal behaviors that Raj does well? What are some of his problems nonverbally? How might Raj improve his verbal choices?

Fundamental Issues in Verbal Communication

We'll address three issues related to verbal communication: characteristics of verbal codes; influences on verbal communication; and problematic aspects of verbal communication.

Characteristics of Verbal Codes

Words are characterized by four important qualities:

- They are arbitrary
- Their meanings evolve
- They're powerful
- Their meanings exist on two levels

First, words are arbitrary, mutually agreed upon labels for feelings, concepts, objects, or events. No direct relationship exists between the word and what it represents. For instance, the letters *c-h-a-i-r* form an agreed upon symbol for the object that English speakers call a "chair." The Spanish word *silla* and the French word *chaise* are equally arbitrary symbols used to represent the same piece of furniture. Figure 4.1 illustrates the semantic triangle (Ogden & Richards, 1923) showing that the word is *not* the thing, but merely a symbol that a community agrees represents the thing.

Although words are arbitrary, they aren't static. Like the communication process, they evolve over time. As time passes, some words are no longer used. For instance, words like *aglet* (the end of a shoelace) and *jiffle* (to fidget or shuffle) are words that used to be part of the English vocabulary that we no longer use. Some words become obsolete because the

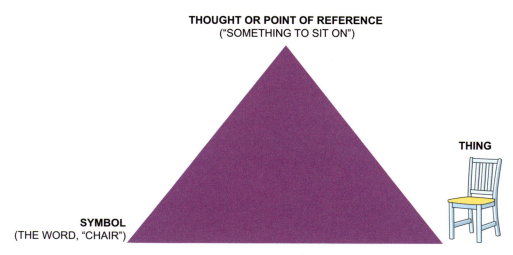

Figure 4.1 Semantic Triangle

activity they labeled ceases to exist. Jeffery Kacirk (2000) provides the example of *upknocking*, a nineteenth-century occupation. Upknocking involved going to the homes of the working class early in the morning, knocking on their doors and waking them for work. Kacirk explains that this job (and the word) disappeared when alarm clocks became affordable.

Occasionally words remain, but their meanings change. For example, over 500 years ago, the word *flirt* meant flicking something open (like a fan) or pushing something away with a jerky movement. Today, *flirt* remains in the English vocabulary but with a different meaning. Additionally, new words come into a vocabulary to label new activities and ideas. For instance, the words *dox* (to publish private personal information about a person without their consent), *lifehack* (a tip, trick, or efficient method for doing a day-to-day task or activity), and *gender-fluid* (relating to a person whose gender identity or gender expression is not fixed, and shifts over time or situation) all can now be found in dictionary.com. An online dictionary has the ability to add new words and remove outdated ones very quickly to keep up with contemporary usage.

Further, words have power and affect people dramatically. Words are arbitrary symbols, so they don't have inherent power; but we give them power. Think about a time that someone said something that pleased or upset you. The emotion you felt was engendered just through the words that were spoken. If someone viciously called Nadine, from our Communication Encounter, a *cripple* she might have a very strong negative reaction. It's just a word, but its effects can be dramatic. The power of words also can be seen in periodic efforts to ban certain words from being used. In 2017, in the United States, the Trump administration told the Centers for Disease Control (CDC) that there were several words they were no longer able to use in official budget documents. These words included: fetus, diversity, and evidence-based. The list and the ensuing outcry from the CDC and on Twitter spoke to the power we've invested in words. Further, words, especially when spoken by those in power, can set off huge controversies. In 2018, when US President Donald Trump reportedly used a vulgar expletive referring to Haiti and countries in Africa, it prompted an explosive discussion in the USA and caused a worldwide uproar. Are there words you wouldn't say in certain contexts? Do you think words are powerful or do people overreact?

Finally, the meaning of a word exists on two levels: denotative and connotative. **Denotative meaning** refers to the literal, conventional meaning that's found in a dictionary. For instance, in 2017, dictionary.com defined the word *hoard* as follows:

Noun
1. a supply or accumulation that is hidden or carefully guarded for preservation, future use, etc.
    a vast hoard of silver

Verb (used with object)

2. to accumulate for preservation, future use, etc., in a hidden or carefully guarded place.

    to hoard food during a shortage

Verb (used without object)

3. to accumulate money, food, or the like, in a hidden or carefully guarded place for preservation, future use, etc.

(www.dictionary.com/browse/hoard?s = t).

Denotative meanings can be confusing; because dictionary.com provides more than one meaning for *hoard*, a receiver must decide if the source is using definition 1, 2, or 3. Further, denotative meanings may differ within different social groups, even groups from the same culture. If you consult the Urban Dictionary, you'll find the definition for *catcall* is: "An insulting and usually sexist remark made in public towards a woman by a man. Not to be confused with compliments" (www.urbandictionary.com, 2015). But, if you consult the Merriam Webster Dictionary Online, you'd find this definition: "a loud or raucous cry made especially to express disapproval (as at a sports event)" (merriam-webster.com, 2016).

The connotative meaning of a term is even more confusing, because they vary from person to person. **Connotative meanings** derive from people's personal and subjective experiences. For example, someone who is a hoarder, or lives with one, would have different connotations for the word than someone who has no personal relationship to hoarding. Nadine's possible negative reaction to being called a *cripple* results from her personal experience. An able-bodied person probably wouldn't have the same connotations for *cripple*.

Influences on Verbal Communication

In this section, we discuss how culture and context influence verbal communication. Although we discuss these factors in isolation, they exist in combinations. For example, a woman of Mexican heritage living in the United States talking to her husband at home uses verbal symbols differently than a Korean American man speaking via Skype to a group of business associates located around the world.

Culture

Culture affects verbal symbols (and vice versa) first, and foremost, because most cultures develop their own language. Thus, people from Spain tend to speak Spanish, and those from Kenya usually speak Swahili. Culture and ethnicity affect verbal communication and perception (see Chapter 3) because the way we talk influences the way we think. Research suggests that being bilingual (or even speaking two dialectics of the same language, like

Black American English and General American English) provides cognitive benefits for people, as thinking expands from having more than one cultural knowledge base (e.g., Adescope, Lavin, Thompson, & Ungerleider, 2010; Antoniou, Grohmann, Kambanaros, & Katsos, 2016).

Further, language creates a shared culture because those who understand the vocabulary and grammar of a particular language are insiders while those who don't are outsiders. Spanish speakers or speakers of Swahili have access to the culture of Spain or Kenya in ways that people who aren't native speakers don't. In co-cultures, such as those formed by generation, we also see how language establishes insiders and outsiders. Jessica Wolf (2016) writes in the *New York Times* that her sons don't like it when she uses "hip" words they use like "dope," "stife," and "Fo'Shizzle." Although Wolf expresses admiration for their vocabulary, she sees it's meant to establish their solidarity and to keep her out. She comments:

> When my older son and his friends are together, listening to them talk is like trying to decipher the clicking of the Bantu. It's all delivered so fast – recognizable words cavorting with the unfamiliar – and there's not even a moment to ground myself in context clues. I think of it as a unique dialect, perhaps specific to our town – possibly even to our high school. (para. 7)

Wolf refers to her sons' language and their disdain when she tries to use it, as a way of establishing a "clubhouse" that includes their generation, and provides a big "Keep Out" sign for her and others of her generation.

Language also solidifies status levels. In England, for instance, upper class speakers are distinguished from those of the lower class by means of vocabulary and accent, even though all speakers are technically speaking the English language. In Paraguay the distinction between classes is made through two different languages altogether. The language of power is Spanish while the language of the streets is Guaraní. Myles McCormick (2018) reported in the *New York Times* that this has been the case for most of the country's history, with teachers even going so far as to brutally punish students who spoke Guaraní in schools. There's a current movement in Paraguay to restore Guaraní and make the country bilingual. If this movement succeeds, perhaps the status differential will be diminished.

In addition, language shapes cultural thinking by naming certain objects, ideas, and experiences while leaving others unnamed. As we'll discuss later, when we don't have a word for something, we may overlook it as unimportant, and literally not worth talking about (Hoijer, 1994; Whorf, 1956). Conversely, having many ways to name and talk about a concept signals its importance. For instance, in the United States, there are many slang words for money (e.g. *dough, cash, Benjamins, dead presidents, bread, bucks, cheddar*) indicating that money holds an important value in mainstream US culture. In China, however, there are fewer terms for money, but many terms for the act of bargaining. These vocabulary differences point to differing cultural values around money and marketplace bargaining, which is infrequently done in the USA and expected in most of China.

A **lexical gap** exists when concepts remain unnamed in a language (Talbot, 2014). In our Communication Encounter, when Nadine tries to tell Randy how she feels about getting around campus, she struggles and words fail her. We could consider the differently-abled a co-culture within the United States; a co-culture that the vocabulary of mainstream English doesn't serve well. Thus, the daily experiences of people in wheelchairs, using walkers, or with some other mobility issue aren't named in English. Nadine literally doesn't have words to express her thoughts and experiences.

The relationship between language and culture is intertwined and, as Alexandra Levine (2016) observes in the *New York Times*, "in many cases a culture dies with its words" (para. 14). The Endangered Language Alliance (http://elalliance.org/why/) notes on their website that "as languages die, thousands of years of accumulated human knowledge, experience, creativity and evolution goes with them" (para. 2). The Alliance cautions that a large percentage of the world's estimated 7,000 languages will be gone by the end of the twenty-first century, and with the loss of these languages we'll lose an enormous store-house of cultural knowledge.

As we've discussed previously, sex and gender are distinct, but overlapping, cultural categories. When researchers ask if sex and gender affect language and verbal symbols, they usually focus on sex (i.e., they study men and women) but their results often reveal the impact of gender (i.e., the expectations for behaving in a feminine or masculine way). Early research by Robin Lakoff (1975) asserted vast differences in the vocabulary of women and men including that women use:

- more color words (e.g., *ecru*)
- more modifiers (e.g., *so* and *very*)
- more expressions of politeness and apology (e.g., *please* and *sorry*)

Subsequent research has questioned these generalizations, and some research examining online language (e.g. Park et al., 2016) finds fewer differences between women and men. Further, some researchers reject the whole enterprise of comparing women and men's speech. These researchers argue that examining people based only on their sex ignores other aspects of their identity like race, sexual identity, and socioeconomic status that intersect with sex and gender to affect speech (e.g., Tariq & Syed, 2017). Yet, other researchers (e.g., Kendall & Tannen, 2003) still argue that women and men form separate speech communities, and have shared experiences based on their sex and gender and thus speak somewhat differently.

Context

Context refers to all the elements surrounding an interaction: the sex of the people involved, the culture, the setting, and so forth. Think of the same statement, "You need to leave now," said in the following situations:

- By a woman sitting on the couch in her living room to her former boyfriend after an argument
- By a homeowner at 8 p.m. to a worker who has been doing construction work on the home since early that morning
- By a parent to a child who is going to be late for school

Although the words remain the same, each of these contexts creates a different meaning for the statement.

The relationship between speakers forms another aspect of context. Imagine two brothers who have a close relationship engaging in the following dialogue:

Sam: "You're crazy if you think I'm going to clean up your mess, bro!"
Mason: (Laughing) "Right, Sam, like you never make a mess!"
Sam: (Laughing) "OK, Mason, don't go there . . . or I'm going to have to mess you up."
Mason: (Laughing) "Yeah, sure, you and what army?"

Now imagine the same conversation between two casual acquaintances and you can see how relationship changes the meaning of the interaction. People with close relationships are permitted to say things to each other that would be off-limits to acquaintances. Of course, even in a close relationship, it's possible to go too far, and then the relationship may fail to buffer the insult.

Problematic Aspects of Verbal Communication

Although verbal symbols aren't inherently positive or negative, people may use words in negative ways. Below we discuss misunderstandings and exclusionary language, which reveal problems in using verbal symbols.

Misunderstandings

Verbal symbols are ambiguous, and because of this, using them often results in misunderstandings. When Ben tells Allen to meet him at the bridge and there are several bridges in town, they may end up in different places. Allysa tells Marcia that she has important news: she's dropping out of school. Marcia doesn't realize that "important" means confidential in this context. Allysa is furious when Marcia tells another friend about her plans. Sometimes, misunderstandings occur despite our efforts to be clear, and other times we wish to be misunderstood. **Strategic ambiguity** (Carmon, 2013) results when we deliberately utilize a word that has multiple or vague meanings so we can avoid conflict. Cecily tells her mother "I see" after hearing her opinions about only dating people of their faith. Cecily hopes "I see" is vague enough to avoid a conflict where she'd reveal that she disagrees with her mother.

Exclusionary Language

Language may be exclusionary in many ways. Here we discuss three:

- sexist language
- racist language
- homophobic language

Sexism in language

Sexist language refers to language that demeans or excludes one sex. The use of the generic *he* in English provides an example. The generic *he* refers to the rule in English grammar, requiring the masculine pronoun *he* be used when the subject's sex is not known. For instance, in the following sentence, using the generic *he* rule, *his* would be the correct word to fill in the blanks: "A person should mind ___ own business in order to keep ____ friends." Researchers argue this rule excludes women because *his* isn't generic; rather, it's masculine and people think of men when they hear *he, his,* and other so-called male generics (Ivy, Bullis-Moore, Norvell, Backlund, & Javidi, 1995; Martin & Papadelos, 2017). Because language evolves, however, grammar rules are changing to allow the plural "their" to be used as a singular. Now most style manuals accept that "a person should mind their own business in order to keep their friends" as correct (Guo, 2016), although not all authorities agree.

Other examples of sexism in verbal symbols include man-linked words and expressions and use of the word *guys* generically. Man-linked words are words such as *chairman, salesman,* and *mailman,* which include the word *man* but are supposed to be generic. Man-linked expressions include phrases such as *manning the registration desk.* In addition, the practice of referring to a group of women and men as *guys,* as in "Hey, guys, what should we do tonight?," seems to reinforce sexism in language. There are alternatives to the generic *he* and man-linked words (Earp, 2012) and this aspect of sexism in language may be easily reduced (see Table 4.2).

Sexism in language is also exemplified in:

- heterosexual marriage practices
- negative terms
- parallel terms

When a woman marries she may take her husband's last name and she's often referred to by the honorific Mrs.; men keep their birth names and remain Mr. regardless of marital status. Some argue that by taking on a new name, women are losing their identity when they marry. The commonly stated "I now pronounce you man and wife" at the end of a

TABLE 4.2 Reducing Sexism in Language

Male Generics	Alternatives
Generic "he" language: "The scholar opened his book	Alternative: "The scholar opened a book."
Man-linked language: Freshman	Alternative: First-year student
Generic "he" language: A person needs his sleep.	Alternative: People need their sleep.
Male generic language: "Hi, guys!"	Alternative: "Hi, everyone"
Man-linked language: Manning the service desk	Alternative: Staffing the service desk

heterosexual wedding ceremony is also seen as sexist because the man isn't identified by his relational role while the woman is. Many couples have changed that phrase to "life partners" or "husband and wife" to avoid the problem.

There's a wealth of negative terms for women, and Peggy Orenstein (2016) points out that while these terms change over time, their negative connotations remain (*strumpet, hussy, tramp, slut, skank, ho*). Orenstein comments that these words demonize girls' sexuality. Many fewer negative terms exist for men, and those that do aren't always focused on sexuality. Further, when examining parallel terms for the sexes, we notice that the term for males often has a positive connotation while its supposed parallel term (for females) has a negative connotation (i.e., master and mistress).

Racism in language

Verbal symbols may also be racist. **Racist language** consists of verbal symbols and practices demeaning people based on race. Today, most, but not all, people avoid overt racial slurs. However, language can be racist in subtler ways. A study published over 40 years ago (Bosmajian, 1974) claimed that English is inherently racist because of the 134 synonyms found for "white" only 10 had negative connotations while 44 were positive. And of the 120 synonyms for "black", 60 words had negative connotations and none had positive connotations. In an effort to see if English has evolved in this regard, we checked www.powerthesaurus.org and found 648 synonyms for "white," many of which were positive (i.e., immaculate, virtuous, unsullied), while only a few were negative (i.e., wan, sickly). Of the over 1000 synonyms for "black" on the site the vast majority were negative (i.e., villainous, depressing, disgraceful, malevolent). Some of the synonyms could be classified as neutral (i.e., onyx, ebony), but none of them appeared to have strong positive connotations. Other practices such as associating the word "black" with some type of negativity in phrases such as "blackening his reputation," "black market," and "blackmail" also contribute to racism in English.

Homophobia, Biphobia, and Transphobia in language

Finally, verbal symbols also express homophobia. **Homophobic language** demeans gays and lesbians, while **biphobic language** and **transphobic language** degrade bisexuals and transgender individuals. Despite the fact that these slurs are recognized as negative and hostile, they're used frequently in the United States. Some research indicates that members of sexual minorities in the USA experience around two instances of homophobic epithets every week (Fasoli et al., 2016). In a study of 9th- to 12th-grade students performed in 2003 (reported in Snorton, 2004), 66 percent of respondents reported that they, themselves, used phrases such as "that's so gay" to describe something they thought was wrong or stupid. Eighty-one percent reported hearing homophobic language in their schools frequently or often. A 2010 study surveying 253 high school students found that homophobic epithets were associated with bullying behaviors on the part of both boys and girls (Poteat & Rivers, 2010).

Changing language bias

Sometimes members of a group may choose to re-appropriate a word that's been used by others to denigrate their group. **Re-appropriation** gives the word a more positive meaning and can be used by the group members to establish group cohesion. The use of the B-word to indicate a powerful woman, using the word *Mary* as a term of endearment among gay men, and the reclamation of the N-word in rap songs are all examples of re-appropriation. However, these words only achieve positive connotations when the user is a group member. Those out-group cannot re-appropriate the word without being subject to negative repercussions.

Theoretical Insight: Linguistic Determinism/Relativity Theory (Sapir & Whorf)

Here we review **Linguistic Determinism/Relativity Theory** created by Edward Sapir and Benjamin Whorf (Hoijer, 1994; Whorf, 1956). This theory links verbal symbols, perception, and culture.

The theory asserts that the words we use determine our ability to perceive and think. Both Sapir and Whorf believed that if your language lacked a word to label something, you would have difficulty perceiving it in your environment and thus, thinking about it wouldn't be possible. For instance, the English language has words for eyes, nose, lips, ears, skin, and so forth. When English speakers look at someone's face they notice these features. However, English doesn't label the space between the nose and upper lip, so generally people don't pay attention to that part of a face. In fact, the theory suggests that English speakers wouldn't even "see" that part of the face.

TABLE 4.3 Examples of Nonverbal Communication Codes

Nonverbal Communication Codes	
Kinesics	Body and head movements, gestures, and body positions and posture
Physical appearance	Clothing, hair and makeup styles, tattoos, piercings, jewelry, accessories, body size and skin color
Facial expression	Smile, frown, raised brow, jutting chin, clenched jaw
Para language	Tone of voice, pitch, cadence, volume, inflection, disfluencies such as 'ah' or 'um'
Haptics	Touches, hugs, pats, nudges, bumps
Proxemics	Use of space and distance, leaning in or backing away
Environment	Aspects of your physical surroundings such as clutter and color
Chronemics	Organization and use of time

Not everyone agrees with linguistic determinism. Benjamin Whorf himself questioned whether language is really deterministic, so he created Linguistic Relativity Theory (Whorf, 1956), which states that language doesn't determine perception, but influences it. But even linguistic relativity has to be modified somewhat because we can recognize new situations and concepts before a word for them exists. We have already discussed how language evolves to accommodate new words. However, the basic premise of the theory still resonates: the words people use, derived from their cultural heritage, have an impact on how they perceive and process the world.

Fundamental Issues in Nonverbal Communication

In this section, two central issues in nonverbal communication are addressed: types of nonverbal codes, and how culture and context influence the production and interpretation of nonverbal communication.

Types of Nonverbal Codes

Let's examine eight commonly researched nonverbal codes: kinesics; physical appearance; facial expressions; paralanguage; haptics; proxemics; the environment; and chronemics (see Table 4.3).

Figure 4.2 What Kinesic Cues are Apparent in this Photo?

Kinesics (Body Movement)

Kinesics, from a Greek word meaning "movement," refers to the study of communication through gestures, posture, and other bodily motions. Gestures can be intentional: Think about seeing a friend enter the coffee shop where you're studying, and waving and gesturing to him to join you. Gestures are also unintentional: Think about threading a pen through your fingers while you're concentrating on a test question. In addition to gestures, body posture and orientation are important nonverbal communicators. Posture generally reflects how tense or relaxed we are. Body orientation refers to how we turn our legs, shoulders, and head toward (or away) from another, and often relates to status. Typically, when people communicate with someone of higher status, they tend to face them directly (see Figure 4.2).

Physical Appearance

Physical appearance encompasses all our physical characteristics: body size, skin color, hair color and style, facial hair, facial features, and so forth. Physical appearance also includes **body artifacts** or how we decorate ourselves. Clothing, jewelry, uniforms, body piercings, tattoos, hair color, make-up, and so forth can communicate many different messages from nonconformity to favorite hobbies to political affiliations. Sometimes these nonverbal body artifacts are augmented with verbal symbols, such as hats and t-shirts that communicate team names and various slogans.

The nonverbal code of physical appearance also includes the communicators' attractiveness. Physically attractive people are often judged as more intelligent and friendly than those deemed unattractive. Further, research documents a positive relationship between physical attractiveness and income. People who are considered attractive earn 20 percent more than those of average attractiveness (Wong & Penner, 2016). This attractiveness premium doesn't differ for men and women, but women's attractiveness is judged more stringently than men's.

Everyday Talk: Different Nonverbal Expectations for Women and Men at Work

Emily Peck writes in the *Huffington Post* (2016, June 1) that a nonverbal cue illustrates that women and men haven't yet achieved equality in the workplace. Peck focuses her column on the differences between the clothing choices of two Facebook executives, Sheryl Sandberg (Facebook's COO) and Mark Zuckerberg (Facebook's co-founder and CEO). Specifically, Peck observes Sandberg's shoes and Zuckerberg's t-shirts, commenting, "women can't just roll out of bed, toss on yesterday's jeans, brush their teeth, and do well at work." To see Sandberg's attire compared to Zuckerberg's go to www.huffingtonpost.com/entry/sheryl-sandberg-shoes_us_574 f3845e4b0eb20fa0c988a. While Peck admits that this is an extreme example, she notes that some studies substantiate the claim that there are different expectations for the sexes in workplace attire.

1. What do these different expectations about the nonverbal presentation of the sexes at work mean to you?
2. Do you think it's a disadvantage for women to be expected to dress more formally and attractively than men?
3. Do you think women and men can be considered equal in the workplace when different things are expected of them in terms of their appearance?

Facial Expressions

More than any other body part, the face provides insight into emotions. Can you keep from smiling when you see an adorable puppy? Can you talk about your grandmother's recent illness and death without looking sad? And the eyes especially communicate a host of nonverbal messages. We may look directly into someone's eyes to communicate anything from interest to anger. We roll our eyes to signal disbelief or disapproval. We cast our eyes downward and avoid eye contact when we are uninterested, nervous, or shy. Our eyes also facilitate interactions. We look at others while they speak encouraging them to keep talking. If we drop eye contact, the conversation may falter.

Smiling also reveals multiple meanings. For instance, Jeff may smirk when he feels he bested Scott in an argument. Edie might sneer to communicate her disdain for David's comment. Belle may smile warmly to encourage her son's conversation. Smiling usually has positive effects; however, smiling during a conflict might aggravate the conflict further.

Paralanguage

Paralanguage refers not to *what* a person says but *how* they say it. **Paralanguage** covers a vast array of nonverbal behaviors such as pitch, rate, volume, inflection, tempo, pronunciation, disfluencies (ums and ahhs), and silence. Paralanguage also encompasses nonverbal behaviors like crying, laughing, groaning, and muttering. One way to understand paralanguage is to say the same sentence with various rates, volume, inflection, and tempo. For example, try saying the following statement to show *praise, blame*, and *exasperation*:

"I didn't expect to see you here."

Rosario Signorello and Nari Rhee (2016) studied the paralanguage of US candidates in the 2016 presidential primary. They found that both women and men were similar in using two different vocal pitches, one indicating inclusion and one authority. You can see a short video of Hillary Clinton, Donald Trump, and Bernie Sanders illustrating these cues at www.cbsnews.com/news/what-can-we-learn-from-the-way-presidential-candidates-talk/.

Haptics (Touch)

Haptics or touch communication represents ultimate access to others. Touch is the most primitive form of communication. When people touch each other, they invade each other's personal space. This may signal affection (when a father touches his daughter's shoulder in approval after watching her play soccer), power (when a supervisor pats an employee on the back after the employee finishes a project), formality (when two strangers shake hands upon being introduced), or intimate relationships (when partners kiss each other goodbye upon leave-taking). Sometimes, touch isn't a matter of choice, but when we accidentally touch someone, in a crowded elevator or when sitting next to them on the train, for instance, we normally offer an apology or an excuse.

Proxemics (Space)

Proxemics is the study of how communication is influenced by space and distance. Proxemics is usually divided into two types: personal space and territoriality. **Personal space** refers to the distance existing between ourselves and others. Personal space is often conceptualized as an invisible bubble around ourselves that we generally don't want others to enter. How do you respond when you perceive that someone is invading your personal space? How close can people approach before you become uncomfortable?

Anthropologist Edward T. Hall (1959) created four categories relating to space. They include:

- intimate distance
- personal distance
- social distance
- public distance

Intimate distance covers the distance that extends from you out 18 inches. This spatial zone is normally reserved for those people with whom you're intimate – close friends, romantic partners, and family members. **Personal distance**, ranging from 18 inches to 4 feet away from you, is the space most people use during conversations. Casual friends or co-workers usually maintain personal distance. **Social distance**, which is 4 to 12 feet, is the spatial zone usually reserved for professional or formal interpersonal encounters. Some office environments are arranged specifically for social distance. **Public distance** occurs at 12 or more feet from you. Hall's categories relate to communication behaviors. Think about the kind of communication in classrooms (public distance) generally. How does it differ from communication conducted at personal or intimate distance? Would you be likely to say "I love you" to someone who was 12 feet or more away from you? (see Figure 4.3).

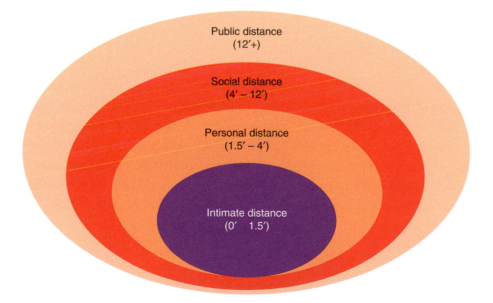

Figure 4.3 Hall's Distances

Territoriality, the other type of proxemics, represents our sense of spatial ownership. When you ask someone to "save your place" in line while you step away briefly, you're expressing territoriality. When you sit in the same seat in a classroom each class meeting, you reflect territoriality. People mark their territories in various ways, usually with items or objects that are called **territorial markers**. For example, perhaps you go to a coffee shop each morning and stake out your table by hanging your jacket over the back of the chair. Or, maybe you grew up in a house that had a fence separating it from the neighbor's. We don't always need to physically mark our territory. We may gain access to a particular space through habit and use, sometimes called *tenure*. Think, for example, about where your family members sit at the dinner table or in a family room. Is there a chair "belonging" to one family member that no one else would ever occupy?

The Environment

The physical environment exerts nonverbal messages affecting the communication taking place within it. The attributes of where you study, sleep, socialize, exercise, worship, and so forth make up your **physical environment**. A number of features, including smell (e.g., restaurant), clutter (e.g., attic, garage, basement, closet), color (e.g., wall paint), lighting (e.g. flattering or harsh), size (tiny houses or McMansions), and sounds (e.g., music, chatter) shape our physical environment. Imagine a conversation about religious beliefs between you and your best friend taking place in your dorm room while your roommate practices on a portable drum set. Now think about the same conversation occurring in your car while you and your friend are driving home from campus for the weekend. How might each physical environment influence the conversation?

Chronemics

Chronemics reflects how we think about and use time. Fifteen minutes seems to last forever when you're waiting to hear from the doctor about test results, but an hour seems like no time at all when you're engrossed in an interesting conversation. Time communicates status because people of lower status are expected to be on time and wait for those of higher status. Doctors can keep their patients waiting, professors may be late for class but patients, and students are expected to be on time. If Kevin is perpetually late meeting you and your statuses are relatively equal, then time will communicate something about Kevin's investment in your relationship and/or his character.

Influences on Nonverbal Communication

In this section, we discuss how culture and context influence nonverbal communication. Although we're discussing these factors in isolation, in practice they exist in combinations, as we mentioned in the verbal communication section.

Culture

Previously, we discussed eight nonverbal codes. In illustrating them, we used a North American cultural perspective. But, nonverbal behaviors convey different meanings across cultures (Burgoon, Guerrero, & Floyd, 2016). For instance, gestures vary across cultures. Mexicans and Italians use animated hand gestures in their conversations, while people in a number of Asian cultures consider such gestures rude. In most Western countries like the United States, a handshake is the approved greeting gesture, especially in business contexts. In Japan, however, the traditional greeting is a bow, and there's a definite ritual associated with bowing. The person of lower status is expected to initiate the gesture, and to bow deeper than the individual with higher status. Bows can indicate the formality of the situation, with more formal contexts requiring deeper bows (Mishima, 2017).

There are cultural differences in eye contact as well. Direct eye contact is usually a sign of respect in the United States, and failure to meet someone's eyes can result in that person thinking you are untrustworthy or unsure of yourself. This judgment is completely reversed in other cultures, such as China, for instance. Meeting someone's gaze, especially a superior's, is considered rude in China, and subordinates are expected to keep their eyes downcast. In addition, judgments of appropriate personal space vary from culture to culture. People from Egypt, India, and many South American countries, such as Brazil, require little personal space in an interaction. Cities such as Sao Paulo, Mumbai, and Cairo are crowded, and perhaps the close proximity in which the inhabitants live encourages lesser personal space needs (Martin & Nakayama, 2018).

Smiling is often thought to have fairly universal meaning, and it's generally believed to be a positive facial expression. Still, some research (Krys et al., 2016) calls that assumption into question. Kuba Krys and his colleagues surveyed over 5,000 people across 44 cultures and found that people from cultures experiencing high uncertainty and high levels of corruption rated pictures of smiling people as less intelligent and less trustworthy than pictures of people with a neutral expression. The researchers conclude that when the future is uncertain it's a sign of stupidity to go around smiling. When corruption is widespread, it is equally stupid to smile, expressing trust. The researchers refer to a Russian adage that states "smiling with no reason is a sign of stupidity", and argue that culture is critically important in interpreting nonverbals. While we cannot be conversant in the practices of all cultures, it's important to be sensitive to how culture impacts the interpretation of nonverbal codes.

Men and women in the United States are widely believed to have different repertoires of nonverbal behavior. Think about the different ways of gesturing, moving, and self-presentation that accompanied Bruce Jenner's transition to Caitlyn Jenner. Marianne

LaFrance and Andrea Vial (2016) report on some of the beliefs that people hold about nonverbal communication based on sex:

1. Women are more nonverbally expressive and responsive than men.
2. Women are better at sending and understanding nonverbal messages.
3. Men are louder and exhibit more restless body movements than women.
4. Men use more "ums" and "ahs" than women.

LaFrance and Vial conclude that while these beliefs are strongly held, they are not consistently demonstrated through research. In some contexts, such as close friendships, for instance, women do exhibit more expressive nonverbal behaviors, and are more accurate decoders, but in other contexts, like on the job, these sex differences disappear (e.g., Santilli & Miller, 2011).

LaFrance and Vial (2016) also note that, in the United States, some nonverbal behaviors are **pregendered**, meaning that people believe the behavior itself is either masculine or feminine (crying is an example of a feminine nonverbal). They conclude that when we see someone performing a behavior that is pregendered our response is different depending on whether or not the behavior matches the sex of the person performing it. This pregendering also influences whether or not we'll perform the behavior ourselves. If we want to be "gender-deviant" we might engage in crying as a male, but if we wish to avoid that label, we'll avoid the behavior. What do you think seeing a man cry or hearing a woman speak assertively? Do you label them as gender-deviant, and what does that mean to you? Do you avoid yelling as a female or crying as a male?

Context

Here we focus on one communication context: communication online. It's important to remember that new technologies impact every generation's communication behavior. For instance, when telephones came into general use in the 1920s and 1930s, people sounded some of the same concerns that we hear today about smart phones and social media. In a book about the history of the telephone, Claude Fischer (1992) summarized the results of a survey taken in 1930 examining people's reactions to telephones:

> Most people saw telephoning as accelerating social life, which is another way of saying that telephoning broke isolation and augmented social contacts. A minority felt that telephones served this function too well. These people complained about too much gossip, about unwanted calls, or, as did some family patriarchs, about wives and children chatting too much. Most probably sensed that the telephone bell, besides disrupting their activities, could also bring bad news or bothersome requests. (p. 247)

So, concerns about how technology affects our lives and communication behaviors are not new. However, our reliance on social media does bring with it some new challenges for nonverbal communication, in particular.

Think about how social media impact the various nonverbal codes we identified earlier. How do we gesture on Instagram? How do we convey paralinguistic cues in a text? Joseph Walther (2011) believes we do use nonverbals online (e.g., emoticons, GIFs, capital letters, and so forth). We'll discuss Walther's theory on this topic in Chapter 8. We certainly use chronemic cues online. Think about how you feel if a friend doesn't respond to your text immediately, or if you wait several hours before a "like" is posted on your Facebook page. The timing of online messages provides critical nonverbal communication affecting our relationships.

In addition, technology impacts nonverbal communication even in face-to-face encounters. For example, when we're walking while looking at our cell, what happens when we forget to look up and bump into another person, impinging upon their personal space? What about when we're out with friends and we text a friend who's not present? How do the friends who are there feel? What about being on an electronic device at dinner with your family? How do they react? How do you feel when friends text or talk on the phone when they're out with you?

Theoretical Insight: Expectancy Violations Theory (Burgoon)

One of the eight codes of nonverbal communication we've discussed is proxemics, or the use of space. Proxemics helps us understand what's communicated when we stand close to others or farther away, for instance. The **Expectancy Violations Theory** (EVT) by Judee Burgoon (1978, 2009) furthers our understanding of the use of distance. The theory helps us understand why we feel uncomfortable when someone invades our personal space, and why we sometimes allow this invasion to occur. EVT states that people have two competing desires: maintaining personal space and maintaining affiliation with others. These two desires are in conflict with each other to the extent that drawing closer to others erodes our personal space.

In EVT, Burgoon utilized Edward Hall's (1966) distance ranges (see Figure 4.3). Burgoon argued that Hall's distances set up expectations for behavior. Generally speaking, we formulate our expectations based on three sets of factors:

- Individual (is the person attractive, older than we are, and so forth?)
- Relational (how well do we know the person, how much do we like them, what is the power difference between us, and so forth?)
- Contextual (are we in a formal setting, what are the cultural norms, what's the environment like, and so forth?)

If a person violates our expectations (if, for instance, a work colleague stands too close while talking with us), our response will depend on a mix of the answers to the questions posed above. If we're in a formal setting, and we do not know the person well, and he is an older man, we'll develop a different reaction than if we're in an informal setting and the person is a woman our age that we know well. The theory suggests that how much we like the person who violates our expectations will strongly factor in to our reaction. If we like them, we'll typically allow a distance violation. We may even reciprocate, and stand closer than expected. If we dislike the person, we'll likely be irritated by the violation and move away. Personal space violations, therefore, have consequences on our interactions.

Enhancing Your Skills

Throughout this chapter we have emphasized how important verbal and nonverbal communication behaviors are for successful communication encounters. However, we've also pointed out the ambiguity of verbal and nonverbal communication, and how they're subject to misinterpretation as well as other, possibly more damaging, outcomes. Thus, it's critical that we become skillful in our use of verbal and nonverbal communication. Toward that end, we explain three specific skills:

- making tentative interpretations
- focusing on your audience
- owning your opinions

After describing these skills, we discuss how to apply one of them, owning your opinions, in two contexts.

The first skill emphasizes your abilities in interpreting the verbal and nonverbal behaviors of others. The second and third skills concentrate on message production and your abilities in sending verbal and nonverbal cues. When we are able to make tentative interpretations, we're acknowledging that the ambiguous nature of communication makes it difficult to be certain in our conclusions. For example, when Kimo visits his boss, Jan, in Jan's office, Kimo may think that Jan doesn't want to see him, even though they have arranged a meeting for this time. Kimo draws this conclusion because Jan is looking down at a desk that's covered in papers, and she doesn't look up when Kimo enters. However, these nonverbal cues may not mean that Jan wants to cancel the meeting. Kimo should ask Jan if this is a bad time, and keep an open mind while hearing what Jan says. Perhaps they will reschedule, but it's also possible that Jan is only momentarily distracted and welcomes the chance to meet with Kimo.

Focusing on your listener means thinking about the impact of your verbal and non-verbal behaviors on those with whom you interact. Focusing on your audience requires you to **self-monitor**, or to reflect on your own behaviors and how they affect others (Gangestad & Snyder, 2000; Snyder, 1979). Self-monitoring means you're aware of the words you use, how you say something, your proximity to others, the extent to which you use touch, your use of silence, and so forth. However, self-monitoring is not easy. For example, think back to our Communication Encounter. Nadine may be so focused on her problems with campus accessibility that she's unaware of how she's coming across to Randy. When Nadine tries to make her point, it's not easy for her to think about *how* she is saying something or whether or not she's smiling nervously when she doesn't mean to smile. Self-monitoring enables Nadine to be aware of what she's projecting both verbally and nonverbally.

Do the Right Thing: Layoffs at Work

Your boss, Ms. Monahan, has asked you to help her compose a company-wide email telling the workforce about an impending layoff that will affect at least 25% of them. Those who aren't directly affected by losing their own job will be indirectly impacted by having to pick up more work because of the downsizing. Ms. Monahan has not asked your opinion concerning the wisdom of sending out this information via email, nor has she asked your opinion about downsizing. But, you have strong feelings about both. First, you can see many ways to economize without having to let so many people go from the company, and second, you are strongly against telling people this information in a group email. You're also skeptical about sending an email saying that the layoffs are "impending". If you were in charge, you wouldn't reveal this information right now, and upset the whole company before you had a chance to think of other ways to handle the situation. But, of course, you're not in charge, and Ms. Monahan is your boss with control over your future in the company. You are very conflicted about helping Ms. Monahan craft this email, yet, she has not asked for your advice about anything besides the wording of the email. You can't think of how to word such a message without sending a lot of very negative unspoken messages as well. You have an appointment to see Ms. Monahan in two days, and she's expecting you to come with a few drafts of the email for her to look over; what do you do?

1. If you used the categorical imperative as your ethical system, how would you proceed?
2. If you used utilitarianism as your ethical system, how would you proceed?
3. If you used the ethic of care as your ethical system, how would you proceed?
4. Specifically, if you had to write out a script for your conversation with Ms. Monahan, what would you say to her?

TABLE 4.4 "I" Messages

How to avoid blame – and own your opinions	
You are so annoying.	I am losing my patience when I hear you complain.
You are constantly late.	I noticed you were 20 minutes late today.
You are very rude.	I am unhappy when you interrupt me.
You are such a slob.	I feel disappointed because the dishes are not washed.

The self-monitoring skill also means that you think about the vocabulary you use and how the people you're speaking with react to that vocabulary. For instance, you might use a lot of swear words when talking with your roommates, but cut those from your conversation when you're home with a parent. If you're giving a speech about photography to people who know nothing about it, you would try not to use a lot of specialized jargon, and you'd be sure to give definitions for any jargon you did use.

Owning your opinions requires you to take responsibility for what you say, and recognize when you are offering a personal opinion and not a fact ("I'm upset with you," rather than "you're doing the wrong thing"). Owning is often accomplished through sending I-messages, or messages where you're clear that your comment is your own opinion, emotion, or reaction. Owning avoids blaming others for your opinions, emotions, or reactions. Table 4.4 presents examples of how to convert blaming messages to I-messages.

Now, let's illustrate how owning your opinions can help your communication in two different situations.

Applying *Owning Your Opinions* at Work

Trisha has been working for a tech start-up for the past 18 months. She's really happy with her job; it allows her to exercise her skills and creativity. Recently, however, she has become uncomfortable with some of her co-workers' conversations. Whenever they are all in the office together (which occurs about twice a month), the joking and banter that goes on seems sexist and racist. She's kept out of the conversations but it's been getting worse over time. Trisha isn't sure how speaking up might affect her job, but these "jokes" are becoming intolerable.

If Trisha decides to speak up, it will be most helpful for her to be sure to own her statements. She might think about talking privately to one person who's been making the offensive comments rather than calling them out in the more public setting when they're all together. Trisha could say, "I wanted to talk to you, because I'm feeling uncomfortable with the joking that's been going on in the office. I'm wondering how we can continue to have a relaxed atmosphere where we can joke around, but not direct our humor toward women and people of other races."

Applying *Owning Your Opinions* with Friends

Monty's roommate, Miguel, recently got engaged to his longtime girlfriend, Teri. Now, all he wants to do is hang out with her. When he's not with Teri, he's talking about her to Monty or to anyone who will listen. Monty likes Teri but misses time with Miguel, and he feels like Miguel's attention is completely taken up by Teri and wedding planning. Lately, he's been avoiding Miguel and hanging out with other friends.

Monty could find a time when he and Miguel are alone, and he could begin by saying, "Miguel, I really like Teri and I'm happy for you both. But, to be honest, I miss hanging out with just you and talking about stuff besides the wedding. I know getting married is a big life event, and I'm there for you, but I'd like it if the two of us could go bowling next week like we used to."

Communication Response: Nadine Hellman and Randy Mitchell

In our Communication Encounter, Nadine Hellman and Randy Mitchell were about to study together for a test. Nadine uses a wheelchair and sometimes tells Randy about how the lack of accessibility on campus frustrates her. On this occasion, she felt Randy just didn't "get" it. She struggled with what to say, and finally decided to let it go; she didn't want to make a big deal out of it. And, Randy, for his part, wasn't sure what to say to his friend. When he pointed out that the campus had curb cuts, it didn't seem to make Nadine feel better. But, she was smiling, so Randy decided to get on with studying too. After thinking about the material in this chapter, answer the following questions:

1. Were the words they used in their conversation clear to each other? Were there times when words seem to "get in their way"? Give examples.
2. What characteristics of verbal communication might be at work in their conversation? What influences (sex, context, etc.) on verbal communication do you observe?
3. What types of nonverbal codes do Randy and Nadine use in this encounter? Are their verbal and nonverbal codes consistent?
4. What advice do you suggest to make their interactions more successful?

Questions for Understanding

1. Define verbal and nonverbal communication and discuss at least two ways they relate to each other.
2. List two influences on verbal and nonverbal communication and provide an example of each.
3. Explain the Linguistic Determinism/Relativity Theory. Distinguish between Determinism and Relativity and discuss how each one adds to our understanding of verbal communication.
4 Explain the Expectancy Violations Theory and discuss how it adds to our understanding of nonverbal communication.

Questions for Analysis

1. What other ways, besides those discussed in the chapter, might verbal communication be destructive rather than constructive?
2. Do you think that language is sexist, racist, and homophobic or is it the speakers of that language who are? Explain your answer.
3. Would you consider silence to be part of nonverbal communication? Explain your answer.
4. How does technology affect nonverbal communication? Do you agree that there's nonverbal communication online? Explain your position.

Suggestions for Further Reading

Burgoon, J. K., Guerrero, L. K., & Floyd, K. (2016). *Nonverbal communication*. London: Routledge.

Carroll, J. B., Levinson, S. C., & Lee, P. (eds.) (2012). *Language, thought, and reality: Selected writings of Benjamin Lee Whorf*, 2nd edn. Cambridge, MA: The MIT Press.

Gamble, T. K., & Gamble, M. W. (2015). *The gender communication connection*, 2nd edn. New York: Routledge.

Hall, J. A., & Knapp, M. L. (eds.) (2013). *Nonverbal communication*. Berlin, Germany: de Gruyter Mouton.

5 Listening and Responding

CHAPTER OUTLINE

CHAPTER GOALS

At the completion of this chapter you will be able to:

- Explain the value of listening in our personal and professional lives.
- Differentiate between hearing and listening.
- Identify and describe the components of the listening process.
- Articulate and exemplify the four personal and preferred listening styles.
- Describe several poor listening habits.

- Delineate the intersection of technology on the listening process.
- Delineate the intersection of culture on the listening process.

- Explain how Working Memory Theory functions in how we listen to others.
- Apply a variety of strategies to improve your listening effectiveness.

COMMUNICATION ENCOUNTER: PROFESSOR NASH AND RODNEY JASPER

Rodney Jasper's angry demeanor was obvious even to those who didn't know his predicament. His lips were pressed, his walk was forceful, and no one could ignore the mumbling that seemed to become even more audible as he got closer to Professor Charlotte Nash's office, after class. When Rodney got there, he asked if he could sit down and speak with her about his grade and paper. After the professor agreed, he jumped right in: "Okay. I hate to be so direct, but you told us that we could have rewrites and now you're saying 'no?!'" The professor sat upright and said firmly: "No, Rodney, I told your class that I'd consider allowing each of you to rewrite your papers. I can't help it if you only listened to the part of the message that suited you and ... " Rodney interrupted her: " ... no. I distinctly remember – and look, I'm a great listener with these things – that I was going to be okay because I've never had a "D" since starting college and wasn't about ... " Professor Nash wanted desperately to tell Rodney, but she knew that he was having a hard time in class and appeared very anxious. She looked at Rodney and figured that now was not the time to inflame an already difficult conversation. She continued: "Mr. Jasper, my policy in the syllabus requires a student to write up a challenge to any grade and I will review it. I know this is an important issue to you. You've told me that you felt that a rewrite was going to happen. So here's what I want you to do: After you've had some time to think about it, please send me an email talking about why you feel a rewrite is necessary and why you challenge the grade you received. I never promised any rewrites; I simply said I would consider the option."

Rodney didn't know how to respond. Deep down, he felt that his professor might be right. But, all he remembered was that she mentioned something about a rewrite and maybe he simply didn't listen to the entire message. Regardless, it was clear that both student and professor were part of a dialogue complete with tension, awkwardness, and passion.

Being an effective listener is one of the most important, yet neglected, skills in our communication repertoire. It may be the most difficult skill because it seems so many view it as simple! After all, we've been told to "LISTEN!" since we started school. Listening plays an instrumental role in the transaction of meaning in the communication process and it has been written about for decades (e.g., Nichols, 1957). And listening has been called a *healing practice to calm your body, clear your mind, and open your heart* (Pransky, 2017). Still, authors have identified listening as a *lost art* (Mipham, 2017) and a *forgotten skill* (Burley-Allen, 1997).

Background
The Importance of Listening

Listening has been promoted as "the most critical business skill of all" (Ferrari, 2012) and organizational leaders identify it as one of the most important global communication skills for meeting success. Moreover, Melissa Daimler of the *Harvard Business Review* (2016) argues that listening is "an overlooked tool that creates an environment of safety when done well" (p. 177). Jessica Williams (2016) views listening as part of a twenty-first-century communication skill. Clearly, listening is a conversational imperative and we explore its many trajectories in this chapter.

Most people think they're good listeners (Worthington & Fitch-Hauser, 2017). Notice how Rodney in our Communication Encounter felt that he's a "great listener." The reality, however, is far different than Rodney's (or others') perception. For instance, Accenture, the management consulting corporation, surveyed over 3,500 professionals from over 30 countries – from entry level to senior management with a relatively equal division of both female and male respondents. The company discovered, among other conclusions, that while nearly all respondents considered themselves to be good listeners (96%), they also openly admit that emails, unexpected visitors, and multiple phone calls – as well as multitasking – interrupt their ability to listen effectively. Over 65% of respondents reported that although many companies value social media platforms such as Facebook and Twitter, these sites make listening difficult. In sum, perhaps communication consultant Harvey MacKay (n. d.) put it best: "Listening is the hardest of the 'easy' tasks; if you want to be heard, you must know how to listen."

It's not hard to see why listening is difficult. Sometimes we think we know what the other person's message will be ("I may have told you this before, but . . ."), other times we find the message useless ("Aunt Maria knitted her daughters three scarves for their birthdays . . ."), at times, we simply don't understand the purpose of the message ("My Instagram profile has pictures that make people smile . . ."), and other messages we simply tune out ("Let me tell you about the new direct deposit process that our bank started . . .").

But poor listening has many negative consequences: unsatisfying relationships, impaired health, loss of productivity at work, among others. Imagine how you'd feel if your counselor didn't listen to you during a session? What might happen if a physician didn't listen to your health concerns? Consider your response to a partner who doesn't listen when you're angry about something going on at home. Or, imagine the effects of poor listening skills on the construction of new roads or bridges? Think about your exasperation with a boss who didn't listen to your concerns about an unethical work colleague.

This chapter discusses the value and importance of listening, presents reasons why we fail to listen effectively at times, and presents ways to overcome some of the ineffective listening habits we've adopted over time. Clearly, your academic achievement, employment success, relationship happiness, and personal satisfaction depend significantly on your ability to listen effectively.

Not everyone has the physical ability to hear or listen. In fact, research shows that hearing loss occurs as people age (Eggermont, 2017) and hearing loss may impact not only what is said, but also the nonverbal components (e.g., pitch, rate, tone, etc.) of speech. Hearing loss, however, doesn't mean one is incapable of achieving meaning in a conversation. Rather than the actual words, some people are capable of encoding and decoding the nonverbal communication to assess one's emotional state (Knapp, Hall, & Horgan, 2013). Professor Nash, for instance, from our opening story was able to "read" Rodney's nonverbal communication and as a result, chose her words carefully.

In addition, many individuals rely on an alternative communication system to create and share symbols: American Sign Language (ASL). ASL is a visual rather than an auditory communication form and as many of you already know, is composed of precise hand and body movements. According to Gallaudet University Library (a school dedicated to educating the deaf and hard-of-hearing), between 500,000 and 2 million people communicate in this manner in the United States and Canada alone. The hard-of-hearing and deaf communities have embraced ASL, and it is used to create and sustain communication within the community. In our examination of the listening process, we believe that impaired hearing doesn't have to equate with faulty listening.

Differentiating Between Hearing and Listening

The two processes – hearing and listening – are often considered synonymous and yet, the two could not be more different. We differentiate between them below.

Hearing

Hearing is, essentially, a biological activity involving receiving sound stimuli. Hearing occurs when a sound wave hits an eardrum with the resulting vibrations (or stimuli) sent to the brain. For our purposes, we define **hearing** as a physical process of letting in auditory stimuli without trying to understand those stimuli. Unless a physical or

STAGES		DEFINITION
Stage 1	Receiving	Attend to message
Stage 2	Responding	Provide appropriate feedback to message
Stage 3	Recalling	Remember the core of message
Stage 4	Rating	Evaluate message

Figure 5.1 The Listening Process

psychological reason exists, hearing is involuntary, meaning that we can't simply "turn it on or off" and it's done rather effortlessly. Concentration is rarely, if ever, required for hearing to occur. We do, however, often select some stimuli over others, a topic we discussed in Chapter 3, and will examine in more depth later in this chapter.

Listening

When we are connected with a message and striving for meaning, we have begun the journey to listening. Unlike hearing, listening is an active process, meaning that we are motivated to achieve meaning. Many people frequently use the phrase "just listen" – in fact, a book by Goulston (2015) is titled with this specific phrase! Yet, as Andy Wolvin (2010) advances, this sort of phrase trivializes and reduces listening to the "non-active, receptor part of human communication" (p. 2). Listening involves the processing of the words of another person and creating messages in response.

Listening is, as you're aware by now, a complex and often challenging behavior and one that we should never take for granted. For our purposes, we define **listening** as a transactional activity that requires us to receive, respond, recall, and rate stimuli and/or messages. It is transactional because it requires both the sender and receiver to be active agents in the process; listening is a "two-way street." The remaining four concepts in this definition – receiving, responding, recalling, and rating ("The 4 Rs") – require a great deal more discussion and we discuss each below. We illustrate these four components by referring back to our opening story of Rodney Jasper and Professor Nash, and Figure 5.1 presents an overview of the process.

Components of the Listening Process

Receiving

The initial step in the listening process is the reception of a message. **Receiving** a message requires us to attend to it and focus attention on it. Receiving involves the nonverbal and verbal confirmation of communication. It is impossible to receive all of the messages that we are introduced to each day. One reason is because our attention spans are short – lasting around 8 seconds (Egan, 2016). Try testing this out by looking at a class of yours for about a minute or so. See how many of your classmates are doodling, looking out a window, texting, or dozing (we know none of you would *ever* do any of these!). And, of course, there is the influence that social media play on how we receive a message. Being preoccupied with Snapchat, for example, will necessarily affect how much attention you are paying to a message that is being presented to you face-to-face. At the core of receiving is the notion of **mindfulness**, a behavior that requires us to pay close attention to an incoming message. Mindfulness is being in the moment, not reflecting on the past or considering the future. **Mindful listening**, then, is a type of listening that includes both being aware of one's internal thoughts and reactions as well as suspending judgments and criticisms of another's words.

Looking back at our opening about Rodney and Professor Nash, we can see mindful listening at play. The professor clearly wanted to respond to her student in the same way he spoke to her, but she considered the feelings that he was having at the time. She also avoided judging his angry approach and instead focused on the content.

Responding

We generally think of listening as simply receiving messages, but responding is an integral part of the process. **Responding** means providing appropriate feedback to another communicator. Responding lets the sender know that you have received the message and understood the message.

Responding occurs during and after the conversation. That is, we provide both verbal and nonverbal communication/feedback (a topic we explored in Chapter 4) to someone as the person speaks with us. Feedback is an essential ingredient in the listening process. For example, Margaret Imhof (2003) differentiated between good and bad listeners in a sample of US and German communicators. Those who were determined to be "good listeners" provided feedback that included frequent eye contact, an open body positioning angled toward the speaker, and rephrasing or restating pertinent conversational details. Those who were defined as "poor listeners" frequently talked incessantly about themselves, jumped to conclusions, and displayed a body position that included closed arms and legs crossed.

Professor Nash illustrates the responding function of the listening process. She physically "prepared" herself by making her posture more attentive, signaling that this conversation has importance to her. Although Rodney's responding was not as effective, he did manage to ask if he could sit down, suggesting that the topic was important enough for him to stay for a few minutes.

Recalling

Those who recall a message are demonstrating understanding by interpreting the message and making sense of it. **Recalling** includes storing a message for future encounters and remembering it later. Of course, because some messages are rather complex, we can't possibly recall each aspect of a message. For instance, imagine a financial aid advisor talking to you about scholarships and grants available to you during your sophomore year. The details of the conversation – whether it's entities such as the US Government or the European Commission – will involve issues like federal distribution guidelines, institutional available aid, family tax declarations, personal tax exemptions, among other areas. There are far too many complexities in this conversation to recall every aspect of it. Robert Bostrom (1990) observes that in these situations, we will recall a "personal version" of the conversation, remembering the essence of the dialogue. Further, much of what we recall will be from short-term memory. According to Nelson Cowan (2016), this information includes information such as digits, words, names, and other items for a relatively short period of time, with the average person holding between four and seven chunks of information.

A study by Michele Tine & Rebecca Gotlieb (2013) tells us that the recall abilities of people can vary tremendously. In her research on rural and urban poverty of sixth-grade students, she showed that low-income rural and urban students showed poorer recall on tasks compared to their high-income counterparts. This research supports the belief that poor economic and environmental conditions affect the listening comprehension of young people, a topic that has remained overlooked in listening research.

Rodney Jasper clearly recalls a "personal version" of what Professor Nash communicated to the class, affirming claims by Robert Bostrom nearly 30 years ago. Although his memory is clearly different than his professor's, he, nonetheless, communicates that he recalls what Professor Nash said and it's clear that regardless of accuracy, he "stored" it for this moment in her office.

Rating

When you evaluate or assess a message, you are **rating** it. Evaluating a message during the listening process includes a number of different experiences, including assessing whether it is organized, verifiable, and significant, among other areas. We may also rate whether the sender has a particular motivation for a message. That is, we often try to assess the extent to which a sender is biased in the presentation of a message. Rodney Jasper is certainly motivated to deliver a message to his professor, whether it relates to his academic integrity or simply his desire to avoid receiving a poor grade on his paper.

In general, we rate messages on two levels: (1) We determine whether or not we agree with a message, and (2) We determine how to place a message in context. First, we often disagree with the messages we receive from others. Understanding a person's field of experience (a topic we discussed in Chapter 1), however, is an important backdrop before evaluating. Rating in this manner will avoid confusing among what is fact, what is inference, and what is opinion. **Facts** are verifiable and can only be made after observation, **inferences** "fill in" a conversation's missing pieces and require listeners to consider things beyond a conversation, and **opinions** are informed judgments based on facts and on a communicator's ever-changing beliefs and values which often change over time.

Rodney and Professor Nash differed on the facts and, according to his professor, he was inferring that a rewrite was automatically granted. Both clearly offered their opinions on the matter, which framed their conversation with a great deal of challenge.

These four stages (receiving, responding, receiving, and rating) of the listening process don't always happen with awareness; in fact, most of these occur without much thought at all. Our conversations usually require us to make snap decisions and so we don't have all that much time to be aware of how we're listening or which part of the listening process is getting shortchanged. But, don't forget the challenge of moving too quickly through the listening process during some important life moments, including a job interview, a doctor's diagnosis, or a marriage proposal!

Fundamental Issues

Thus far, we have provided you an examination of the difference between hearing and listening, the components of the listening process, and various influences on the listening process. We now turn our attention to how listening exists in our personal lives. To do so, we explore various types of listening that we find in our personal and professional relationships.

Personal and Preferred Listening Styles

Each day, from when you open your eyes to when you close them, you are exposed to a variety of listening opportunities. You listen to your family, your partner, the car radio, the television, YouTube, roommates, your boss, your friends, and to other students, on Skype, to video, among many others. In fact, most research shows that we can spend up to 55 percent of our waking time listening to others. Clearly, listening is an activity that consumes our lives and yet, we all don't have the same listening style.

Typically, we adopt a style of listening in our interpersonal interactions (Bodie, 2015). A **listening style** is a preferred approach to the messages we hear. We adopt a style to make sense out of a speaker's message. In general, listening requires us to think about the relationships we have with others and the tasks that are assigned to us. Providing a template for these listening styles, Charles Johnston, James Weaver, Kittie Watson, and Larry Barker (2000) have identified four distinct styles: People-centered, Action-centered, Content-centered, and Time-centered. Using this model, a "P-A-C-T" takes place between and among communicators.

- **People-centered listeners** (PCL) are concerned with other people's feelings or emotions. People-oriented listeners try to compromise and find common areas of interest. Research shows that these listeners are generally not as apprehensive in groups, meetings, and interpersonal situations as other types of listeners. PCL instinctively notice others' moods and provide clear verbal and nonverbal feedback. Those who work in mental health engage in a great deal of people-centered listening.

- **Action-centered listeners** (ACL) want messages to be highly organized, concise, and error free. These people help speakers focus on what is important in the message. Action-centered listeners want speakers to keep the conversation on point and are often frustrated when people tell stories in a disorganized or random fashion. ACL also tell others that they want unambiguous feedback. Electricians, plumbers, and other professional tradespeople are skill-centered and in most cases, desire action-centered listening.

- **Content-centered listeners** (CCL) focus on the facts and details of a message. Content-centered listeners consider the various sides to an issue and prefer to listen to information from credible sources. Consequently, CCL are likely to play the role of devil's advocate in conversations. Attorneys and others in the legal profession are likely to favor this style of listening in their jobs.

- **Time-centered listeners** (TCL) are preoccupied with messages that are economically presented. They let others know that messages should be presented with a consideration of time constraints. That is, TCL discourage chattiness from speakers and set time guidelines for conversations, such as prefacing a conversation with "I have only 5 minutes to talk." Many time-centered listeners constantly check their watches or abruptly end encounters with others (e.g., a person waiting for a train or ferry).

Which listening style is the best? It's not a trick question because it all depends on the situation and the purpose of the encounter. At times, you may need to adapt your preferred style to meet the needs of another person. Think about a roommate who is going through some financial problems; it's probable that you will be quite person-centered. After leaving your dorm room, however, you may be walking briskly to work or rushing to catch the bus. In that case, time-centered listening is valuable. Knowing your preferred style of listening is important, but remaining flexible in your style helps you to respond appropriately to the communication situation.

Poor Listening Habits

By now, we're sure you understand that listening is not an easy process, but rather a communication activity that demands quite a bit of us. There are times when despite our best efforts, our listening is interrupted by the habits we've formed over the years – habits that are often problematic. We now present five of these poor listening habits that people have found themselves engaged in at one time or another. We focus on five of the most common: (a) ambushing, (b) selective listening, (c) omnipotent listening, (d) defensive listening, and (e) talkaholism. After identifying each, we provide one skill to consider if you find yourself predisposed to the habit. At the end of this section, see which one(s) you are susceptible to practicing. Table 5.1 provides a summary of each habit.

TABLE 5.1 Poor Listening Habits

Habit	Example
Ambushing	Cross-examination of witness *"And let me refer you to what you stated just a few minutes ago ... "*
Selective Listening	A teenager receiving a curfew from her dad *"I told you, Alec, that we 'might' think about letting you stay out till 11, not that we 'will.'"*
Omnipotent Listening	A physician talking with a patient *"Look, you don't have to finish telling me about the med's side effects on you; I know what the prescription does."*
Defensive Listening	An employee speaking to a gourmet market customer *"I'm sorry our soup doesn't measure up to what your Nana used to make."*
Talkaholism	A sibling talking to a sibling about their mom's 70th birthday party *"First, we should get all kinds of 70th birthday stuff, then we should get the old pictures ... I'm probably the best to do this because I'm pretty organized. Being organized should be on everyone's minds these days. And what difficult days these are because ... "*

Ambushing

When a communicator accumulates the words of another and saves them for an attack, **ambushing** has occurred. Ambushers want to retrieve information to discredit or manipulate another person. Ambushing usually requires careful listening, so it's likely the receiver is attentive to the particular message and then, almost without warning, attacks the speaker. This type of listening obstacle is quite common when politicians debate.

Why would someone engage in ambush listening? A primary reason why this "gotcha" type of communication exists relates to the person doing the ambushing. Consider a couple going through a nasty divorce. Both communicators may find themselves as targets of ambushing because both are often uncertain, anxious, frustrated, and/or angry. Ambushing, therefore, is simply an extension of feelings that are both ineffective and unproductive. Further, an ambush listener may also feel contempt for another, providing even more "ammunition" when a communication episode takes place.

In order to avoid ambushing, and despite the anger, you should clearly avoid any personal attacks on the individual. Make sure that your feelings about another matter don't find themselves in your conversation with someone. For example, if you've been fired from a job, don't ambush your close friend because you're experiencing hurt and frustration.

Selective Listening

Filtering out bits of a message while disregarding other parts is **selective listening**, sometimes called spot listening. In general, we selectively listen to those parts of a message that interest us or that are compatible with our beliefs, attitudes, or values. Consider our opening dialogue between Professor Nash and Rodney Jasper. One reason that Rodney had so much angst when approaching his professor is because he selectively listened to the portion of the message of Professor Nash that suited him ("rewrites") rather than the entire message ("[I may offer] rewrites [to you]").

Selective listening can be influenced by your perception of another communicator. Supposed that you believe that your group member, Carly, is too preoccupied with her new boyfriend and not holding up her share of a group project. You may subsequently only listen to messages that support your attribution (a topic we addressed in Chapter 3). Regardless of whether or not Carly is an astute group member, as a selective listener you are likely to attend to those parts of her communication that align with your perception.

It should be obvious that avoiding selective listening requires you to wait and engage the entire message of the sender. Make eye contact, if possible, and don't doze off during a conversation. It's easy to pick out specific parts of a message; it's more difficult to listen to the complete message before reacting.

Omnipotent Listening

Most of you recall the classic movie *The Wizard of Oz*, which features the "great and powerful Oz" who is considered to be "all knowing". This sort of self-declaration is at the heart of **omnipotent listening**, or the type of listening that occurs when a receiver tries to complete the message of a speaker, even before that speaker has sent a message. In a sense, omnipotent listeners "fill in the gaps" in that they believe that they can correctly guess the rest of a story a speaker is sharing. These gap fillers assume that they know how a message will unfold and often interrupt, prompting the sender to either stop the message and/or for the omnipotent listener to alter the message.

Filling in the gaps of a message can be corrected by making sure you are not led astray or lose your concentration throughout a message. That means that, at times, you need to repeat or summarize the speaker's message to demonstrate attention and not allow your attention to wane.

Defensive Listening

When a listener listens to words that a speaker communicates as personal attacks or hostile expressions, they are acting out **defensive listening**. Even though a speaker did not intend to insult or threaten via a message, a receiver may perceive the message and threatening or as a personal affront. For instance, think about the challenge that Georgina, the owner of a small bead and necklace shop in the mall, faces with one of her employees. As Georgina and her employee, Rafta, unpacked a shipment of new beads, Rafta suggested: "Georgina, the beads are great, but it seems like you could branch out and get some interesting gems, too. I mean, the girls love those things and I know there's a Gem and Bead Show in June." Georgina shot back: "My dear Rafta: I've owned this business for 10 years. I've had no one tell me how to be a successful businesswoman. And while I could appreciate your perception, you've only been here six months and you're already telling me how to make more money!"

Cleary, Georgina's defensive listening suggests that an "innocent" recommendation by Rafta was taken as a personal criticism of not only Georgina's leadership, but also of her business expertise. The owner may not have any animosity toward her employee, but still misinterpreted Rafta's suggestion. And, similar to other obstacles to listening, this defensiveness will likely add more tension and awkwardness to the interpersonal relationship.

One antidote to defensive listening is to make sure that you approach a conversation with confidence and avoid being caught up in thinking that people are naturally antagonistic. Although you may encounter a speaker who may not care about your well-being, it's more likely that speakers are trying to be as authentic as you.

Talkaholism

When people become consumed with their own communication and ignore another's view, they are considered to be talkaholics (Sidelinger & Bolen, 2016). **Talkaholism** is a form of communication that prompts a listener to redirect the conversation to himself/herself. Think of it as egospeak. Talkaholics are compulsive talkers who hog the conversational stage and monopolize the various encounters in which they find themselves. Talkaholics simply do not either take the time or have the time to listen to the words of others. Rather, they usually enjoy talking about themselves (egospeak) with one behavior most frequently undertaken: interrupting. Consider Uncle Jimmy, the talkaholic in the Lannigan family. Each Thanksgiving, there is a dread that falls upon many members of the family as they prepare for Uncle Jimmy because all he ever does is talk. And talk. Family members can't get a word in at all. Regardless if the topic is football, turkey, or shopping, the chatty uncle has an opinion on it and incessantly expresses it. Talkaholics could never be effective listeners because they don't take the time to listen.

Whether you are a talkaholic or prone to egospeak, one sure way to avoid this poor habit is to repeat what the speaker said so as not to immediately jump in with your opinion or life experience. When you are talking, you are not listening. Therefore, enhance your listening by reiterating the points of the sender.

The previous five poor listening habits – ambushing, selective listening, omnipotent listening, defensive listening, and talkaholism – are primary challenges to becoming an effective listener. Despite our awareness of these incompetent listening behaviors, we may find ourselves practicing them without fully realizing their impact upon others and their perceptions of us.

Influences on Listening: Technology and Culture

Before providing you several skills to improve your listening effectiveness, it's first important to explain two major influences upon the listening process: technology and culture. Regardless of where you're reading this chapter right now, you can't escape the role that these two areas play in listening. We devote a portion of the next section to how social media, in particular, affect your listening and then to the interface of culture and listening. We conclude the chapter by exploring a skill set to consider as you think about your own listening expertise.

Technology and the Listening Process

It's cliché to state it at this point, but the world is saturated with discussions of technology. Today, the word "virus" relates to both biology and technology. When we "swipe," we refer to both our credit cards and potential dating mates. Talking about "traffic" now suggests both vehicles during rush hour and the "audience" viewing various websites. And, we've made up many new terms such as "clickbait", "F2F", and "hashtag". Regardless of language or the diversity around the globe, technology pervades the human condition in ways still not fully known.

With such a reach, it's impossible to ignore the intersection of technology and listening. Think, for example, about social media. In fact, around the globe, social media is an international technological *du jour*, with billions (with a "b") of Facebook users, Twitter followers, Linked In accounts, and Pinterest pinners. These numbers cannot be ignored when discussing listening styles.

Those prone to relying upon digital technology often forget that face-to-face communication, and consequently, listening to others, is quite different and demands a different communication approach (Sumner & Ramirez, 2017). Sherry Turkle (2011, 2015) reminds us that a technological reliance on social media causes people to confuse postings, likes, and online sharing with genuine communication. She claims our "smartphones" are not that smart when it comes to establishing and maintaining our relationships with others. Taking this one step further: Listening cannot be achieved if we allow our technology to interfere with our face-to-face communication. Turkle argues that whether we are at work, at home, in love, or in the political arena, we need to "reclaim our conversations" and put away the cell phones, iPads, and watch phones and instead, try to engage another with full attention. Turkle (2015) highlights this point by quoting a college sophomore: "If someone gets a text and apologizes and silences it (their phone), that sends a signal that they are there, they are listening to you" (p. 30). Turkle sums up the student's sentiment this way: "technology gives us the illusion of companionship without the demands of friendship" (p. 50).

Still, we understand that we live in a digital world and to ignore that world can be perilous in some ways. Yet, what we – and scores of other communication writers – encourage is an understanding that while you may prefer to communicate with others online, that communication (sending, receiving, listening, etc.) is limiting. The key is to ensure that your listening style remains flexible across both face-to-face and electronic encounters.

Culture and the Listening Process

Chapter 2 showed us that we are all members of both a larger culture and several co-cultures. We've learned that culture permeates nearly every communication situation and whether you reside in Wales or Washington, our cultural backgrounds affect our listening abilities (Worthington & Fitch-Hauser, 2017). To be sure, the most populated country on earth, China, views listening (*tinghua*) as one of the key principles in Chinese (Mackenzie, 2013), clearly suggesting that the oldest written language in the world values listening

YOU

EYES

EAR

UNDIVIDED
ATTENTION

HEART

Figure 5.2 Chinese Symbol for Listening

greatly. Among the features of the character are the ears, eyes, heart, and undivided attention (Figure 5.2).

It's impossible to provide a complete picture of how culture affects listening. Nonetheless, despite listening being viewed as a universal communication activity, it is not understood nor practiced similarly across cultures. Space prohibits us from discussing the cultural influences upon listening in detail, but that information can be gleaned from other sources (e.g., Brownell, 2013; Ferrari, 2012). Still, in order to give you a general understanding of the culture-listening interplay, we provide you a snapshot of three different themes: country-of-origin, sex/gender, and race. In doing so, we hope you will sense that the topic of listening has been studied in varied and diverse ways.

Country-of-Origin

Significant amounts of writing have been undertaken related to the influence that a person's native country has upon listening between and among people. Much of the research, however, is based on one person's life experience in a country, underscoring one person's field-of-experience rather than a more holistic understanding. Among those who have studied and experienced many cultures across the globe, however, is Richard Lewis (2006).

Lewis (2006) posits, among other things, the notion of "listening cultures" (p. 32). People from countries such as Japan, South Korea, Taiwan, and Finland are rather deferential during conversations, preferring to listen to the sender and suspend interruptions and judgment while messages are being conveyed. Citizens in listening cultures tend to listen in silence and remain patient while listening. Silence allows one to "listen and learn" (p. 7) and listening cultures contend that conversations should be opportunities for reflection and respect. However, those from Germany, the USA, France, and Peru find that a conversation is "a two-way process, where one person takes up where the other one leaves off" (p. 7). In these cultures, being loquacious, or chatty, is a sign of confidence and cleverness.

Several other conclusions regarding country-of-origin and listening merit consideration. Many Arab countries, such as Iraq, listen for facts in a conversation and prefer some "personal touches" (e.g., calling one out by name, referencing a commonly understood event, etc.). Spanish and German listeners generally prefer to listen for information, with Spaniards often taking things literally in a conversation and Germans attending to the nonverbal displays of the communicator. Lewis (2006) also has found that Swedes are cooperative listeners who often whisper their feedback in a conversation in order to retain dialogue flow. Just as different cultures employ different speaking habits and language, listening habits vary, too. As always, we need to caution against painting broad cultural strokes when discussing listening across the globe.

Sex, Gender, and Listening

The role that sex and gender play in listening behavior has been studied for decades. But, none of that research shows that one sex is more equipped or more competent than the other in terms of listening effectiveness. Some of the earliest communication research in this area, however, was reported by Deborah Borisoff and Lisa Merrill (1991). They were among the first to note that women were more sensitive to the nonverbal cues that others provide during a conversation, suggesting that women take these into account when interpreting messages from others. Decades later, Deborah Tannen (2017) concludes that women typically are adept at listening to the answers to their questions, demonstrating an "ethic of care" that other researchers (e.g., Gilligan, 1982) previously discovered. Other scholars have noted that women tend to display more eye contact while listening while men are prone to engaging a message verbally (Tannen, 1991).

Listening scholars have also examined the four preferred listening styles we identified earlier in the chapter. The research is rather consistent. In one study, women reported being more comfortable with people-centered listening while men preferred the action-, content-, and time-centered listening styles (Johnston, Weaver, Watson, & Barker, 2000). Consistent with this finding is the research by Stephanie Sargent and Richard Weaver (2012) that showed women preferring people-centered listening. In addition, researchers have also examined the preferred listening style of feminine and masculine individuals (Villaume & Bodie, 2007). Action- and content-centered styles of listening were more associated with masculine personalities, in addition to high motivations for control.

Finally, Corine Jansen, the Chair of the Global Listening Board at the Global Listening Centre, cautions that we need to ensure that we don't rely on stereotypes while discussing this topic. And yet, many conclusions seem aligned with cultural expectations of women and men in developed countries. Jansen reports that there are few, albeit significant differences between men and women:

- *Men are often impatient listeners.*
- *Women check their surroundings for other messages during a conversation.*
- *Men are not as focused on their surroundings during a conversation as are women.*
- *Women tend to listen to the emotional content of messages more than men.*
- *Women often interject conversations with small acknowledgments such as "I see" and "mm-hmm" to demonstrate their listening.*
- *Men tend to listen silently, interjecting usually to seek clarification.*

Again, as mentioned in Chapter 2, it's important to avoid casting broad cultural generalizations, especially when discussing women and men. Still, the preceding provides you some foundation to consider regarding this area of listening and sex and gender.

Racial Identity and Listening

In addition to sex and gender, the relationship between race and listening has also been investigated. Among the various racial groups studied, the Native American (or American Indian) communities emerge over others for their understanding of, and appreciation for, listening's value. A number of Native American communities have centralized listening as a critical skill as they discuss various issues related to tribal relations. There have been conferences (National Indian Nations Conferences) that have featured sessions dedicated solely to listening. In addition, the 2014 White Tribal Nations Conference highlighted the value of listening by showcasing a "School Environment Listening Tour" dedicated to supporting Native American students and school issues such as bullying, offensive imagery and symbolism, disproportionate discipline, among other topics. Further, some Native American communities have come together to form an "Intertribal Monitoring Association on Indian Trust Funds" (IMAITF) with the sole purpose of having "listening conferences". Representatives from various tribal nations gather to listen to how the federal government is adhering to Trust Fund Standards, to provide tribal forums, and to keep up-to-date on policies and regulations on federal initiatives, among others. These listening conferences have been taking place for over 20 years.

In addition to the IMAITF, Donal Carbaugh (1999) offers additional information on ways that culture and listening work together within Native American communities. Looking at listening as a personal opportunity to interrelate with the environment, Carbaugh cites an example of the Blackfeet Indians:

Blackfeet listening is a highly reflective and revelatory mode of communication that can open one to the mysteries of unity between the physical and spiritual, to the relationships between natural and human forms, and to the intimate links between places and persons. (p. 265)

Clearly, Native Americans remain among the most respectful of the listening process in their personal and professional endeavors.

Theoretical Insight: Working Memory Theory (Baddeley)

Listening scholars have examined the topic from a number of different theoretical frameworks. Because listening involves both cognitive and behavioral functions, the theories related to listening are often complex. We delineate one that resonates across the literature: Working Memory Theory by Alan Baddeley.

The notion that our cognitive systems hold information temporarily in order to retrieve it is the foundation of **Working Memory Theory**. The idea that the mind is like a computer was posited back in the 1960s (Baddeley, Eysenck, & Anderson, 2014). In some ways, working memory is similar to short-term memory, except Baddeley (2007) clarified that short-term memory was simply a storage "facility" where we recall information over a brief period of time. On the contrary, working memory allowed information to be modified and altered. Differentiate between short-term memory and working memory by referring back to our opening with Professor Nash and Rodney Jasper.

The Working Memory model is conceived of as having three major components: the central executive, the phonological loop, and the visuospatial sketchpad. We discuss each briefly below.

The central executive is similar to the nucleus of an environment; it serves as the conduit to all other functions. The **central executive** prompts the memory to attend to relevant information while ignoring or suppressing irrelevant information (Baddeley, 2007). When the mind is asked to perform more than one task (recall and rate, for instance), the central executive moves into high gear and determines how to accomplish the tasks simultaneously. The central executive is like the principal of a high school telling students and staff what to do during a fire drill. There need to be directions of where to go, for how long, and other matters to ensure everyone's safety.

Embedded in the central executive are two components: the phonological loop and the visuospatial sketchpad. Both sound very complex, but both really are quite easy to understand. The **phonological loop** refers to the auditory nature of a message, including both the physical sound as well as how that sound is being received. Baddeley (2007; 2014) contends that this loop functions in two ways: as an "inner ear", which "remembers" speech sounds in their chronological order and an "inner voice", which "repeats" words and phrases on a loop so that they are not forgotten. Think of when you were a young child

Connections: Listening and Group Communication

It's fair to say that a phrase repeated often between people is "You never listen!" This phrase reflects frustration and sometimes anger. The work place is especially prone to listening challenges because those with seniority think they've "heard it all" and newer employees are usually too busy with projects to worry whether or not their communication is affecting other people. Consider the interrelationship between listening and group communication as you think about the following situation:

As a 26-year-old senior, Simon knew that not only was his age "nontraditional", but also the fact that he read all the material assigned. So, it came as a surprise to no one when he volunteered to be the leader of the group project in Research Methods. But, what Simon wasn't ready for were those team members who simply chose to focus on other things and ignore him. First, there was Louie, doing everything he could to attract the attention of Jenny, a third group member. Jenny was more than happy to accommodate Louie's overtures, especially because she was so fond of saying: "This class means nothing to me; I only need a C to pass it!" Because the other members were so focused on other issues, Simon simply couldn't facilitate any dialogue related to the assignment. And when the fourth member, Lizzy, responded, she did nothing but attack Simon because she thought he was a "know-it-all" because he "has kids and stuff." Simon couldn't possibly do all the work himself, but felt that his group members did not have the motivation to do anything. They were much too preoccupied with interpersonal matters that were external to the group.

Describe how this situation demonstrates the interrelationships among listening, group communication, and interpersonal relationships. If you found yourself in Simon's circumstance, how would you respond to your group members? Explain how listening, in particular, might be addressed to rectify the difficult relational challenges for Simon.

---

trying to remember words. This vocabulary acquisition is at the root of the phonological loop. The child receives words (the inner ear) and hears those words repetitively (the inner voice), resulting in the acquisition of language.

The **visuospatial sketchpad** is a pathway in the brain that stores the visual and spatial information. The visual component represents color, taste, and shapes; the spatial component is the location. This is a "sketchpad" because these are the mental "maps" that people construct as they are introduced to a message. Both the loop and the sketchpad work simultaneously to process stimuli. And, as we alluded to earlier, all of this happens within a few seconds in a conversation!

With this understanding of Working Memory Theory, think about the number of distractions you experience as a college student. Somehow and in some way, you need to deal with these distractions and accommodate them as best as possible. Consider a few of these interruptions and think about how your memory is able to organize them and ultimately, how you're able to make sense of them.

Enhancing Your Skills

In this chapter, we've reiterated the fact that listening is a vitally important part of communication. But unlike writing and speaking, it is a skill that is rarely if ever taught. A few schools, including the University of Kent, the University of Northern Iowa, and the University of Maryland, provide courses on listening and yet, this is not a growing list of schools! Thus, we now turn our attention to a group of skills that you should consider in order to improve your listening: practice active listening, prepare yourself to listen, provide non-judgmental feedback, honor silence, and listen with empathy (see Figure 5.3). We close with the application of how one of these skills (listening with empathy) functions in a how family relationship.

Our first listening skill is active listening, a behavior we highly recommend. We define **active listening** as a transactional process in which a listener reinforces the message of the

Figure 5.3 The "Three Mystic Apes" Communicate the Interplay among Speaking, Listening, and Nonverbal Communication

Do the Right Thing: Getting Tips for Being a Listener

The fact that you have to work three jobs in order to pay for college doesn't bother you as much as the fact that one of your jobs is a server at a diner. One night, near the end of your shift, Bruno, one of your best customers, called you over to his table and said: "Look: Over the past few months, you have listened to me every time I came in this place. I went through a divorce and you were there. I lost my dog and you were there. I sold my favorite painting and you were there. You are a great listener and I appreciate it!" Just then, Bruno tucked a $100 bill in your hand, thanked you, and said: "Don't say anything; I know you're supposed to share tips but keep this for yourself." When Bruno left, you went to the restroom to look at the money more closely; you had never seen nor held a bill that large. But, just then, reality hit! You don't want to say anything because you need the money, but you know the restaurant policy. Still, you wonder both how many times other servers put in personal tips and how many times the others may have kept the tips. Your dilemma couldn't be more difficult.

1. If you used the categorical imperative as your ethical system, how would you proceed?
2. If you used utilitarianism as your ethical system, how would you proceed?
3. If you used the ethic of care as your ethical system, how would you proceed?

speaker. When we practice active listening, we are showing both verbal and nonverbal support of another person and demonstrating an authentic interest in both the message and the messenger. Active listening includes behaviors like (a) asking questions, (b) paraphrasing messages, so both sender and receiver are communicating with similar intentions, and (c) staying other-centered throughout a conversation. The value of active listening is especially important in such situations as when a close friend is talking about her sister's surgery, a family member is disclosing a job promotion, or a teacher is talking about paper rewrite options, as Rodney in our opening example has learned.

Second, preparing yourself to listen can improve your communication competency. It may seem odd to you, but like Professor Nash, we need to get ready to listen to another person. If you're hearing impaired, you may ask for some assistance to ensure message meaning. If and when possible, place yourself physically closer to the sender to avoid interference. If you're an individual who is easily distracted, then remove any technology such as laptops or phones. Imagine, for instance, the challenge of Kian when he tries to tell his mom that he may have to retake a course because he's failing it. While describing his situation, Kian's mom, a realtor, continues to receive calls from potential clients for a house that she is showing in a few days. It's clear that Kian's mom is ill-prepared to listen since her cell is not only available, but the ringer is turned on. Many of us have been accused of being poor listeners because we either text during a conversation or look at our phones or laptops while another person is speaking.

In addition to being supportive and prepared, the kind of feedback we provide others is also significant in listening. It's consequential that we provide non-judgmental feedback,

Everyday Talk: The Interplay between Listening and Technology

In the *Huffington Post*, Mary Donohue (www.huffingtonpost.ca/mary-donohue/technology-etiquette_b_6191230.html) discusses the challenges related to technology and listening. Looking at the workplace, in particular, she contends that one of the most pressing problems is that people "don't have time to listen to each other." Donohue blames the rise in technology, providing evidence that the average worker receives about 125 emails a day, and 13 of them are spam. She concludes that this technological reliance results in workers spending about 2.5 hours a day on emails alone! The rise in technology has resulted, according to Donohue, in a corporate climate of being "rushed" to complete projects, rather than listening to co-workers who may have more innovative ways of accomplishing tasks. She observed that Microsoft, for instance, "stood by" and watched tech giants like Google and Apple "ride a wave of innovation" because the software company failed to listen to the innovators in its midst. But, Donohue warns, all companies need to caution against relying too much on technology because the human voice will slowly be diminished in value. She concludes: "Turn off your technology and pay attention when someone is speaking to you."

1. Identify some examples when technology has interrupted the listening process with a friend or family member.
2. How do you feel when someone reads a text message while you're talking with them? Are you offended? Why or why not?
3. Is the listening process always jeopardized when technology is involved? Explain with examples.

the third skill recommendation we identify. At times, we communicate with others – especially those with whom we're especially close such as family members – with little, if any, regard for their feedback. But, if we're too busy judging a circumstance, we are then ignoring the message. Let's say your roommate confides in you that he is thinking about talking to his parents about wanting sex reassignment surgery. There are appropriate and effective ways of providing feedback (e.g., "I'm sure there will be so many challenges for you, but you seem strong enough to handle them") and inappropriate and judgmental ways of providing feedback ("Well, I'm sure you haven't thought about the fact that others will think that you're a hot mess if you tell them about your plans"). Suspending judgement remains critical.

Fourth, recalling the Native American communities that we discussed earlier in the chapter, we should respect and honor silence in our conversations with others. It may seem odd to talk about silence in a book on communication, particularly because self-help sections on Amazon proudly proclaim to "communicate!" in so many of their titles. Further, silence is, as we know, influenced by culture and various societies and co-cultures incorporate it into their discourse in different ways. And yet, we believe that without silence, listening becomes jeopardized.

It's true that people can use "the silent treatment" (Schrodt, Witt, & Shimkowski, 2014), resulting in a spiral of relationship conflict. But, **silent listening**, or a type of listening that requires us to stay attentive and respond nonverbally when another is speaking, can be quite effective during challenging dialogues. The great Chinese philosopher Confucius once said: "Silence is a true friend who never betrays." Many of us should get to know this "friend" more intimately!

Finally, when we listen with empathy, we are essentially telling another person that we value what they are saying. **Empathy** is a process of trying to identify with the beliefs and actions of another person (we address this further in Chapter 6). When we are empathic, we are not placing ourselves in another's situation, but attempting to co-create the experience. You are empathic when you and your partner work together toward understanding. Judi Brownell (2002) puts empathy this way: "You do not *reproduce* the other person's experiences. Rather, you and your partner work together to *produce*, or co-create, meanings" (p. 185). Consider Maureen and Calvin, two work colleagues who have cubicles next to each other. Maureen is angry that her annual review did not come with a bonus – after 15 years of being employed at the same company. Examine the following two dialogues:

MAUREEN: It ticks me off that I work so hard here and the company makes so much money and they can't even give me a $1000 bonus. Zip!
CALVIN: I'd write them a note telling them "thanks for nothing."

Now, let's look at Calvin's response showing empathy:

MAUREEN: It ticks me off that I work so hard here and the company makes so much money and they can't even give me a $1000 bonus. Zip!
CALVIN: You sound so frustrated and I completely understand. It seems like you want to quit. I know it's rough for you now, but hang in there. You're a great worker!

Clearly, in the latter scenario, Calvin shows he's responsive and empathic and instead of instigating more anger (as in the first dialogue), he becomes less antagonistic and more concerned with Maureen. Now, apply this skill to Facebook or other social media sites.

With these skills in mind, let's take a deeper look into one of these skills – listening with empathy – exemplified with a romantic partner

Applying *Listening with Empathy* in the Family

Bonnie and Helen have been dating a little over a year and are in their mid-40s. One night at dinner Bonnie asked a very direct question: "Do you want to get married?" Helen put her wine glass down: "Are you serious?" Bonnie proceeded to reaffirm how much she loved Helen and told her marriage was a "natural next step." But Helen couldn't agree. She had so much on her mind – from her finances to her mother's rheumatoid arthritis diagnosis to not knowing how to deal with Bonnie's children. She responded: "I'm sorry, honey. There's just no way I can," and then tried to explain why. Bonnie sat there, not knowing what to say or do.

Although Bonnie had thought about the marriage proposal, she clearly wasn't prepared for rejection. To demonstrate empathy and avoid a potential conflict, Bonnie might say that she can't imagine how tough it must be having your mother in constant pain. Bonnie's empathy for Helen's situation might be surmised in this manner: "Listen, Helen. I know you're hurting and frightened in a lot of ways and I want you to know, I'm always here for you. Never gonna leave you alone."

Communication Response: Professor Nash and Rodney Jasper

In our opening Communication Encounter, we find Rodney Jasper challenging Professor Nash's interpretations of rewriting a poorly written paper. Rodney thought he recalled his professor saying that she'd allow rewrites and his professor clarified that she told the class that she'd *consider* the option. In the end, although Rodney started to rethink his recall accuracy, Professor Nash offered him an opportunity to write up a rebuttal to his grade indicating why he didn't deserve the grade he received. After reading this chapter devoted to the listening process, respond to the following questions:

1. Describe the moments when effective listening behaviors were present.
2. Describe the moments when ineffective listening behaviors were present.
3. What advice would you give to Rodney so that he can improve his listening skills in other classes?
4. Illustrate how nonverbal cues play a role in the conversation between the student and professor.

Questions for Understanding

1. Explain the difference between hearing and listening and provide an example to justify your position.

2. Define active listening and provide three examples of when it would be quite important in your relationships.
3. Identify a social media platform (e.g., Facebook, Snapchat, etc.) and describe whether or not listening functions within that platform and if so, how.
4. Explain the four personal and preferred listening styles and provide an example of how each works in a business setting.

Questions for Analysis

1. Why is listening a skill that is rarely taught?
2. Defend or criticize the following statement: "Some of the worst listeners are those with the most passion." Use examples.
3. Explain at least two situations where time-centered listening may be a preferred personal style.
4. Suppose you were asked to talk to a high school student about why listening is an important communication behavior. What would that dialogue look like?

Suggestions for Further Reading

Baddeley, A. D. (2014). *Essentials of human memory*. New York: Psychology Press.

Brownell, J. (2017). *Listening: Attitudes, principles, and skills*. New York: Routledge.

Raina, R., Roebuck, D. B., & Lee, C. E. (2014). An exploratory study of listening skills of professionals across different cultures. *World Review of Business Research*, *4*, 1–13.

The International Listening Association, http://www.listen.org

Wolvin, A. (2013). Understanding the listening process: Rethinking the "one size fits all" model. *International Journal of Listening*, *27*, 104–106.

PART II

Communication Types and Contexts

6 Interpersonal and Relational Communication

CHAPTER GOALS

At the completion of this chapter you will be able to:

- Provide definitions of interpersonal and relational communication and explain how the two differ.
- Distinguish among three types of relationships.
- Identify ten relationship development stages.
- Exemplify relational communication practices including self-disclosure, expression of affection, and conflict.
- Examine the impact of technology on relational communication.
- Clarify how relational dialectics theory explains relational communication.
- Apply a variety of strategies to improve skills in interpersonal and relational communication.

COMMUNICATION ENCOUNTER: MARSHA AND TAMI NEIMANN

Tami will soon be leaving her home in Denver, Colorado, to enter a grad program at the prestigious London School of Economics. Today, she and her mom, Marsha, are in her room beginning to pack her things for London. Although they're excited Tami earned this incredible opportunity, they're also sad about the impending separation. Marsha's been a single-mother since Tami was three-years-old, when she and Tami's father, Nathan, divorced. Nathan died in a car accident shortly afterwards, and Tami really had no memories of him. Although Marsha had dated other men, she was committed to Tami's upbringing. She rarely brought a new man into Tami's life, and never seriously considered remarriage. The two of them formed a solid unit – their friends jokingly called them "The Neimann Girls" in a reference to the TV show "The Gilmore Girls". Tami had even chosen to do her undergraduate work at the University of Denver, so she could see her mom often. One of Tami's professors had encouraged her to apply to the London School of Economics, and she did so without really believing that she stood a chance of getting accepted. When she received the acceptance letter, she and her mom celebrated, but privately each worried about how this new stage in their lives would work. Now, as Tami asked Marsha whether she should pack anything dressy, she thought she saw tears in her mom's eyes. But, as usual, Marsha didn't cry, and instead answered with a joke about how Tami might want something nice for when she socialized with William and Kate and Harry and Meghan at Buckingham Palace. Tami hugged her mom and felt tears stinging her own eyes. She depended on her mother all the time for emotional support and practical advice;

she just hoped Skype, texting, and email would do the trick until she came home for the holidays in December. Her voice trembled a little as she told her mom she loved her; Marsha responded with her usual "love you more" comeback.

In Chapter 1 we described eight types of communication. Interpersonal communication was one of these, and relational communication forms a critical sub-type of interpersonal. Think about the conversations you've had today with friends, family members, and romantic partners. While perhaps none of them had the import of Tami and Marsha's interaction, they all served some purpose: to exchange information, affection, support, or conflict. And, they all served to develop, unravel, or affect in some way the important relationships in our lives.

Background

We begin by providing definitions for interpersonal and relational communication. Then, we outline ways to distinguish between them. The two areas are intertwined. Just try to think about one of your relationships *without* thinking about the communication you share with that relational partner. Or, try to imagine an interaction you've had with someone *without* hanging a relational label on the two of you (e.g., friends, family, co-workers, acquaintances, and so forth). Most of the rest of this chapter focuses specifically on relational communication, but it's important to understand that interpersonal encounters occur between people who do not have, or seek to have, a developed relationship with one another.

Definitions

We define **interpersonal communication** as "the process of message transaction between two people to create and sustain shared meaning" (West & Turner, 2017, p. 6). Thus, interpersonal communication includes casual encounters between people who ask and receive directions from one another, between two people who see each other daily in a coffee shop and exchange friendly hellos, as well as between two people who have known each other for a lifetime, and are talking about a meaningful topic, such as Tami and Marsha Neimann. Generally, interpersonal communication takes place within **dyads** (two people), and this differentiates interpersonal communication from group communication, for instance, where more people are involved.

Relational communication, which also occurs within dyads, refers to communication occurring within the context of a developed relationship. Scholars studying relational communication assume that communication creates relationships. This assumption references the "constitutive" nature of communication, or the idea that communication creates

Figure 6.1 Relational Communication Usually Takes Place in, and Creates a Sense of, a Developed Relationship Like a Family

and sustains relational life (e.g. Rogers & Escudero, 2014). Thinking this way shifts the focus from the individual to the relationship as a whole, and from one individual's utterance to the interactions between people in the relationship (see Figure 6.1). When trying to understand Tami and Marsha's communication, the relational approach advocates examining the "interacts" or the back and forth between the two, rather than just what one of them says. For instance, meaning is derived from the fact that Marsha responds "I love you more" when Tami says "I love you". A much different relationship emerges if one person says "I love you" and the other person replies "Prove it" or ignores the comment.

Distinguishing between Interpersonal and Relational Communication

In 1975, Gerald Miller and Mark Steinberg suggested that communication varied on a continuum from impersonal to interpersonal. We'll explain this continuum changing *impersonal* to *interpersonal* and *interpersonal* to *relational*. Miller and Steinberg argued that locating relationships on this continuum was based on three different types of information: relational history, relational rules, and relational uniqueness. Figure 6.2 illustrates how these three types of information relate to the continuum we're calling interpersonal to relational communication.

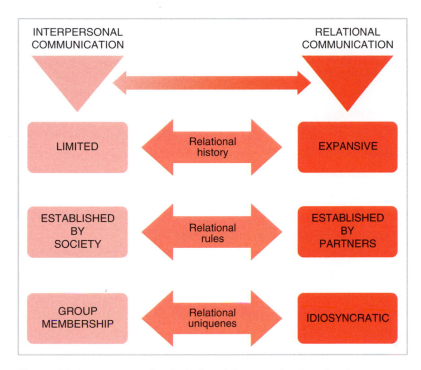

Figure 6.2 Interpersonal to Relational Communication Continuum

Relational history refers to prior interactions shared by communicators. Your father, for instance, who raised you since you were born, has an extensive relational history with you. A professor who teaches you a required class for one semester has a rather shallow relational history with you, especially if it's a large lecture class and you don't spend time in the professor's office or after class, seeking help. Someone that you speak to only once at a coffee shop has the least relational history with you. The continuum shows that the more elaborate the relational history, the more likely the communication is relational.

The second type of information discussed by Miller and Steinberg is **relational rules**, or specifically the rules established to govern the relationship. The continuum illustrates that the more the members of the relationship, themselves, construct their own rules for functioning, the more likely the communication is relational. Think about a close friendship. Who decides how frequently you meet or how you address one another, or what topics are off-limits? Now think of someone you may see frequently but who isn't a friend: a checkout person at a store you go to a lot, or the receptionist in your college's office with whom you exchange friendly greetings. When you ask who sets the rules for communicating in each case, you'll probably come up with different answers. You and your close friend create your own rules usually; in the second situation the rules are likely set by social and cultural norms. Of course, we're all somewhat constrained by culture (see Chapter 2), but friends often break social norms and do things their own way. That's less likely to happen in more casual relationships.

Finally, placement on the continuum is influenced by **relational uniqueness** or how much a given relationship differs from others you have. Communication in unique relationships belongs toward the relational end of the continuum. For instance, Maddy's relationship with one of her brothers is unique to them; it's even different from the relationships she has with her other brothers. Maddy and her brother Joe share certain ideas, experiences, and beliefs in common that make the interactions between Maddy and Joe different from those she participates in with anyone else. Also, Maddy and Joe share inside jokes based on their past experiences together. A person's relationship with a server at a restaurant, however, is much less likely to be unique. Most of the communication we have with servers in restaurants sounds roughly similar.

Miller and Steinberg (1975) argued that as you combine these three sources of information (relational history, rules, and uniqueness) you'll be able to place a given relationship on the continuum, and this placement reveals the communication that will take place within it. This system is useful; however, it's not perfect in predicting all communication within relationships. We know that we often exchange rather impersonal communication even in close relationships. Think about coming home from school and having a sibling or parent ask how your day was, and you replying "fine." It's also the case that sometimes we exchange rather personal information within the context of a relationship that has no uniqueness or history. Think about having a conversation with a seatmate on a plane about your feelings concerning a recent break-up.

Despite these confusions with the continuum, it's a useful way to begin thinking about interpersonal and relational communication. Another related approach focuses on differentiating among types of relationships, and examining the communication within them. We discuss this next.

Research suggests that people's relationships fall into three general categories: role relationships, interpersonal relationships, and close relationships (Guerrero, Andersen, & Afifi, 2018). **Role relationships** consist of relationships that facilitate tasks. People in role relationships are important to one another because they exhibit **behavioral interdependence**; their behaviors affect one another. Yet, role relationships consist of people who are replaceable. Think about a student, James, who's in class with you and with whom you study for exams. You and James work together toward a shared goal, getting a good grade in the class, but you don't spend much time getting to know each other personally; anyone who had a study ethic similar to yours and wanted to do well in the class could probably serve as your study partner just as well as James does. You and James have a role relationship. If you think about the people you know and interact with regularly, many of these relationships probably fall into this general type. A receptionist at your doctor's office, a sales clerk, a study partner, and a realtor all are people you have a relationship with for a time, but your interactions are routinized and even if you like the people, you could find someone else with whom you could accomplish the same outcomes.

When you add mutual influence to behavioral interdependence, you move to the next relational type: interpersonal relationships. **Mutual influence** means that the people in the relationship affect each other emotionally or socially. If you and James begin talking about things other than the class, and his opinions begin to influence yours and you're spending time during study sessions boosting each other's confidence, then you've developed an **interpersonal relationship**. In interpersonal relationships, you see the other person regularly and your interactions become more unique. James seems to be less replaceable; you could study with Monica and accomplish your goal, but you wouldn't have the private jokes or the sense of support you're getting from interacting with James.

Finally, **close relationships** exist when you have all the qualities of the other two plus a strong sense of attachment and irreplaceability. There's more emotional attachment in close relationships than in the other two types. The functions that the other person serves in close relationships seem impossible to replace with anyone else. In our communication encounter, Marsha and Tami are engaged in a task: packing. Anyone could help Tami pack, but only her mother can provide the understanding, support, and affection that Tami requires. Further, just occupying the role of "mother" doesn't guarantee a close relationship; Marsha and Tami have to develop this. A close relationship contains all kinds of communication behaviors, including those found in role and interpersonal relationships. But, unlike those two, close relationships also exhibit unique communication patterns.

Research (Hinde, 1995) suggests that, in North America, communication in close relationships is characterized by:

- variety (partners do and say many different things together)
- depth (partners move beyond surface interactions to discuss topics in detail)
- affection (partners tell and show each other that they care for each other)
- conflict (partners disagree)
- self-disclosures (partners tell each other personal information)
- idiosyncratic interactions (partners speak to one another in ways that others don't understand)

Everyday Talk: Expressing Love in Different Cultures

Tara Parker-Pope writes in the *New York Times* (2010, May 24) about research illustrating that while different cultural norms may affect how people express love, the brain functions in the same way across cultures (at least across China and the USA) when people report being in love. Parker-Pope reports on research conducted by Dr. Art Aron showing that while the Chinese talk about romantic love much differently, and more negatively, than people in the USA do, brain scans reveal the same patterns for people who say they're in love. When the researchers showed people pictures of their beloved while scanning their brains they found that "love lights up the brain in the same manner, regardless of ethnic background" (para. 7). Parker-Pope concludes with Dr. Aron's observation that love is not simply a cultural construction, but the way we think about love, talk about it, and express it to loved ones is shaped and influenced by our cultural backgrounds. You can see the full article at http://well.blogs.nytimes.com/2010/05/24/love-on-the-global-brain/

1. What does this report suggest to you about the relationship between love, expressions of love, and culture?
2. How difficult do you think it would be to change your thinking about love if you engaged in a close relationship with someone of another culture?
3. If a Chinese person, with a more negative feeling toward romantic love, based on cultural expectations, dated a person from the United States with a more positive cultural feeling about romantic love, how do you suppose that would affect their communication of affection to one another?

These three general relationship types give us additional information, but they aren't necessarily discrete. Role relationships can become interpersonal or close as people evolve and continue communicating. And, as we mentioned, simply having the role relationship of "mother" or "father," for instance, doesn't determine the kind of communication (or relationship) that exists between the participants. However, thinking about these three types of relationships provides another way to understand interpersonal and relational communication.

Fundamental Issues

Many issues permeate a discussion about communication in close relationships. Scholars from fields such as interpersonal communication, psychology, family studies, and sociology have studied the subject for decades, and have uncovered a variety of issues on the subject. Here we review three: relationship development, communication characterizing close relationships, and technology's impact on relational communication.

Relationship Development

Stage models provide one way of describing relationship development. Mark Knapp and his colleagues (Knapp, 1978; Knapp, Vangelisti, & Caughlin, 2014) present a stage model illustrating five stages of coming together and five stages of coming apart. Table 6.1 provides a summary of the model.

TABLE 6.1 Relationship Development Stages

Coming Together	Coming Apart
Initiating	Differentiating
Experimenting	Stagnating
Integrating	Avoiding
Bonding	Terminating

Some scholars think stage models don't describe the messier aspects of relational life, such as when relationships go back and forth between episodes of breaking up and reuniting (Vennum, Lindstrom, Monk, & Adams, 2014), or what happens when one partner wants to move to the next stage but the other partner doesn't. Further, other researchers (e.g., Fox, Warber, & Makstaller, 2013) note that Knapp's model hasn't had sufficient empirical testing and argue that it cannot account for online relational development; although one study (Velten & Arif, 2016) did find some support for the model in examining communication on Snapchat. It's certainly true that stage models simplify a complicated process, and Knapp's model may not completely apply to relational development online. Yet, despite that, a stage model shows us something important about relationship development: the ways it's related to communication behaviors. We'll briefly discuss each of the stages in the Knapp model and the communication that's related to each stage.

Initiating

In the **initiating stage** two people indicate that they're interested in making contact. Initiation depends on **attraction**, or a motivation to act positively toward another person. Attraction could be physical (you like their looks), social (they look like someone you'd want to hang out with), or task (you think they could help you accomplish something). In this stage, people exchange smiles and very low-level communication. Conversations are short and routine ("It's been really hot lately!" "That's for sure."). Some relationships stay in the initiating stage. You can have a relationship that's long lasting but never moves out of the initiating stage. Can you think of any of your relationships that fit this description?

Experimenting

In the **experimenting stage**, people engage in **small talk**, those types of interactions that are relaxed, pleasant, uncritical, and casual. Small talk includes gossip, comments about work and school, sports or other low-threat topics. Think about conversations you have with people at a party; they're usually filled with small talk. Many of our relationships stay in the experimenting stage.

Intensifying

The **intensifying stage** refers to a deepening intimacy. In this stage, partners self-disclose, address each other informally, perhaps using nicknames or terms of endearment ("Hi, Babe" "How's it going, honey bunny?"). Relational partners now refer to "we" or "us." They may say things like "We like horror movies" or "It's time for us to take a study break." Partners may also develop a **private language**, or idiosyncratic words and phrases based on past experiences. For instance, Theo and his wife still say "it's as good as done" to each other when things are out of control, because that's what Theo said when he forgot to do something important that his wife requested. Partners also speak specifically of their affection and commitment in this stage ("I really love doing stuff with you." "I feel exactly the same way!").

Integrating

In the **integrating stage**, the partners form a clear identity as a couple; they talk about themselves as a unit ("We're the girls from Bolton Hall"). This stage is often acknowledged by the pair's social network, who also speak about them as a duo. They're invited to places together, and when friends think about one of them, they usually think of the other.

Bonding

The **bonding stage** refers to making a public commitment. Bonding is easier in some types of relationships than others. For romantic relationships, both gay and straight, the marriage ceremony is a traditional bonding ritual. There are some bonding ceremonies for other relationships as well, such as sorority and fraternity initiations and ceremonies to welcome new babies to a family. Relationships that do not have a traditional bonding ritual may make up one for themselves. Before gay marriage was legalized in the United States, gay couples often engaged in commitment ceremonies, for example.

Differentiating

The first stage in coming apart is the **differentiating stage**, which refers to talking about how the partners differ. In the coming together stages the partners talked about their similarities, but now their differences are highlighted. Conflict may occur in this stage, but people can differentiate without conflict. For example, differentiation occurs when someone simply says they don't like sushi as much as their partner does. In this stage, people talk more about themselves as individuals ("I") than as part of the couple ("we").

Circumscribing

The **circumscribing stage** establishes topics that the pair avoids for fear of conflict. This results in less interaction between them. This stage is characterized by silences and comments like "I don't want to talk about that anymore," or "Don't go there." All relationships may experience some communication that's typical of circumscribing. But when people spend most of their time declaring topics as out of bounds, that's a sign the relationship is likely coming apart.

Stagnating

The **stagnating stage** consists of extending circumscribing so far that the partners no longer talk much. They believe there's no use in talking because they already know what the other will say. "I won't even bother bringing this up – I know he'll disagree" is a common theme during this stage. People feel "stuck," and their communication is unsatisfying.

Avoiding

In the **avoiding stage** partners stay away from each other. They make excuses for why they can't see one another ("Sorry, I have to study tonight"). They may change their routines so they don't run into their partner like they used to. For example, if people used to walk on a route where they'd see their friend, they'll walk a different way to avoid the friend now. Sometimes it's not possible to physically avoid another. If siblings still live in their parents' home, for instance, it's difficult for them to be completely separate. In such cases, partners in the avoiding stage simply ignore one another or tacitly agree to use their living space at different times.

Terminating

The **terminating stage** refers to ending a relationship. Terminating some relationships might not require much communication. People may simply stop speaking and seeing each other. For other relationships, a lot of interaction may be required, and mediators and lawyers may be involved.

Communication Behaviors Characterizing Close Relationships

Throughout our discussion we've referred to some communication behaviors found in close relationships. Here we discuss three specifically: self-disclosure, expressing affection, and conflict.

Self-Disclosure

Self-disclosure has frequently been associated with positive relational outcomes such as greater emotional involvement in a relationship, a more positive attitude toward oneself and one's partner, as well as improved access to social support (Catona, Greene, & Magsamen-Conrad, 2015). Think about the last time you confided personal information to a relational partner. Did it create these types of positive outcomes?

Self-disclosure is an important and complex communication behavior, so first, we'll define it, and then review four important principles of self-disclosing behavior.

Interpreting self-disclosure

Self-disclosure is personal information, shared intentionally, that another person wouldn't know without being told. When you say, "I'm afraid my parents might be getting a divorce," or "I'm really proud of how well I did on my last exam" you are probably engaging in self-disclosure. Most self-disclosures are verbal behaviors. However, we reveal information about ourselves nonverbally – for example, by wearing a hijab, a wedding ring, religious jewelry, like a cross or a Star of David, and making facial expressions. Our definition highlights four important features of self-disclosing:

1) intentionality and choice
2) personal information
3) risk
4) trust

When you engage in self-disclosure, you're intentionally choosing to let another person know something personal about you. Although disclosures sometimes slip out unintentionally (when someone is drunk or overly tired, for instance), these "slips" don't meet our definition for self-disclosure. When you tell your best friend, Rob, that you have been feeling envious of his success in business because you're struggling to get a job that you like, you're self-disclosing.

You can see from this example both the features of personal information and risk. Self-disclosures involve information that listeners wouldn't know unless they were told; it's private information rather than public. **Public information** consists of facts we make a part of our public image – the parts of ourselves that we present to others. **Private information** reflects the self-concept, and consists of evaluations, both good and bad, that we've made about ourselves. Private information focuses on our personal values and our interests, fears, and concerns. When you tell Rob about your feelings and your struggle to find your own place in the business world, you're sharing something that he wouldn't know otherwise, and you're taking a risk. Maybe Rob will have a negative response to the information, perhaps he'll taunt you later about not being a success, or maybe he'll want to avoid feeling guilty around you and he'll pull back from your friendship. These are the inherent risks in self-disclosing, and before you tell Rob your feelings, you'll probably assess how likely it is that any of these negative outcomes will occur (Afifi & Steuber, 2009). But, no matter how much you consider the risks, self-disclosing always involves a leap of faith.

The last feature, trust, explains why we go ahead and take that leap. When Rob is a trusted friend, we're willing to take the risk. When we have trust in our relational partner, we become more confident and our desire to be known to them becomes more important than the risk. Our perception of trust is a key factor in our decision to self-disclose.

Principles of self-disclosure

Next, we'll discuss four principles of self-disclosure. First, close relationships are the context for self-disclosing, so *self-disclosures occur between two people in a close relationship*. Although it's possible to tell personal information to small groups of people (or even to large groups, such as on social media sites), generally researchers have believed that self-disclosure occurs between two people in a close relationship.

However, there are exceptions to this principle. One is called "the bus rider phenomenon" or "strangers on a train" (Thibaut & Kelley, 1959). The name comes from the fact that such self-disclosures often occur on public transportation where two people are confined together for a period of time with not much else to do but talk. It's possible that we're willing to share in this context because we're *not* in a close relationship with the other person, and so none of the risks we discussed previously apply. The more we use social media, the more we may discover other exceptions, because people post personal, risky information on Facebook, for example.

The second principle states that *self-disclosures are reciprocal*. **Reciprocal** means that people mirror each other's behaviors: when one person self-discloses, the other will likely do so also. Further, the **dyadic effect** states that we won't simply self-disclose, but we'll match our partner's disclosure in intimacy level. So, if Marie tells Tania she's thinking of getting a divorce, Tania wouldn't respond by saying she's enrolling in night school, but would probably confide some problems she's had in her romantic relationship. In this way, relationships develop in closeness as each member invests relatively equally in the relationship and becomes known to the other.

However, conversations involving self-disclosures don't need to contain immediate reciprocity. A partner may simply listen with empathy while the other discloses. Actually, research suggests that expressing empathy may be a more desirable response than instantly providing a matching self-disclosure (Berg & Archer, 1980). People in close relationships don't have to engage in immediate reciprocity, but they should reciprocate at some point to keep the relationship in balance.

Thirdly, disclosures generally happen incrementally over time as the relationship develops: *self-disclosures occur over time*. We usually tell a low-level self-disclosure to a relational partner first and then increase the intimacy level of our disclosures as time goes by and our relationship with that person continues and deepens. Finally, *self-disclosing is a process*. Disclosures aren't discrete, finite events; rather, they are processes that occur in an ongoing fashion (Thoth, Tucker, Leahy, & Stewart, 2014). Self-disclosures can be seen as unfinished business; there is always something more to tell as relationships deepen.

Expressing Affection

Expressing affection is one of the most important communication behaviors characterizing close relationships. **Affectionate communication** involves:

> an individual's use of verbal statements (e.g., expressing verbal sentiments such as "I love you" or "Our relationship is important"), nonverbal gestures (e.g., engaging in nonverbal behaviors such as holding hands, sitting close, kissing, or hugging), and social support behaviors (e.g., helping partners with their problems, sharing private information, and praising a partner's accomplishments). (Myers, 2015, pp. 302–303)

Research supports several positive outcomes from engaging in affectionate communication. People in all kinds of relationships report more satisfaction when there is a high level of affectionate expression (e.g., Floyd, 2002; Morman & Floyd, 1999), as well as better physical and mental health, and an overall sense of well being (Myers, 2015).

Some research suggests that there are sex differences in expressing affection. Julia Wood and Natalie Fixmer-Oraiz (2017) note some evidence demonstrating that women prefer, and are more adept at, the verbal statement dimension of affectionate communication than men. Daniel Weigel (2003) found that newlywed wives, more so than husbands, favored saying "I love you" as a way to establish affection and commitment in their relationship.

Expressing Conflict

Conflict is hugely important to relational life; it appears in the Differentiating Stage of Knapp's model, and some scholars suggest that a developed relationship alternates between periods of integrating/intensifying and differentiating. Conflict is a well-researched topic, and we cannot do it justice here. But, because of its importance, we address it to introduce some basics. We first provide a brief definition, and then specify six types of relational conflict.

Interpreting Interpersonal Conflict

Interpersonal conflict is commonly defined as "the interaction of interdependent people who perceive incompatibility and the possibility of interference from others as a result of this incompatibility" (Folger, Poole, & Stutman, 2016, p. 4). This definition has four key terms:

- interaction
- interdependence
- perception
- interference

We'll explicate each briefly with an example.

Interaction means that conflict is rooted in verbal and nonverbal behaviors, like yelling, talking about differences, crying, or icy silences. If Kylie is angry with Jeff, but she doesn't say or do anything indicating that's the case, they don't have interpersonal conflict, and Jeff can be forgiven for believing everything is fine between them. Conflict only occurs when Kylie says or does something to indicate she's upset.

Interdependence means that people don't bother engaging in conflict with someone unless they have relational connections with them. Kylie and Jeff are dating, so they're dependent on one another for a variety of things. If Jeff were someone Kylie simply saw occasionally at school and he annoyed her, she wouldn't engage in conflict with him, because she doesn't depend on him to satisfy any of her relational needs; if we're not interdependent, it's relatively easy to avoid conflict.

Perception, as we discussed in Chapter 3, refers to the psychological process involved in sensing meaning. Our definition of conflict specifies that conflict exists when interdependent people *think* they have some type of incompatibility or some difference in goals. So, if Kylie thinks that Jeff is interested in her sister and that's been bothering her, they could have conflict even if she's wrong, and Jeff has no interest in Kylie's sister whatsoever. Conversely, if Jeff is starting to look at other women, but Kylie hasn't noticed, they might not engage in conflict.

Finally, interference is a two-part issue. First, the seeds of conflict are sown when people don't share the same goals (i.e., if Kylie wants to have more freedom to do things with her friends, and Jeff wants the two of them to spend more time together). And conflict occurs when people see others interfering with their goal achievement (i.e., every time Kylie makes plans with her friends, Jeff starts talking about an important topic making it difficult for Kylie to leave).

Do the Right Thing: Telling the Truth?

You've been friends with Alma since college. Recently, she told you she was applying for a teaching job at the same school where your husband teaches, although in a different department. You encouraged Alma in her application and were happy for her when she received a call for an interview. Alma texted you the other day saying she didn't get the job. She wondered if you'd ask your husband and find out why. As it happens, your husband had had lunch with one of the people who interviewed Alma, and he knew the reasons that an offer hadn't been extended. Your husband heard that Alma had alienated several people on the hiring committee by seeming to be really "full of herself" and uninterested in anyone else. They watched her teach a class as part of the interview and felt that she was disinterested in the students. They generally didn't care for her style or her self-presentation. You are upset to hear this because you think highly of Alma and you don't think of her as conceited or unconcerned about others.

You can't understand how the interviewers got that impression. Alma has been leaving you messages inquiring as to whether you found out why she failed to get an offer; what do you do?

1. If you used the categorical imperative as your ethical system, how would you proceed?
2. If you used utilitarianism as your ethical system, how would you proceed?
3. If you used the ethic of care as your ethical system, how would you proceed?
4. Specifically, if you had to write out a script for your conversation with Alma, what would you say to her?

Types of Conflict

People engage in conflict on myriad topics. What's the last thing you and someone else argued about? Although the topics are endless, we focus on five specific types of conflict, regardless of subject matter:

- **Content conflicts**. These are conflicts centered on a specific subject, and involve questions of fact and opinion. When we ask if democracy is the best form of government or we question whether drones are safe, we're asking content type questions.
- **Image conflicts**. These conflicts occur over differing perceptions, often about self-images. When Niles believes his mother still treats him like he's a child, he may engage in a conflict with her about that. If Lara believes that her friend treats her in a condescending manner, they may clash over their differing images of Lara's competence.
- **Relational conflicts**. This conflict type occurs when people perceive something is wrong with their relationship, disagree about their relationship definition, or have a clash about the way they're conducting the relationship. Rachel could complain that her wife, Bella, doesn't spend enough family time with her and their adopted son. Joel might desire a romantic relationship with Kirsten while she wants a friendship.
- **Serial conflicts**. These occur when relational partners engage in the same conflict repeatedly, almost as though they were reading from a script. Serial conflicts are usually unwanted by the participants, who seem powerless against the force of these repeated patterns. For example, Ned keeps a lot of boxes of papers in the attic of his house. His husband, Todd, regularly asks Ned to clean out the attic, and each time they fall into a serial conflict about the boxes. Todd mentions that Ned never looks into the boxes, and Ned responds that he might want to some day, and they're off for an hour's worth of repeated arguing.
- **Meta-conflicts**. These are conflicts about a conflict, or a way of conducting conflict. That sounds abstract, but if you think about it, you probably can remember a time

when you engaged in a meta-conflict because it happens frequently. When you tell your roommate, in the midst of a conflict about cleaning the apartment, that you don't like to be interrupted so much, and she responds that she hardly ever interrupts, you may be beginning a meta-conflict.

Although these types are discrete, they may overlap, and one of them may contain elements of several others. Can you think of one relational conflict exemplifying all these types? Table 6.2 presents examples of the communication characterizing these types.

TABLE 6.2 Types of Conflict

Content Conflict: Jane: "I think Donald Trump is a horrible president" Joan: "Are you kidding? He's doing so many important things to keep our country safe. He's a great president."
Image Conflict: Phil: "I am going to build a cabin on some land I just bought." Dave (Phil's father): "I think I should help you. That's a lot to take on." Phil: "Seriously, Dad, do you think I'm still a teenager?"
Relational Conflict: Tess: "I'm not sure why we never get together anymore, Nancy. Our friendship doesn't seem as important to you as it does to me." Nancy: "It's not that it's not important to me, but you have seemed awfully needy lately. I just needed a break."
Serial Conflict: Morgan: "Jeff, why can't you keep the food on the fridge shelves where I put it?" Jeff: "Your organization makes no sense to me – I just put things back where's there's room." Morgan: "I knew you'd say that." Jeff: "I knew you'd say that too – we keep repeating ourselves everyday about this stupid refrigerator. I'm sick of it." Morgan: "Me too."
Meta-conflict: Ida: "Kay, you keep yelling at me." Kay: "I don't think I'm yelling, but I want to get my point across." Ida: "I don't like to be yelled at." Kay: "That's not what I'm doing."

Technology and Relational Communication

It's not possible to discuss relational communication without reflecting on technology. One third of marriages in the United States began online and those relationships were slightly less likely to break up and slightly more satisfactory than those begun offline (Cacioppo, Cacioppo, Gonzaga, Ogburn & VanderWeele, 2013). More and more of our relationships are formed, maintained, and even terminated online. Researchers are considering whether our beliefs about relational communication, which were developed based on face-to-face encounters, still hold true online. What do you think about this question?

Some research suggests that we don't self-disclose as much online as we do face-to-face, while other researchers argue that because online disclosures are often anonymous, people actually disclose more online, and still others maintain that the channel doesn't really make all that much difference in amount of self-disclosures (Nguyen, Bin, & Campbell, 2012). What are your experiences online? Do you self-disclose more or less on Twitter or Instagram than in person? If you do, why do you suppose that's the case?

Some research focuses on the ways that social media bring relational partners together, providing positive relational outcomes (e.g., Lin & Utz, 2017). These positive outcomes include such things as allowing partners to feel closer, increasing their sense of connectivity, feeling less inhibition, and helping them to maintain their relationships. Think about Tami and Marsha Neimann. They hope to bridge the geographic distance between them when Tami's at school in London through Skype and other digital communication technologies. One study (Drouin & Landgraff, 2012) found that texting between partners was associated with more secure relationship styles. However, this same study also examined **sexting**, or the practice of sending sexually explicit texts, within the context of a relationship. The researchers posited a preliminary conclusion that sexting was similar to casual sex behaviors, and seemed symptomatic of people who wanted to keep their relationships more distant and less intimate.

Some researchers express concern that relationships maintained online are less successful than those maintained face-to-face. One study (Nesi, Widman, Choukas-Bradley, & Prinstein, 2017) examined how adolescents' romantic relational competency related to their use of technology-based communication. The study included 487 teenagers who participated at two time points, one year apart. The results of this self-report study showed that teens who said they used a lot of texting and social media sites to communicate with their romantic partners also reported lower competencies, in areas like conflict management, compared to teens who communicated more through "traditional" channels like the phone and face-to-face. This was especially true for the boys in the study (who comprised 42 % of the sample). Do these results seem reasonable to you?

Other research suggests that some circumstances make terminating relationships online appropriate. Brandon De Hoyos (2017) notes on his AboutTech website that there are some criteria to indicate when it's acceptable to breakup online: the relationship was short-lived, it was abusive, it was a long-distance relationship, or it was formed online. Further, De Hoyos advises that the online platform used for breakups should be a private one (not Twitter, for instance) and he cautions that not everyone will be satisfied with an online break-up.

Another study (Lukacs & Quan-Haase, 2015) investigated how young people using Facebook reacted after the break-up of a close relationship. The researchers hypothe-sized that one of the benefits of social media, connectivity, would lead to increased anxiety and depression after a break-up. Their results showed a more complicated picture of social media and break-up distress. They found that after a break-up, many partners remained Facebook friends, and for those whose break-ups weren't problematic, that was a good option. However, for those whose break-ups were traumatic, unfriending the former partner seemed to be a better idea. People with highly emotional break-ups tended to engage in excessive surveillance of their former partner, contributing to their overall distress. Using social media to search for information about an ex appears to be a common practice. A Pew Research Report noted that 24 % of internet users did so (Smith & Duggan, 2013).

Another study examined the practice of **phubbing**, or snubbing a partner who's in your presence by concentrating on your phone (Roberts & David, 2016). This study examined adults' reactions to phubbing and found that, although not all the participants took offense to the practice, phubbing was related to depression and lessened relationship satisfaction. What do you think when a friend takes a call or texts when they're with you? Do you engage in phubbing? Another study (Chotpitayasunondh & Douglas, 2016) suggested that phubbing's becoming "normal," even though it is often associated with negative effects on relationships.

In the face of all this complex information, it's sometimes difficult to assess the impact technology has on relational communication, competencies, and satisfaction. It may be best to conclude for now, as Lynne Webb (2015) states, that communication technologies are tools, and as such, they have both positive and negative impacts on our relationships depending on how they're used. It's our responsibility to figure out how digital and social media impact our relationships, so we can maximize the good effects and minimize the negative ones. Further, researchers need to keep testing to see if our theories and beliefs about relational communication hold true when a substantial amount of it takes place online.

Theoretical Insight: Relational Dialectics Theory (Baxter)

Many theories help us understand how communication operates in close relationships. Here we review one: Relational Dialectics Theory by Leslie Baxter.

Relational Dialectics Theory (RDT) is a theory that's evolved over time. The original theory was advanced by Leslie Baxter and Barbara Montgomery (Baxter & Montgomery,1996), and expanded by Baxter in 2011. Originally the theory explained relational life as a series of tensions resulting from people's desire to have two opposing things simultaneously. According to the original conception of RDT, relational life is about managing the tensions between seemingly incompatible goals. RDT conceptualizes this as a way to have *both/and* rather than *either/or* in a relationship.

Much of the past research employing RDT focused on three common tensions that permeate relationships:

- autonomy and connection
- openness and protection
- novelty and predictability

The contradiction in an **autonomy and connection dialectic** centers on our desire to be independent (autonomous) while simultaneously wanting to feel a connection with our partner. Have you ever had a friend with whom you wanted a close relationship, but then you sometimes regretted how people always thought of the two of you as a pair? If so, you've experienced the autonomy and connection dialectic.

An **openness and protection dialectic** means we want to self-disclose our innermost secrets to a friend, but we also want to protect ourselves from the chance that we'll then be vulnerable to that friend. Have you ever experienced wanting to tell a friend about something that makes you feel inadequate? For instance, you might want to confide that you're unsure if you're really cut out for college. You want your friend to empathize with you, but you're worried about how the friend will look at you when they know about your insecurities.

The tension in a **novelty and predictability dialectic** results from our simultaneous desires for unpredictability and stability. Zoe isn't completely happy with her relationship with Rina. They are more distant than Zoe wishes they would be, and they tend to always do the same things when they're together – shopping and going out to eat. Yet, she's pretty secure with the friendship, and she's afraid if she tries to change the status quo, it's possible the relationship won't last. It would be fun to try something different, but it's scary too. Table 6.3 presents a summary of these three dialectics.

TABLE 6.3 Three Relational Dialectics

Connection–Autonomy	I want to be close, but I want to be my own person too
Openness–Protection	I want to tell you all about me, but I don't want to be too vulnerable
Predictability–Spontaneity	I want the comfort of routine, but I want the excitement of novelty

Connections: Relational and Verbal Communication

When thinking about relational communication, it's important to remember that it relates to most of the other concepts we discuss in this text. Think about the following scenario:

Darla's been estranged from her father, Rich, and stepmother, BethAnne, for several years. Darla couldn't think of anything specific that precipitated their estrangement, they simply stopped keeping up with each other. Since they lived a thousand miles apart, it was easy to do. But now that it's gone on for so long, Darla's unsure what she'll say when she sees them at a family wedding this summer. She's been worrying about this for a while, and has been thinking about the time before communication ceased. They'd had a pretty good relationship, she thought, and she wondered what had happened. She'd been going over their past conversations in her head, trying to figure out if she'd said something to cause the breach between them. She couldn't think of anything, really. There had been that time when she texted her stepmother, jokingly calling her and Darla's dad "do-gooders," and saying that she'd read on her Facebook page about their "liberal" causes. BethAnne had responded to that text, Darla was sure, and she hadn't seemed angry. But now Darla is second-guessing her use of the words "do-gooder" and "liberal." Maybe her dad and BethAnne had negative reactions to those words and just decided to stop speaking to her.

How does this scenario illustrate principles of verbal communication in the context of relational communication? How can Darla identify problematic language that could have put her relationship with her dad and step-mother in jeopardy?

RDT asserts that the tension we experience from our conflicting desires never completely goes away, but there are several coping strategies we could use to reduce the tension. These include: cyclic alternation, segmentation, selection, and integration (Baxter, 1988, 2011).

- **Cyclic alternation** manages tensions by featuring the oppositions at alternating times. If Tami Neimann disclosed a great deal with her mother, Marsha, through college but then keeps more information private when she is in London for grad school, that would exemplify cyclic alternation. By choosing some times to be open and other times to keep some secrets, cyclic alternation allows Tami to satisfy both goals.
- **Segmentation** allows people to isolate separate places, rather than times for the oppositions. If Tami chooses to be extremely close to her mother when they are at home, but to become more independent when she's away, she's using segmentation to satisfy both goals.
- **Selection** means that you choose one of the opposites while ignoring the other. If Tami just decides to be close to her mother at all times and places, regardless of her desires for independence, she'd be using selection.
- **Integration** means making an effort to combine the oppositions more fully than the three previous strategies. Integration takes one of the following forms:
  - **Neutralizing** involves compromising between the two oppositions. If Tami and her mother have been arguing because Marsha feels that Tami is leaving her out of her life and not telling her anything, then Tami might decide to use neutralizing with her mom and disclose more than she had been, but perhaps less than Marsha would like.
  - **Disqualifying** allows people to cope with tensions by exempting certain issues from the general pattern. Tami might make some topics such as worries about her performance at school off limits for disclosure with her mom but otherwise engage in a lot of self-disclosure.
  - **Reframing** means rethinking the opposition. For instance, Tami and her mother may agree that they feel closer to each other if they don't tell each other everything. Reframing is illustrated in the belief that if they keep some information private, that makes what they do tell each other more significant.

Table 6.4 provides a summary of these coping strategies.

In Baxter's more recent work (e.g., Baxter & Norwood, 2015) she's highlighted the notion that everything we say in a relationship is in dialogue with all the past things that have been said in that relationship. This makes the tensions of relational life "a discursive struggle among competing discourses" (Baxter & Norwood, 2015, p. 1). Baxter argues that future studies using RDT should be qualitative in nature, should critically expose power

TABLE 6.4 Coping with Dialectics

Cyclic alternation	Ted is close to his sister, Mary, in their old age, but was distant during their youth.
Segmentation	Jon is open with Claudia when they are at home, but not when they are out with friends.
Selection	Rosie and Malia decide they are very close, ignoring their needs for individuation.
Integration: Neutralizing	Michael and Joel compromise on how much spontaneity to have in their relationship: more than Michael wants; less than Joel wants.
Integration: Disqualifying	Frankie tells her mother everything about her life away at college, except her sex life.
Integration: Reframing	Jill and Caitlin agree that they're a closer couple when they spend some time apart pursuing separate interests.

relationships, and should focus less on uncovering specific tensions like autonomy–connection in favor of illuminating how discourses of individualism and community interrelate to form meaning in a relationship.

Enhancing Your Skills

Throughout this chapter we have focused on explaining the communication within interpersonal and close relationships. Relational communication is an extremely important part of our lives, and research shows that people with satisfying relationships are happier and more well adjusted than those without those types of relationships. To achieve these outcomes, we need a skill set. As we discuss the critical skills needed for competent interpersonal and relational communication, we draw on some classic work by other researchers (e.g., Gibb, 1970; Grice, 1975). However, it's important to note that, as Christina Sabee (2015) cautions, although communication competence is a widely researched area, it's complex, and researchers don't agree completely on what constitutes skill or competence. Further, it's often the case that what seems effective in one relationship doesn't translate well to another. So, with that caveat in mind, we present the following skills:

- being appropriate
- being truthful
- being relevant
- being clear
- developing a supportive communication climate

Being appropriate means only telling the other the amount of information needed to convey your message. For example, when Nora tells her brother, Sam, about a problem she's experiencing with her roommate, Angie, being appropriate suggests that she be succinct in her comments. She could go on for hours, but she should pick only the most important details in her history with Angie, when telling Sam about the problem.

Being truthful means to avoid negative, unproven gossip and deception when communicating with others. While Nora tells Sam how angry she is with her roommate, she shouldn't embellish the story, and make up anecdotes, making herself look better and Angie look worse. Nora needs to be truthful about what her own part in the conflict might be as she talks to her brother.

Being relevant requires you to stick to the topic at hand without unnecessary observations. If Nora's upset that Angie isn't paying her share of the rent on time, it's not relevant to the current problem to share that Angie's been leaving campus a lot, and Nora thinks she has a boyfriend at another school. Nora should stay on the current topic to be effective in her communication about this problem.

When you're being clear, you avoid ambiguity in your comments. Nora should use words that Sam understands and that fully express her feelings. If Nora says "It's interesting that Angie seems to have a lot of money for clothes but not rent," Sam might be confused as to whether that means Nora's angry, uncertain, or genuinely interested.

Developing a supportive climate for communication involves six other skills:

- being descriptive
- being provisional
- being spontaneous
- being problem oriented
- being empathic
- embodying equality

We explain each of these skills below.

- Descriptive communication sticks to facts avoiding evaluations ("You have left your clothes on the bathroom floor every night this week" rather than "You're such a slob!").
- Provisional communication allows for tentativeness in your conclusions, as opposed to expressing that you're absolutely sure of your opinions ("I think Professor Bayer

grades women differently from men. What do you think?" rather than "No question about it. Professor Bayer is sexist.")

- Spontaneous communication expresses how you're feeling at the moment, rather than being calculated and strategic ("I'm so appreciative of how you handled that problem!" rather than: I should plan to compliment her at least three times a week.).
- Problem oriented communication focuses on solving a problem with the other ("Is there some way we can do what you want tonight and then what I want tomorrow?" rather than "I never get my way in this relationship – we're always doing what you want, and that has to stop!").
- Empathic communication indicates that you're trying to understand how the other person feels even if you do not feel that way yourself ("I see that you're upset about this. Would it help to talk?").
- Equal communication reflects that you see yourself and your partner as sharing power in the relationship rather than reflecting a power hierarchy ("What do you think? I really want to know your opinion" rather than "I earn the most money in this relationship, so it's going to be my way or the highway.").

Now, we'll discuss how one of these skills, being descriptive, can help relational communication in two different contexts.

Applying *Descriptive Communication* at Work

Andy had been working with Melanie for four years and they were very comfortable with one another. Andy liked and respected Melanie a lot, and he wondered if there was a chance that they could spend some more time outside of work together. He was concerned about dating a co-worker, but their company had no rules prohibiting it, and he liked Melanie enough to take a chance. The next time he saw her, he asked if she'd like to stop for a drink after work with him. Melanie looked a bit shocked, laughed, and shrugged, saying "Are you kidding?"

While it's likely that Andy isn't happy with Melanie's response, he should resist the urge to evaluate it. An evaluative comment would be something like, "What's your problem? I just was trying to be nice, but you're completely rude." Instead of that, if Andy uses description, he could say, "Melanie, I'm confused. I see you laughing at the idea of going out with me, and you looked pretty shocked that I asked you to go for a drink. Can you explain what's going on?"

Applying *Descriptive Communication* in the Family

Fontana is a single mother of two teenage sons, and she's admittedly a clean freak. While she understands that teenage boys don't have the same standards of cleanliness that she does, she's getting really tired of picking up after her sons. She can barely stand going in their rooms; she's only half kidding when she says that the neighbors could report her to the health authorities because the house is a disaster area. Every time Fontana has tried to talk to her sons, it's ended in a screaming match or with one or both of them running out the door before she finished talking.

Fontana should sit down with her sons at a time when all three of them are calm and have the time to talk. She could begin by saying that she realizes that she has a different definition of a clean house than they do. However, she's concerned that the boys are establishing habits now, and she wants to help them create good ones. When she describes their rooms, she needs to avoid words like "disaster area" and focus instead on specific comments. For instance, if she's concerned that they leave the clean clothes she brings up from the laundry on the floor, she should describe that clearly and avoid labeling their behavior as slovenly or calling them names like "slobs." Being clear and descriptive about what the boys are doing now, and how she wants them to change, will be helpful.

Communication Response: Marsha and Tami Neimann

In our Communication Encounter, single mother Marsha and her daughter Tami were preparing for Tami to leave home for the first time, and attend graduate school in London. It's a huge step for them, as they have rarely been separated. Tami had even attended the university in her hometown so that she and her mother could see each other frequently and continue their close and loving relationship. As they pack for Tami's departure they are juggling a lot of bittersweet emotions. Marsha is overjoyed that Tami has this exciting opportunity, and she's very proud of how hard Tami has worked to get accepted to such a prestigious graduate program. But, of course, she will miss Tami terribly and she's very sad to see her go. Tami, for her part, is excited and nervous about this opportunity, and she's wondering how she'll navigate the demands of the program, meeting new people, and getting along in a foreign country without the loving support of her mother. After thinking about the material in this chapter, answer the following questions:

1. How do Marsha and Tami express their feelings of affection toward one another? Give examples of what they said and did.
2. What stage would you say their relationship occupies (using the Knapp and Vangelisti model)? How useful is this model for understanding Marsha and Tami's relationship? Explain your answer.
3. How can Relational Dialectics Theory help us understand Marsha and Tami's interaction? Which relational dialectics are in play in their encounter?
4. What do you predict will happen when Tami attends school in London? How do you predict Marsha and Tami will negotiate their long-distance relationship?

Questions for Understanding

1. Define interpersonal communication, and discuss how it differs from relational communication.
2. Discuss at least two communication behaviors that characterize close relationships and give an original example of each.
3. Explain how self-disclosures maintain and deepen close relationships.
4. Explain Relational Dialectics Theory. Discuss how it purports to explain communication in close relationships.

Questions for Analysis

1. Do you agree that interpersonal communication is distinct from relational communication? Explain your position.
2. Do you believe that conflict has both positive and negative effects in close relationships? Explain your answer.
3. Compare the stage model of relationship development to Relational Dialectics Theory. What are the underlying assumptions of each? Do you see these assumptions as compatible or not? Explain your answer.
4. How does technology affect close relationships? Do you believe that close relationships can be sustained without much face-to-face interaction? Explain your position.

Suggestions for Further Reading

Baxter, L. A. (2007). Mikhail Bakhtin and the philosophy of dialogism. In P. Arneson (ed.) *Perspectives on philosophy of communication*, pp. 247–268. West Lafayette, IN: Purdue University Press.

Baxter, L. A., & Norwood, K. (2015). Relational dialectics theory. In D. O. Braithwaite & P. Schrodt (eds.) *Engaging theories in interpersonal communication*, 2nd edn. Los Angeles, CA: Sage.

Greene, K., Derlega, V. J., & Mathews, A. (2006). Self-disclosure in personal relationships. In A. Vangelisti & D. Perlman (eds.) *Cambridge handbook of personal relationships*, pp. 409–427. Cambridge, UK: Cambridge University Press.

Guerrero, L. K., & Bachman, G. F. (2010). Forgiveness and forgiving communication in dating relationships: An expectancy-investment explanation. *Journal of Social and Personal Relationships, 27*, 801–823. doi: 10.1177/0265407510373258

The Gottman Institute, www.gottman.com.

7 Communication in Small Groups and Organizations

CHAPTER OUTLINE

CHAPTER GOALS

At the completion of this chapter, you will be able to:

- Provide a clear definition of small groups and organizations.
- Explain the characteristics of communication used in small groups and organizations, and illustrate how they differ from other types of communication.
- Discuss the roles people often assume within small groups.
- Elaborate the process of problem solving and decision making in small groups.

- Examine the utility of Groupthink in understanding small group communication.
- Discuss the concept of leadership in the organization.
- Clarify the findings on managing work–family time.
- Examine the utility of Organizational Culture Theory in understanding organizational communication.
- Apply a variety of strategies to improve skills in small group and organizational communication.

COMMUNICATION ENCOUNTER: NORRIS WRIGHT AND FAYE REYNOLDS

Norris Wright looked up from his laptop late on a Friday morning, and was surprised to see his boss, Faye Reynolds, standing in his office doorway. "Hi, Norris" Faye said smiling. "Do you have time to talk?" "Sure, Faye, come on in" Norris said, and smiled back but inside he was feeling a bit apprehensive. The company had made some management changes recently, and it seemed like the new management team had different ideas about running the company than the old leaders had. He'd recently heard that the product manager, Franklyn Newman, had been fired. Rumor had it that Franklyn came in at 8 a.m. one day, got called into his boss' office, and by 1 p.m. he was packing up his things, and was escorted out the door by security. The rest of the employees in Franklyn's division had been on edge ever since. Now, Norris eyed Faye nervously as she sat in his visitor's chair. "Norris," Faye began, "I know you've heard about Franklyn leaving the company." Norris nodded and Faye continued. "I know it's upsetting when someone leaves, but, we're a well-oiled machine here, and we can respond to changes pretty well. His departure actually is a good opportunity for us to reorganize, and we'd like to have you take over Franklyn's duties. We'd make you the group leader over Charlene, Tina, and Freya creating a new division of product research. What do you think?" Norris paused. He was delighted, concerned, and scared all at the same time. "Faye" Norris finally said, "I'm flattered you think I am ready to lead a group, and I'm ready for the challenge. Of course, I'll need to see a job description and we'll have to talk about responsibilities and compensation." "Certainly, Norris" Faye responded. "Let's meet on Monday to hammer out all the details, and in the meanwhile, please think about how you'd like to structure the work group. We're promoting you for your creativity, so come in Monday with some fresh ideas." "Sure thing" Norris responded. He was happy, but he wasn't sure how it would work to become the group leader of his former colleagues. He also wondered if it was a good time to be a leader in this company. And he couldn't help worrying about how long it might be before he'd be facing the same fate as Franklyn. He'd just have to work extra hard to be sure that didn't happen.

Background

Nearly everyone has worked in a group and/or an organization, and, thus, engaged in small group and organizational communication. You may be reading this at your college or university, which is an academic organization. In some of your classes, the professors might divide the students into groups for specific assignments. You could also belong to a religious organization (church, mosque, synagogue); you might serve on a committee for fundraising or for hiring the building maintenance person. You may have (or have had) a job at some organization where you probably worked in groups like the one Norris (in our Communication Encounter) is being asked to lead. Groups and organizations are woven into most people's daily lives, and depend on communication activity. Larry Frey (1994), a small group scholar, commented on the centrality of communication to small groups by saying "communication is the lifeblood that flows through the veins of groups" (p. x). And, in 2013, the EK Blog noted that "communication serves as the foundation of every facet of a business" (para. 2).

We begin this chapter by first offering definitions for small groups and organizations, and then discussing characteristics of communication in each context. Keep in mind that entire books are written on the subjects of small group and organizational communication. This chapter is a brief overview of these topics, and we hope you'll do further reading and discover more about these relevant, important areas of communication.

Interpreting Small Groups and Organizations

Sometimes people define groups by counting the number of people present. If there are more than two (or a dyad) and fewer than 15 or so (the outer limit isn't always clear), then they're designated as a small group. But, a better method for defining **group** is based on the social characteristics that distinguish it from other collections of people. These characteristics include:

- goal orientation (the members share a common goal or purpose)
- interdependence (the members need one another to accomplish their goal; everyone must play their part for the group to be successful)
- interpersonal interaction (the members must engage in communication with one another to accomplish their goal)
- perception of membership (the members all acknowledge that they are part of the group)
- structured relations (the members have a known way for interacting; for instance, they begin and end meetings in the same way, and group members assume roles to further the group's goal)
- individual motivation (all the group members need to feel a sense of commitment to the group and be ready to do their part to accomplish the group's goal)

These characteristics together form a good definition of a small group. A collection of people who are standing together waiting to buy tickets for a concert, for example, is not a group as we're thinking about it here because they do not satisfy all the social characteristics of a group discussed above. Groups can form from collections of people, however. For instance, if seven people are seated together in a hospital waiting room while their partners are receiving cancer treatments, they are not a group as we're defining it. But if they should start to talk with one another and decide to band together to get better services for their partners and others, they transform themselves from a collection of people to a small group by our definition.

There are a variety of types of small groups. Our discussion here focuses on task groups that exist to solve a long-term problem (formal groups) or those working on something short term (advisory groups). We're defining **formal groups** as groups that have a long-term task, or a series of tasks (such as a debate club, or a standing committee in an organization) and are structured in a formal way, meaning that membership is restricted (not everyone can be on the committee, for instance), and the structure is clearly outlined. There is a designated leader and there may be other officers as well. **Advisory groups** are very similar in definition but their task is a short-term one. A committee charged with planning a fund-raiser for a fraternity or sorority, a jury, a group of faculty members who need to pick departmental award winners for the year all illustrate advisory groups.

We're talking about groups and organizations together in this chapter because **organizations** have often been defined as groups of groups working together toward a common goal. Organizations are more complex than small groups because they contain within them a number of groups, all with somewhat different responsibilities, working together for the same overall purpose. Like groups, organizations have been defined by their essential characteristics (Mumby, 2013; Redding, 1988) including:

- interdependence
- differentiation of tasks and functions
- a goal orientation
- control
- communication

We'll examine each of these characteristics briefly. First, organizations are *interdependent* because the work of any one individual affects the other members in some way. When upper management decided to make a change in personnel and fired Franklyn Newman in our Communication Encounter, that decision affected Franklyn, of course, but it also rippled through the organization, making an impact on Faye, who had to decide how to reorganize the team, Norris, who may become the new group leader, and Charlene, Tina, and Freya, who will probably be working for their former colleague. This newly formed group within the organization will undoubtedly also affect other organizational members when they begin contributing ideas to the company. Mumby (2013) comments on the independence of organizations by saying "all complex organizations consist of intricate webs of interconnected communication activities, the integration of which determines the success or failure of the organization" (p. 6). Interdependence, then, is animated by communication in the organization.

The organization's complexity is illustrated in part because of its second characteristic, *differentiation of tasks and functions*. This characteristic might also be called division of labor and it reflects that organizations depend on specialization. Division of labor results in organizations having a variety of different departments, each doing a different aspect of the overall job of the whole organization. What jobs have you held in the past? Think about how the specific job description you had fit into the overall picture of the organization. Did you ever work on an assembly line? The assembly line is perhaps the clearest expression of the characteristic of division of labor.

The third defining characteristic of organizations is *goal orientation*, meaning that organizations emphasize a common purpose. Organizations are focused on a common goal that's often reflected in a mission statement. While organizations subscribe to a single, specific mission, because they are complex, some divisions may find themselves in conflict with others. An organization's goal is usually general, and parts of the organization may find their interpretation of the mission disagrees with the way other parts define it. People who work in university admissions may see themselves as counselors. They may believe that their goal is finding the best fit between their school and prospective students. From this perspective, admissions workers might not "sell" even a great student on their university, if they believe the fit isn't there. But those who work in finance for the university might believe that the admissions people should be marketers, finding a way to prove to prospective students that there is a fit between them and the school.

The fourth characteristic, *control*, refers to the fact that organizations must exert efforts to keep employees and departments functioning toward the goals. Precisely because of the potential conflict among different divisions within an organization, leaders must exercise control, assuring coordination among the different areas and providing a clear path to the overall goal.

Finally, *communication* helps us understand an organization. We take the position that communication and organizations are intertwined, and that communication creates organizations through a variety of practices such as repeated patterns, rituals, and metaphors. This is the **CCO approach**, or the idea that communication constitutes organizations (e.g., Mumby, 2013; Putnam & Nicotera, 2008). This approach is illustrated in our Communication Encounter when Faye tells Norris that their company is "a well-oiled machine" that can respond to change. When organizational members utilize metaphors to describe their organization, they are both capturing and creating the sense of its identity simultaneously. Later in the chapter, we'll discuss Organizational Culture Theory, a theory that's congruent with the CCO perspective.

Communication in Small Groups and Organizations

Because we adopt the CCO perspective, we'll address some specific characteristics of the communication shaping small groups and organizations. Some researchers believe that group and organizational communication are just interpersonal communication in different contexts. While that view is an oversimplification, as we discuss below, it's true that many of the same principles we've discussed about perception, verbal and nonverbal communication, listening and so forth are relevant to group and organizational communication.

Small Groups

Communication within small groups is generally more formal than communication among friends, and sometimes the communication in a group is strictly rule-governed. Communication practices differ by group type. If you belong to a legislative assembly (formal group), there may be rules such as that people have to be acknowledged by the chair to gain the floor and give an opinion, people may not speak twice on a subject until everyone has had a chance to speak once, and there may be time limits on an individual's contributions. If you belong to a sorority fund-raising committee (advisory group), the rules are probably not as strict, but the communication within the committee is still more formal than a group of friends chatting about issues in the sorority. The members are expected to stay on the topic and, if they digress, they'll be reprimanded and asked to stick to the problem at hand.

Connections: Listening and Communication in Groups and Organizations

Reflect on how listening relates to communication within organizations. Think about the following scenario:

Micah is beginning his first job after graduating from college with a degree in engineering. He's excited about the company and believes that there's a great fit between him and management. In his final interview, the interviewer expressed how much the company believed in collaboration across divisions within the organization. The interviewer gave Micah several examples of how this type of collaboration had enriched projects that they had completed in the past. Micah agreed wholeheartedly, and he was happy to begin working with a company that stressed values and beliefs that were congruent with his. Imagine Micah's surprise when he tries to pitch a collaborative project to his immediate supervisor and is dismissed quickly with the comment that his idea is too "out there" for the company to consider. Thinking that perhaps his initial idea needed more development, Micah tried to remember the examples the interviewer had mentioned when discussing collaborations that had been effective in the past. For some reason, he can only remember one of the examples and as he reflects on it, he can't understand why his own idea got shot down. He thinks it resembles the example in many regards. Micah makes an appointment with the interviewer to check his memory. When he speaks with her, he's unhappy to discover that he'd remembered the example incorrectly and his idea was completely different from what she'd said the company endorsed in the way of collaboration. Micah leaves the appointment concerned about his place in the organization, but determined to find a way to work it out.

How does this scenario illustrate connections between the material we discussed about listening and the material in this chapter about groups and organizations?

Communication within groups may also follow a ritualized pattern. Some groups adopt a "catch-up" time at the beginning of each meeting where members volunteer things they've done or thought about since the last meeting that could affect their contributions at the current meeting. It's also possible to have a "debriefing" session at the end of a group meeting where members offer feedback, both positive and negative, about how the meeting went and provide suggestions for improvement. Groups often follow an agenda, and in some groups a member is appointed (or self-appoints) to keep the discussion on track. Sometimes the group or a single member allots a specific amount of time for the group to talk about each agenda item.

Being effective in a group requires that members understand and follow the rules governing their communication behaviors, or suggest modifications to make the rules more effective. For instance, when Selena believes that the time limits in the agenda are stifling full discussion about an item, she speaks up and tells the group they need to spend more time on a particular point.

Organizations

Communication structures, and reflects the structure of, an organization. In organizations that operate with a hierarchical chain of command, workers get a great deal of information about how to do their jobs by listening to their supervisors. Messages coming from a higher power individual in the organization sent to those with less power are called **downward communication**. Downward communication may be used to explain rules in the organization and to require workers' compliance. This type of communication usually is formal, although some workers may have an individualized relationship with their boss and this can affect the formality. Downward communication may take place face-to-face or via email, phone calls, voice messages, or texts. In our Communication Encounter, Faye Reynolds engages in downward communication when she lets Norris know that she's interested in promoting him to lead a work group, and she's expecting him to come up with some creative ideas for shaping a new direction for the group. But she also illustrates that her relationship with Norris is personalized because she comes to his office and asks if he has time to talk, rather than summoning him to her office.

The opposite of downward communication, **upward communication**, refers to those messages sent from a subordinate to his or her superior. Aside from the directional flow of the communication, the messages in this type of communication differ from downward communication as well. Subordinates don't explain or enforce organizational rules to their superiors; rather they ask for clarification, make suggestions, respond to superiors' requests and questions, and they may give feedback or share important information. Upward communication also occurs when an employee learns something important about the company from interactions with customers or observations of colleagues that they feel is necessary to share with supervisors. When Norris tells Faye that he's interested in negotiating with her about the new position, he is engaging in upward communication.

A third type of communication, **horizontal communication**, refers to the interactions between co-workers or peers on the same power level in the organization. Although initially most research on organizational communication focused on upward and downward communication, soon scholars realized the need to study communication between and among co-workers. Horizontal communication takes place in formal settings such as a meeting among group members working on the design for a new company logo, but it often occurs in more informal ways, such as in hallways, the break room, and even outside of the workplace in coffee shops or one another's homes. In a study about a hospital's cancer clinic, Ellingson (2005) found that the clinic was characterized by a lot of informal horizontal communication, a process she called *backstage teamwork*.

Even in what some people call the "gig" economy (Schwartz, Collins, Stockton, Wagner, & Walsh, 2017), where more people work remotely and independently from home, people remain concerned about having a community of colleagues. The company, WeWork, offers independent workers a sense of community by providing desks and carrels in a communal space where independent workers gather. The founders of WeWork posted the following on their website:

> *When we started WeWork in 2010, we wanted to build more than beautiful, shared office spaces. We wanted to build a community. A place you join as an individual, 'me', but where you become part of a greater 'we'. A place where we're redefining success measured by personal fulfillment, not just the bottom line. Community is our catalyst. (www.wework.com/mission)*

Think about a job you've held. Do you think conversations with co-workers were important to your sense of your job and the organization as a whole? Would you be comfortable working in isolation and not having any co-workers to talk to?

An additional type of communication, called **boundary spanning,** occurs when members of the organization speak to others in a different company, or to someone served by the organization. Boundary spanning occurs when you call another company to order supplies, take a call from an angry customer, collaborate with other organizations to set up a community benefit, or do market research by interviewing prospective clients. This type of communication, external to the organization itself, connects the organization to its publics and to the community in which it exists (see Figure 7.1).

Now that we have a sense of how to define small groups and organizations, as well as the communication characterizing each of them, we turn to an examination of fundamental issues and theoretical insights first in groups and then organizations.

Fundamental Issues in Small Group Communication

As we've mentioned, small group communication is a large topic and there are many important issues we could discuss. Here we focus on two that have been researched extensively and have important consequences for the effective functioning of small groups: group roles and group decision making and problem solving.

Group Roles

Many years ago, Robert Bales (1950) proposed that some people in groups are rational and task oriented, while others are more oriented toward the relationships among group

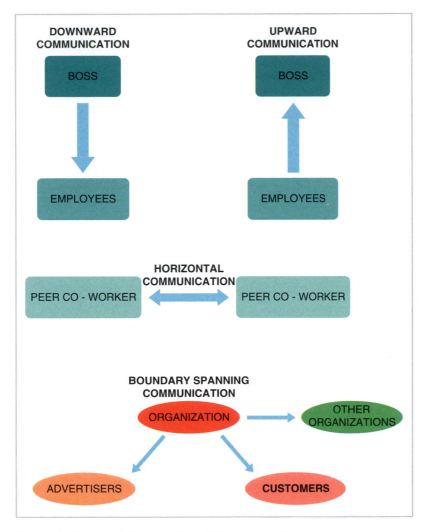

Figure 7.1 Types of Organizational Communication

members, and still others contribute dysfunctional behaviors to the group. Bales argued that this means there are three types of roles in groups:

- task completion
- relational maintenance
- dysfunctional.

The first two role types are functional for the group; the third is not. When people play task-oriented roles, they contribute behaviors such as helping the group define its task, asking for information needed to solve the problem the group's addressing, providing that information, and recording information needed for future meetings.

Bales called the output from task roles **productivity**. When people play socio-emotional roles, they support and encourage the contributions members make, they make sure that everyone gets heard in the group ("Angel, we haven't heard from you, what do you think?"), and they mediate when group members engage in conflict ("Let's take a break for a minute to cool off; then we can come back to discuss this"). The output from socioemotional roles is known as **cohesion**, or a measure of how much the group likes each other and enjoys being part of the group. Later we'll discuss the theory of Groupthink that focuses on how too much cohesion may harm the group's ability to make a good decision. Finally, Bales acknowledges that some behaviors such as excessive joking and off-topic comments and silence or a refusal to engage in the group's work aren't functional. When you have participated in small groups, have you noticed people exhibiting any of these behaviors? A complete list of the roles is found in Table 7.1 along with a brief example of the communication displayed in each role.

Bales acknowledged that the behaviors defining roles may be exhibited by more than one person in the group and may not be played consistently by any one person. So while Rafe may be dysfunctional and clowning around in the group one day, he might act in a functional manner at another meeting. Also, roles may be shared so that both Niles and Rona help the group define its goals, and more than one group member could provide key information for the group to consider.

Group Decision Making and Problem Solving

One of the main reasons that groups are often tasked with decision making or problem solving is the assumption that when people work on a problem together, each individual's thinking will be enriched by hearing the others' comments. As the members build on each other's ideas, **synergy** results and a group's decision will generally be of a higher quality than any individual's alone would be. This is only the case, however, when groups are not beset by the problems that hinder decision-making abilities, and also when the problem they are working on doesn't have one specific solution, requiring an expert's judgment. If a group of consumers, architects, and city planners is trying to design a shopping mall, the group will benefit from the synergy of multiple ideas voiced in the meetings. But, if a group is trying to decide on the rank order of materials needed by explorers climbing a mountain, an expert mountain climber could solve that problem better than a random group of people.

Groups approach problem solving and decision making in many ways, but they often follow similar stages that researchers have attempted to model. One commonly utilized model is B. Aubrey Fisher's (1970) four-stage progression of: Orientation, Conflict, Emergence, and Reinforcement. In the **orientation stage**, members get to know one another and figure out their goal; they adopt some role behaviors that they

TABLE 7.1 Roles and Behaviors in a Small Group

Roles	Behaviors Exhibited
Task	
Leader	Helps group define and achieve goals
Initiator	Offers ideas and suggestions
Information seeker	Requests information germane to the problem
Information giver	Provides data for group to consider
Recorder	Keeps group records
Questioner	Prods group so they don't become complacent with their ideas
Socioemotional	
Encourager	Provides praise for ideas
Tension Reliever	Helps resolve conflicts; uses humor and acts as mediator
Gatekeeper	Manages the flow of communication; watches to see that no one dominates
Feelings Monitor	Checks to be sure no one feels left out or "unheard"
Dysfunctional	
Isolate	Withdraws from the group and won't contribute
Clown	Goes beyond tension relief and engages in practical jokes and comic routines that distract the group members
Blocker	Objects to every idea that is raised
Cynic	Displays a negative attitude; acts like a "downer" and brings group morale down

might maintain for subsequent meetings. They may elect or appoint a leader and a recorder. The orientation stage may last for several meetings or be accomplished during a single group session. The heart of the group's work is accomplished during the **conflict stage** where members engage in discussions about the feasibility of a variety of solutions. They test solutions against criteria they develop, and argue about what will work best. As the group closes in on a solution, they enter the **emergence stage**. Finally, the group congratulates itself on finding a solution and begins to praise their work in the **reinforcement stage**.

Fisher's model illustrates how communication and the stages have a reciprocal relationship with each other. The stage produces a certain type of communication and the communication voiced by members propels the group into a particular stage. For example, if someone says, "I think if we combine the last two suggestions we've been discussing, we'll have a creative solution" and others voice agreement and there's nodding all around the group, that would characterize the emergence stage, as well as clue members to the fact that the group was finished with the conflict stage and was starting to be ready to propose a solution.

This model suggests a rational approach to how small groups make decisions and solve problems, but we know from our experiences working in small groups that the process isn't always rational. M. Scott Poole and his colleagues (Poole & DeSanctis, 1990; Poole & McPhee, 2005; Poole, Seibold, & McPhee, 1996) advanced a multiple sequence model that represents the more complicated approaches groups utilize. The multiple sequence model acknowledges three major decision-making paths, including the rational approach:

1) the unitary sequence path
2) the complex cyclic path
3) the solution-oriented path

The **unitary sequence path** is the rational approach and the pathway is like the sequence proposed by Fisher discussed previously. However, a study (Poole & Roth, 1989) found that most groups didn't use the rational approach. Only about 23 % of groups studied followed the unitary sequence path. Far more (47 %) utilized the **complex cyclic path**, which involved the group beginning one approach to problem solving only to abandon it and take up another. In this path, the group interaction consisted of multiple problem-solution cycles. Finally, in the **solution-oriented path**, used by 30 % of the groups, the members simply began to solve the problem at hand and devoted no time to discussing the parameters of the problem or analyzing it. As you think about groups you've been in, which model seems most accurate to describe the way your group made a decision?

Do the Right Thing: Dealing with Difficult Topics in Groups

You have been placed in a work group in your American history class whose task it is to create some type of multimedia presentation about an aspect of the history you've been studying in the course. Your professor, Dr. Su, arbitrarily created the groups and your group contains four other students you do not really know. One of them, Jed Hastings, is someone who speaks out a lot in class and you've been disturbed by some of the things he's said. When the class was discussing the Civil War, you thought some of the comments Jed made bordered on racism. Further, Jed made a point of saying that he understood why people wanted to keep up statues commemorating Southern resistance in the Civil War. Jed was angry that statues that had been around since the 1800s and reflected the history of the US had to go just to "pacify the feelings of some of the people living there now." Dr. Su let Jed talk about this for a while before cutting him off saying that his comments didn't reflect on the topic at hand, although it was an interesting discussion for another day. When your group first meets, the topic comes up again because Jed wants to focus your project on this issue. One of the other members of your group is an African American woman, Maya Weston, and you can see she is uncomfortable with this idea, but she doesn't voice an opinion. You are not sure what to say in response to Jed's comments in the group, and you're unhappy that he's jumped in to take over as the group leader. Also, you want to encourage Maya to speak up, but you don't want to make her a token black voice. No one else in the group has said anything besides Jed. You can't imagine working on this topic and you know you need to say something. What do you do?

1. If you used the categorical imperative as your ethical system, how would you proceed?
2. If you used utilitarianism as your ethical system, how would you proceed?
3. If you used the ethic of care as your ethical system, how would you proceed?
4. Specifically, if you had to write out a script for what you should say in the group, what would it be?

Theoretical Insight: Groupthink (Janis)

We now review a theory focusing on the concept of group cohesion: Irving Janis' (1972) Groupthink theory.

We've discussed how a small group can be very effective in solving certain problems, due to synergy. But, we know from our experiences in groups that sometimes things go awry and often we leave a group meeting feeling frustrated. Further, sometimes synergy does not occur and a group actually makes a bad decision, one that an individual might have been able to do better. Have you ever had to do a small group assignment for one of your classes where each member of the group received the same grade? If so, you might have believed that if you'd done the assignment yourself you would have gotten a better grade than what the group achieved. Irving Janis' theory of **Groupthink** is one well-known explanation for these feelings, and the actual occurrence of poor problem solving within groups.

Groupthink occurs when group members become more concerned with **consensus** (a decision-making process where all can agree) than with critically assessing all options for solutions to the problem or problems they are considering. When groups become highly cohesive, and they emphasize the socioemotional aspect of their deliberations, they may also become less concerned with the task at hand. Janis advances that this occurs because the group members would rather encourage each other than debate with each other over unpopular or minority opinions. According to the theory, when this happens, the members make premature decisions, some of which will be problematic and could have long-lasting and calamitous consequences. Have you ever been in a group where you kept quiet even when you had a different opinion from the majority just because you liked the group members and you didn't want to rock the boat? If so, you know what Janis was thinking about in developing this theory.

In creating Groupthink Theory, Janis examined policy decisions made by US presidents and their advisors that had negative consequences for the United States. These decisions included the US Navy's policies leading to a lack of preparedness prior to the bombing of Pearl Harbor in 1941, the decision by President Kennedy to invade Cuba at the Bay of Pigs in 1961, President Johnson's decision to pursue the Vietnam War in 1964, and President Nixon's decision to participate in the Watergate cover-up in 1972. Janis interviewed many of the people who were part of these groups and concluded that the poor quality of all these decisions was a result of groupthink.

The theory outlines eight symptoms of groupthink that occur in three categories. The first category, called *overestimating the group*, contains two symptoms:

- the illusion of invulnerability
- unquestioned belief in the morality of the group

When group members believe that they are special and they know more than most other people, they begin to think they can't make a mistake. This contributes to their sense of essential correctness, that Janis calls the **illusion of invulnerability**. When group members share the belief that they're good and moral, they believe that the decisions they make are good and moral as well, and this promotes the **unquestioned belief in the morality of the group**. For instance, when Bihkar joined a student protest group dedicated to preventing speakers with offensive views from speaking on campus, he believed in the cause. The longer he belonged to the group, the more convinced he was of the morality of their goals and the special quality of the members and the group itself. Bihkar is overestimating the group. If all the other members engage in this type of thinking, the group may make problematic decisions. Can you think of a time when you belonged to a group and you believed it was special and morally correct in all ways?

The second category is *closed-mindedness* and its symptoms include:

- stereotyping those outside the group
- collective rationalization

Out-group stereotypes consist of characterizing those outside the group in rigid and often negative ways. For instance, if Bihkar and his group believe that anyone who disagrees with them is ignorant and short-sighted, then out-group stereotypes are developing. **Collective rationalization** takes place when group members ignore information that's contrary to their beliefs. They don't listen to anything that might prompt them to reconsider their position and alter their decision. Together the members of the group convince each other that they have made the correct decision and they shouldn't revisit it.

The final category, *pressures toward uniformity*, involves the following symptoms:

- self-censorship
- mindguards
- the illusion of unanimity
- pressure applied to dissenters

Self-censorship occurs when group members have dissenting ideas but stop themselves from expressing them to the group. No one has to argue with Bihkar, he simply stifles his doubts himself. **Mindguards** are group members (usually self-appointed) who actively work to keep contrary information from the rest of the group. If a member of Bihkar's group reads a compelling argument about free speech for all, but decides not to call it to the group's attention, that member is acting as a mindguard. The **illusion of unanimity** exists in the group when silence is interpreted as agreement. Sometimes group members are not sure how to express their disagreement with a decision that the rest of the group seems to support. In this case they may be silent and let the more vocal members of the group push the decision through. **Pressure applied to dissenters** may take several forms. Sometimes dissenters are asked to leave the group or are made to feel so uncomfortable that they resign. Other times members simply provide verbal and nonverbal feedback to convince dissenters that they should conform to the rest of the group's will. Table 7.2 illustrates these aspects of groupthink.

Several researchers including Janis have discussed how to avoid groupthink and make more productive decisions. Here we review Paul 't Hart's (1994) recommendations.

't Hart suggests four ways to prevent groupthink:

TABLE 7.2 Symptoms of Groupthink

Category	Symptoms
1) Overestimating the group	*illusion of invulnerability
	*unquestioned belief in morality of group
2) Closed-mindedness	*stereotyping outsiders
	*collective rationalization
3) Pressures toward uniformity	*self-censorship
	*mindguards
	*illusion of unanimity
	*pressure applied to dissenters

1) impose external oversight and control before groups start work on problem solving
2) encourage members to voice concerns and develop a questioning culture within the group
3) allow group members to opt out of a decision if they find it morally objectionable
4) balance the desire for consensus with recourse to majority rule

't Hart argues that implementing these four suggestions will instill a questioning attitude within the group, as well as provide external inputs to the group that will help counteract groupthink.

Fundamental Issues in Organizational Communication

Organizational communication researchers study myriad issues, and here we address two of them: leadership and managing work and home demands.

Leadership

Leadership is one of the most studied aspects of organizations, no doubt because leaders are assumed to be extremely important to the functioning of organizations. Early leadership research focused on the single person as a great leader and examined traits that an effective leader embodied. Distilling the literature on the **trait approach to leadership** suggests that the important qualities a leader should possess include: intelligence, self-confidence, determination, integrity, and sociability (Miller & Barbour, 2015). If you think about CEOs like the late Steve Jobs or political leaders like the Prime Minister of Canada, Justin Trudeau, do you think they fit the traits listed above?

Over time researchers became disenchanted with the trait approach to leadership, because it didn't seem accurate. Can you think of jobs you've had where the bosses were very different from one another but yet were all successful leaders? If Carla is soft-spoken and Mick is loud and boisterous isn't it possible that they both can be effective leaders for their companies? Researchers began to reject the trait approach in favor of the **situational approach to leadership**. This means that in some situations, someone who's soft-spoken might be the perfect leader; in a different situation a louder, more forceful speaker might be needed. Some people are effective with small groups while others are more effective at directing large groups. One type of leadership is effective in start-ups, and a different type of leadership is needed in an established corporation.

Researchers have examined leadership and followership in conjunction with one another. This focus on the relationship between leaders and followers brings communication to the forefront as communication explains how relationships are formed and sustained (Gardner, 2003). This approach has several facets; we'll talk briefly about one of them: the **transformational approach.** This approach suggests that the leader and the follower interact in such a way that both are changed by the relationship. As Miller and Barbour (2015) observe, transformational leaders embody the values and the mission that they wish to instill in their followers. Through their interactions, both have the potential to change. According to Bryman (1996), transformational leadership requires "an active promotion of values which provide shared meanings about the nature of the organization" (p. 277). Although this approach to leadership is different from the trait approach, it does suggest that the transformational leader is likely to be charismatic and inspirational (Bass, 1990). However, how a transformational leader appears depends a great deal on the perceptions of followers. This approach focuses on leadership as a "co-production" between leaders and followers (see Figure 7.2). Have you ever worked for someone you'd call a transformational leader? What was the experience like?

Managing Work–Home Issues

If you and your partner/roommate both work, how do you decide who does the grocery shopping, who maintains the car, who dusts, who cooks, who takes the dog to the groomer, as well as the many other responsibilities of running a home? If you recently

Figure 7.2 Leadership and Followership May Work Together in Some Organizations

lived at home with two parents, how did they divide up work and home chores? Issues of work and home affect people world-wide; however, the communication about these issues differs across cultures, in part because of differing cultural values about the important of work and personal life (Kirby, Wieland, & McBride, 2013). Some cultures make it relatively easy for workers to juggle the responsibilities of work and home life. In these cultures, the state takes over some of the burdens of caring for working families. This is referred to as **familiazation** (Esping-Andersen, 1999). Scandinavia is one region where the culture supports equality and full employment for both men and women. To aid in these goals, the Scandinavian governments provide generous leaves for both parents after the birth of a child as well as a dependable public childcare system (Kirby & Buzzanell, 2014).

The situation in Scandinavia contrasts with that in the United States where work-home issues are seen as private problems to be negotiated by individual workers, sometimes in conjunction with specific workplaces. This approach is congruent with the cultural value of individualism that prevails in the USA. (Recall our discussion from Chapter 2.)

In the United States, support for workers is sometimes provided by their organizations. The Society of Human Resource Management (SHRM) report by Solis & Day (2017), states that some US organizations offer family-friendly benefits such as childcare centers, on-site breastfeeding rooms, paid family leave, and access to a coach who'll help with home-work issues. Further, the SHRM noted that workplace flexibility is vital to an effective workplace; SHRM recognized nearly 300 US businesses for providing pioneering benefits addressing home–work concerns.

However, even when benefits exist, there may be informal norms preventing employees from taking advantage of them in the USA. Buzzanell and Liu (2005) found that employees knew that using family leave was seen as burdensome and out of the norm by their organizations. Thus, the benefits were under-used in the opinion of their respondents. In a study investigating how family-friendly policies were used in institutions of higher learning in the United States, the researchers found that "cultural expectations about what is considered 'appropriate work'" prevented employees from taking advantage of the family-friendly benefits that were offered (Townsley & Broadfoot, 2008, p. 137). Lynda Ross (2016) suggested that most careers in the USA and Canada have implicit expectations that restrict employees', especially mothers', ability to utilize family-friendly benefits.

Managing issues of work and life outside of work is an enduring struggle for all people who hold a job. The values of some cultures make this struggle easier, by providing a great deal of support from the government to workers, especially when the issues of their lives outside work need attention. Other cultures make the struggle more difficult by withholding this state-sponsored support. Sometimes individual companies step in to offer support (see Working Mother's list of the most family friendly companies to work for in 2017; www.workingmother.com/best-companies). However, even when the policies of a company provide support for workers, the culture of the company, influenced by the national culture, might discourage workers from taking advantage of certain policies. If you work for a company, what policies are offered to support you in your life outside of work?

Everyday Talk: How Work Impacts Your Health

In 2016, Nicole Fallon reported on the website Business News Daily about the many ways a person's job may impact their health (www.businessnewsdaily.com/2382-job-health-impact.html). Fallon commented that several work-related habits (many encouraged by organizations) take a toll on both the physical and mental health of workers. For instance, Fallon notes that being a workaholic and not taking enough vacations as well as habitually working overtime not only was related to depression, but also was correlated with heart-related problems. The sedentary nature of much office work resulted in many health ailments ranging from diabetes to back and neck aches. Fallon also observes that workers who check on emails multiple times daily experienced stress. She reports on a study conducted by researchers at the University of British Columbia that found a correlation between stress and frequency of checking emails. The researchers found that when workers were restricted to consulting email only three times during the work day, they reported less stress, although they also reported it was extremely difficult to resist looking at email more often.

1. If you work in an organization, have you noticed any relationship to your work habits and your health?
2. Do you think employers encourage work habits that lead to the negative health outcomes that Fallon reports?
3. How do you think the workplace can be improved to make it a healthier place for workers?

In addition to how much a workplace aids employees in juggling work and home responsibilities, workers report that how their workplace relates to the larger community is also important to them. According to Desda Moss (2016), there's a strong relationship between worker satisfaction and the amount of support their organization provides to the community. Moss states:

> the 2016 Cone Communications Employee Engagement Study found that nearly 75 percent of employees say their job is more fulfilling when they are provided opportunities to make a positive impact at work, and 51 percent won't work for a company that doesn't have a strong commitment to addressing social and environmental issues. Interest in making a significant social impact cuts across generations, and even small efforts can yield big gains. (para. 1)

When you think about your workplace (or future workplace), do its contributions to the community make a difference to you?

Theoretical Insight: Theory of Organizational Culture (Pacanowsky & O'Donnell-Trujillo)

In this section we review one of the many theories explaining communication within the organization: Michael Pacanowsky and Nick O'Donnell-Trujillo's **Theory of Organizational Culture**.

Pacanowsky and O'Donnell-Trujillo (1982, 1983, 1990) built on the ideas of the anthropologist Clifford Geertz, and applied a cultural lens to organizations to understand the communication within them. The theory assumes that organizations construct a unique culture through their practices, especially their communication practices. When you arrive at a new organization, one of your initial tasks is to become socialized to the organization's culture. The organization's culture has been created by the mission statement the founders developed as well as the climate generated by all the members of the company. It's important to note that organizational culture is created through the communication of all its members, not just the bosses, supervisors, or investors. Although as a new employee or student you come in to a culture that's been developed, your behaviors contribute to maintaining, expanding, or revising the culture as you work or study there.

One of the problematic issues within an organization is when the culture changes. When a company merges with another, merging their two different cultures successfully is critical. This can be especially challenging if the cultures are very dissimilar. Norris, from our Communication Encounter, is concerned that the organization he has known since he began working there may be changing when he sees how his colleague Franklyn was treated. On the other hand, some changes in the culture can be very positive, and Norris may have a chance to be more creative within the organization's evolving culture.

To understand the concept of culture as employed in this theory, think about the organizations to which you belong; they probably differ from one another in many ways based on a variety of things such as mission, size, history, location, and so forth. Making this more concrete, imagine you began your higher education at a community college near your home. After two years there, you transferred to a large state school from which you graduated with a B.A. in communication studies. Now imagine that after graduating you worked for a small nonprofit dedicated to promoting the arts scene in a medium-sized city. After four years there, you apply to and are accepted by a private university where you spend two years getting a Master's degree in arts administration. With your M.A. in hand, you move to a larger nonprofit in New York City doing essentially the same work you'd done previously but with a more established company with more employees, in a much larger market.

In this scenario, you have been a member of five organizations, and each would have "felt" very different to you based on Pacanowsky and O'Donnell-Trujillo's (1982) concept of organizational culture, or the essence of the organization. The theory states that as we attempt to study an organization's culture, we need to examine its symbols, which can be divided into three categories: physical; behavioral; and verbal (Hatch, 2006). **Physical symbols** include things like logos, building architecture and décor, and material objects around the office. **Behavioral symbols** are things like traditions within the organization, including the annual family picnic, the holiday party, and gifts that are given to people upon their retirement. Finally, **verbal symbols** include stories, jokes, nicknames, and legends that members hear when they first join the organization and then they tell to others joining later.

Applying these symbols to our previous scenario would lead you to think about your first job located in an old, crumbling building that needed a lot of repairs. People shared desks and no one had a private office. The members of the nonprofit always had Friday drinks together after work each week, and spent a lot of time joking with one another. You might be able to induce a sense of the culture from those symbols and understand how it differed from your next job in a new high-rise building with large glass windows affording a beautiful view of the city. The employees had carrels and the supervisors had private offices. People didn't socialize much at work, but they did gather in the break room often to tell horror stories about donors who withdrew funding without notice and prima donna artists who were hard to work with. How would you describe the culture of these two workplaces based on a brief analysis of these symbols?

Enhancing Your Skills

In this section, we briefly discuss four skills enabling us to work more effectively in both groups and organizations. Then, we'll apply one of them to both an organizational context and a group situation. These skills include:

- clearly articulating the common goal
- listening carefully before speaking
- fostering a creative climate
- developing openness to feedback

Clearly articulating the common goal means understanding what is bringing the group or organization together, and expressing that goal in language that all members understand and accept. Because a common purpose is central to the definitions of groups and organizations, it's critical that every member understand, accept, and put that goal into practice. This skill also means that you are aware of all the skills we discussed in Chapter 4 about verbal and nonverbal communication. You must think about the vocabulary you use and how the person or people you're speaking with will react to that vocabulary. When discussing the group or organization's mission, you have to be sure you don't use jargon that some members don't understand, for instance, and you need to be careful that your verbal and nonverbal behaviors are congruent, to avoid misunderstandings.

All of the skills we discussed in Chapter 5 about listening will enable us to be productive group and organizational members. When we listen carefully before speaking, we are making sure that our contributions add to the conversation and don't take the group off on a tangent because we failed to understand what someone else had just said. When we practice good listening skills in groups or organizations, we maximize the chances that when we do speak, we'll be making a productive contribution to the discussion.

Communication should be used to foster a creative climate within the group or the organization. This means using the skills we discussed in Chapter 6, such as being descriptive rather than evaluative, speaking tentatively, allowing for others to contribute, speaking in a problem oriented manner allowing everyone to focus on the goal for the discussion, and expressing empathy where it's useful, letting others know you understand their positions; rephrasing what you've heard them say and allowing them to correct you if you've misrepresented their position. A creative climate depends on members feeling free to bring up "out-of-the-box" ideas, knowing that they won't be ridiculed, and their ideas will be used as springboards for imaginative thinking.

Finally, developing openness to feedback requires you to hear others' reactions to what you've said. You need to express your thoughts while recognizing that your ideas can be improved when others provide feedback to you. As we discussed in Chapter 4, you may want to engage in I-messages in meetings and discussions, indicating that you know your opinion is not a statement of fact. Openness to feedback is also accomplished when you ask others what they think and avoid dominating the meeting with your own thoughts. Asking "Can you let me know what you think?" or "What's your take on this?" signals to other group members that you want to hear from them. And, of course, you have to be willing to hear that people disagree with some of your ideas, or have thoughts about how to improve them.

Let's now discuss the application of one skill, openness to feedback, to the organizational and group contexts.

Applying *Openness to Feedback* in the Organization

Caleb works for a small tech start-up and he's been satisfied with his job, but it's now time for his first performance appraisal, and he's not looking forward to it. His supervisor, Hannah, is nice enough, but he thinks he's actually more qualified than she is. He worked at another tech company for three years before coming to this job, and this is Hannah's first job out of college. When she comes in to talk to him, he's already prepping for how he'll counter any criticisms that she has of his work.

While it is widely acknowledged that performance appraisals are difficult conversations for both supervisors and employees, they can be productive if both participants work together. Caleb needs to stop anticipating that his performance appraisal will be negative and spend time thinking about how to get the most out of the conversation. He should forget about his feelings about Hannah's qualifications and instead of preparing his defense, prepare a list of questions for which he'd like Hannah's feedback.

Applying *Openness to Feedback* in a Small Group

Sumana is a new faculty member in the Communication Studies department at Metropolitan University and she's excited to go to the faculty meeting this month. That wasn't always the case; she'd been on the job for a semester, and most of the department meetings were pretty boring. But this month, she thought would be different because the department had just received a sizeable gift from an alum, with no strings attached. They were free to use the money any way they wanted, and Sumana had what she thought was a great idea. She came into the meeting and handed everyone a sheet with her idea for spending the endowment. After they'd read it, she asked for feedback. Mona, the most senior member of the department, smiled in a way that Sumana thought was patronizing, and said that it was a good enough idea, but the department had tried it many years ago and it just didn't fly. Sumana asked a couple of questions about what they'd done, and Mona answered quickly, suggesting they should move on. Sumana left the meeting thinking she'd never speak up again.

Sumana began appropriately by preparing her idea and asking for feedback. But, perhaps she needed to let the faculty members have more time to digest the idea, and so she should come back the next time asking to continue the discussion. She certainly shouldn't give up after one negative reaction. However, she should think about what Mona said; she might be tempted to reject Mona's objections out of hand and dismiss her concerns as the result of "old-fashioned" thinking, but she needs to really listen to the feedback and see if there are any ways she might modify her plan to respond to it.

Communication Response: Norris Wright and Faye Reynolds

In our Communication Encounter, Faye Reynolds told Norris that the company wanted to promote him to a leadership role in a reorganization promoted by the recent firing of one of his colleagues. This promotion would result in Norris becoming the group leader for three people who were currently his peer colleagues. Norris was pleasantly surprised to hear his boss's request; when she first entered his office, he thought for a moment he was about to be fired himself. He was a bit apprehensive, because he wasn't sure it would be easy to supervise peers, but he was willing to try. He still had to negotiate with Faye, but he knew this promotion was a good thing and should mean a raise and perhaps other perks. So, overall, Norris was pleased, but some issues definitely gave him pause. Aside from supervising former peers, the atmosphere at work that resulted in such a quick firing of his colleague was concerning, and he knew that this promotion put him under a spotlight and he'd have to deliver. After thinking about the material in this chapter, answer the following questions:

1. How will the culture of Norris' organization make a difference in his success or failure in his new position? What kind of organizational culture might facilitate success for Norris? Why do you think this?

2. What aspects of leadership discussed in this chapter do you think would be helpful for Norris in his new position? Explain your answer.

3. What advice do you suggest for Norris to make his interactions with Faye and his former colleagues successful?

Questions for Understanding

1. Define group and organizational communication and discuss at least two ways that they relate to each other.
2. List two task roles and two socioemotional roles that people play in groups. Give an example of the kind of communication that characterizes each role.
3. Distinguish among trait, situational, and transformational approaches to leadership.

Questions for Analysis

1. Construct your own model of group decision making.
2. Create an argument for and an argument against studying communication in small groups and organizations. Defend or refute the position that the principles of interpersonal communication are the same whether they are practiced in a group, an organization, or any context.
3. Provide some policies you think organizations should extend to workers in the United States and elsewhere to support them in their lives outside of work.

Suggestions for Further Reading

Bullis, C. (2005). From productivity servant to foundation to connection: One history of organizational communication. *Management Communication Quarterly*, *18*(4), 595–603.

Buzzanell, P. M. (2014). Work and family communication. In L. H. Turner & R. West (eds.) *The SAGE handbook of family communication*, pp. 320–336. Thousand Oaks, CA: Sage.

Frey, L. R. (ed.) (2002). *New directions in group communication*. Thousand Oaks, CA: Sage.

Henry, A. (2013). The best collaboration tools for small groups and teams. Lifehacker.com. http://lifehacker.com/the-best-collaboration-tools-for-small-groups-and-teams-1477548590

Lambertz-Berndt, M. M., & Blight, M. G. (2016). "You don't have to like me, but you have to respect me": The impact of assertiveness, cooperativeness, and group satisfaction in collaborative assignments. *Business and Professional Communication Quarterly*, *79*(2), 180–199.

8 Social/Mass Media and Communication

CHAPTER OUTLINE

CHAPTER GOALS

At the completion of this chapter, you will be able to:

- Provide clear definitions for mass media and social media.
- Recount the history of mass media.
- Elaborate the issues involved as a result of the ways that women, people of color, LGBTQ people and others are represented in and by mass media.

- Examine the utility of Agenda Setting Theory in understanding mass communication.
- Examine the utility of Social Information Processing Theory in understanding social media.
- Apply a variety of strategies to improve your skills as consumers and producers of mass and social media.

COMMUNICATION ENCOUNTER: BETH WILDER AND CHAO LI

When Beth Wilder left home for college she hadn't interacted with many people who were different from her. She grew up in Baxter, Minnesota, which was over 90 percent white and where the vast majority of the families were of German, Swedish, or Norwegian heritage. All her friends and the guys she dated looked, acted, and worshipped like she and her family did. One of the reasons Beth was anxious to go to the University of Minnesota was to encounter difference – different people and different ideas. Beth was excited for the adventure to begin. On her very first day, during freshman orientation, she met a young man named Chao Li who was Chinese American. He and Beth started talking about how confusing the requirements for freshmen were and they became friends. Beth was embarrassed to admit that before meeting Chao, the closest she had come to a Chinese person was watching a Jackie Chan movie on Netflix. And, she'd read on her news app that the USA and China had an "iffy" relationship, and that maybe China couldn't be trusted as a US ally. Chao was born in the United States to immigrant parents who'd succeeded in the "American Dream," and raised their children in Eden Prairie, Minnesota. In Eden Prairie the Li's were a definite minority, so Chao was familiar with white people who only knew his culture from the media, and he was pretty accepting of some of the questions he got asked as a "token" Chinese man. In their junior year, Chao told Beth that he was starting to have romantic feelings for her. He was thinking of applying to graduate schools, and before he moved away, he wanted to give the two of them a chance to have a more serious relationship. Beth had to admit her feelings for Chao were growing as well. They dated happily for the next year before Chao left Minnesota for New York City. While apart, the two kept in touch using Skype, FaceTime, and texting. In some ways their connection deepened while they communicated online. Some of the little things that they disagreed on (like being neat and getting to appointments on time) weren't important on Skype. But, now they were about to have their first face-to-face reunion, and both were a little apprehensive about how it would go.

Background: The Importance of Media in Everyday Life

Media, both traditional mass media and social media, play enormously important roles in contemporary life. You can see in our Communication Encounter above that Beth and Chao are affected in multiple ways by mediated communication. Beth forms impressions (maybe stereotypes) about Chinese people from media sources, Chao's parents probably saw mediated versions of the "American Dream" that influenced them to immigrate, and Beth and Chao maintain their relationship using media when they live over a thousand miles apart.

When you think about your own life, multiple mediated sources of communication probably occur to you automatically. You might think about listening to podcasts, streaming videos, texting with friends, posting on Snapchat, or taking a class online, to name just a few ways media intertwine with daily communication encounters. It's rare in the twenty-first century to ever be out of range of mediated communication. It can happen, but you would have to work at it, by going to some remote site that's not served by the internet, and being sure to leave all your screens behind. The Pew Research Center (2017) reports that 95 percent of people in the USA now own some type of a cell phone, and 77 percent own smart phones (up from 35 percent in 2011), making accessing the internet easily done while on the move rather than from a stationary source (i.e. a desktop computer) as in the early years of the twenty-first century. As we're writing this chapter, we have interrupted ourselves frequently to check an incoming email, text on our phones, or verify a source online!

There's been an explosion of commentary about how people use (and may be used by) media and technology. For example, the website, The Daily Journalist (http://thedaily journalist.com), is an international site devoted to reporting the news online and commenting extensively on how society is shaped by media and mediated news sources. They've published articles discussing cyber security and developments in artificial intelligence. Shelly Palmer, an advertising, marketing, and technology consultant, also produces a newsletter about the ways humans interface with technology in addition to the future of media (see TV may actually die soon, 2017, http://adage.com/article/digital next/tv-die-stay-tuned/308618/).

Because mediated communication is such an enormous topic, we cannot begin to cover all of its characteristics and nuances here. Our goal is to provide an overview of the two main media arenas addressed by communication scholars: mass communication, or mass media, and social media. We begin this chapter by discussing several fundamental issues in mass media. Next, we provide a theoretical insight explaining the relationship between mass communication and the audience. Then, we turn to a consideration of fundamental issues in social media, and offer a theory explaining how relationships are formed and maintained using social media.

Fundamental Issues in Mass Media

We begin with definitions. Although some of the terms we're using (like "mass") might be questionable as we think about mediated communication today, it's useful to have a definition of mass media to frame our discussion. We then present a brief history of mass media, and finally, we address how a variety of groups are represented in mass media.

Interpreting Mass Media

We adopt the traditional definition advanced by many scholars (see, for example, McQuail, 2010; Vivian, 2017; Wilson & Wilson, 2001). **Mass media**, a term coined in the early twentieth century, refers to using technological means for professional communicators to communicate with many people (the public) at the same time over large distances. There are several important aspects to this definition that both help to delineate what mass communication is, but also complicate our application of the definition in today's media landscape. Key terms within our definition include:

- technological means or technology
- professional communicators
- the public

We'll discuss each of these briefly.

First, mass communication relies on some type of technology allowing many people across large distances to engage in the process. **Technology** means using the practical application of knowledge to accomplish a task, and it requires the conversion of knowledge into some type of tool (like a telephone, a camera, etc.). It's important to note the evolution of technologically assisted communication relative to our definition. Initially the invention of the telephone did not allow for professional communicators to communicate with many people (the public) at the same time, so it wouldn't have been considered a tool of mass communication. Yet, today, of course, smart phones can be used to watch TV or movies and to consult the internet. Phones also allow us to make a conference call, connecting a large group. In these cases, the phone does become a technology for mass media. Below we provide a chronological list of forms of technology traditionally considered to contribute to mass communication. Later when we discuss the history of mass media and the evolution of social media, we'll elaborate on these technologies and the specific media they enabled.

- The earliest technology was printing, and the invention of moveable type allowed books, newspapers, and so forth to reach a large audience.
- Chemical technology spread photography and film.
- Television is a product of electronic technology.
- The Internet resulted from digital technology.

The second term in our definition, **professional communicators**, refers to a clear separation between producers of messages and consumers of messages. For instance, not everyone can write a book, and authors must hone their art through some type of formalized training. They might study at a university or on their own to become skillful enough to publish their work. Journalists have to study their craft and perfect a set of skills allowing them to produce newspapers and broadcasts. Operating the large equipment initially required to make photographs, films, and television programs entailed a set of skills that had to be learned and practiced. Are you thinking about how social media have upended this traditional approach to mass communication?

Finally, the term, **public**, in our definition presumes a mass audience that tunes in to the same radio and television programs and reads the same books. Early theories of mass communication suggested not only that people were all tuning in to the same messages, but that these mediated messages exerted similar effects on the viewing/listening public. This position presumes a very powerful media and a relatively passive public. This is known as the **Hypodermic Needle Theory** of media, or the belief that media "inject" ideas into the mind of the compliant public.

Mass media theory no longer advances this hypodermic needle approach. Currently, most mass communication scholars conceptualize the audience as active, and capable of thinking critically about ideas presented in the mass media (think about the viewers of Fox News and MSNBC, for instance). This approach led to the **Reception Theory of Mass Communication** (e.g. Jensen, 2012), which suggests that different audience members will have different responses to the same mediated messages based on their differing backgrounds. This means the audience shapes messages along with the media producer.

Connections: Perceptions and Media

As we think about media and communication, it's important to remember that all the principles of communication apply. Reflect on how perceptions relate to mediated communication. Think about the following scenario:

Jesse gets on the train to go home from work. He has his headphones on and he's watching the news on his smart phone. They're talking about how theft, mugging and pickpocketing have increased in the city lately and people should be extra vigilant, especially in crowds. Jesse doesn't think that television affects him; he has always felt much too smart for that because he studies media at the local community college. He closes the news app, and begins thumbing through his email as a stranger enters the train. The train is full, so the stranger sits in the only open seat, the seat next to Jesse. Jesse sizes up the stranger, and has a vague feeling of uneasiness. For some reason the stranger reminds him of the pictures of a convicted pickpocket he'd just seen on the news. Jesse has ridden the train every day, and never had a problem, but today he starts to feel uncomfortable. He puts his phone away, and places his hand on his wallet pocket. The stranger notices his discomfort, and stands up and holds onto the railing instead. Jesse gets off at the next stop, and takes a cab the rest of the way home.

How does this scenario illustrate connections between the material we discussed in Chapter 3 about perception, and the material in this chapter about the influences of mediated communication?

The concept of the public all watching the same media is still important to the definition of mass communication, however. That concept is troubled by the internet, social media, and streaming services like Netflix and Hulu which allow the audience to order media "on demand". As measured by Nielsen ratings (a survey done to establish the number of households tuning in to specific programs), the percent of households tuning in to the highest rated show in the 1950s was much greater than the percentage for the highest rated show in the 2010s (see Table 8.1). We still have some sense of a public, but it's probably more accurate to refer to *publics* to acknowledge the fragmenting of the audience that has occurred in contemporary society.

Reception theorists talk about publics as **interpretive communities**, meaning that groups of media audiences are constituted by demographics, social roles, and by ways of thinking about reality that contribute to making sense of mediated messages. Some people have argued that this fragmentation leads to an "echo chamber" effect where you're only exposed to people and messages that you already agree with. This echo chamber is thought to contribute to intolerance and lack of civility. Do you think that's the case?

TABLE 8.1 Nielsen Ratings for Highest Rated Shows by Decade

Decade	Show Title	Episode	Household share	Date aired	Network
1950s	The Ed Sullivan Show	Elvis Presley guest starred	82.6%	Sept. 9, 1956	CBS
1960s	The Fugitive	"The Judgment" Part 2	45.9%	Aug. 29, 1967	ABC
1970s	Roots (miniseries)	"Part VIII"	51.1%	Jan. 30, 1977	ABC
1980s	M*A*S*H	"Goodbye, Farewell and Amen" series finale	60.2%	Feb. 28, 1983	CBS
1990s	Cheers	"One for the Road"	45.5%	May 20, 1993	NBC
2000s	Friends	"The Last One"	40.2%	May 6, 2004	NBC
2010s	Undercover Boss	"Waste Management, Inc" (Series Premiere)	29.4%	Feb. 7, 2010	CBS

History of Mass Media

A good reason to examine the history of mass media comes from theorist Marshall McLuhan's (1964) often-quoted phrase, "the medium is the message." What McLuhan meant was that far from simply being a container for a message, the medium actually shapes the message. McLuhan (1964) illustrated this belief with the example of a light bulb, which contains light but has no content. Yet, it sends a message by lighting up areas that were previously dark, and enables social change in doing so (i.e., people can go out at night, seeking entertainment, as well as stay up later in their homes). Other media that do contain content (newspapers, TV, and so forth) either expand the message of the content or compete with it in some way, and through that interaction new meanings emerge.

Think about the following example: If Graham wanted to break-up with his boyfriend, Anderson, and chose to do so through a text, Anderson might react more negatively than had Graham spoken to him face-to-face or even communicated the break-up over the phone. A text doesn't convey the message of a personal encounter, and sends an additional message along with the content message of "I want to break up." The additional message could be interpreted by Anderson as something like "And, I don't even care enough about you or the time we've been together to break up with you in person – I want out fast." On an episode of the TV show *9-1-1,* in 2018, a character correctly guesses that a woman calling him is older than he is because she prefers to call rather than text or Facetime.

We begin the history of mass media with the advent of the printing press that led to the printed book. Before the printing press, in the early medieval period, hand-lettered books were repositories for wisdom and religious beliefs, and were only in the hands of priests and the aristocracy. In keeping with McLuhan's assertion, the medium of printing affected content, and over time books became more secular and popular and accessible to the common person.

After the book, the printing press led to newspapers. Newspapers were created to be adversarial to the sources of established power and to print articles exposing corruption and deception perpetuated by the powerful ("telling truth to power"). This message from the medium affected the content published within newspapers, again making McLuhan's point. It's interesting that in the United States, President Trump took an adversarial position toward newspapers and the established press. He suggested that his use of Twitter illustrates that he's using media in a modern way. Do you agree? Do you think that this adversarial relationship between newspapers and those in power is still a useful one? What does it mean when the powerful are the ones adopting the adversarial role that previously had been reserved for the press?

In addition to books and newspapers, other publications were enabled by the printing press: plays, songs, tracts, series novels, poems, and so forth were all part of the mass media that the public consumed in the eighteenth century. By the beginning of the twentieth century many people viewed films and listened to the radio. Although film began as technological novelty, it soon became an important source of entertainment, as it was able to tell stories in an involving format that, according to McLuhan (1964), required little exertion from the viewer. People enjoyed films because their meanings were essentially provided to them so that they could relax and enjoy the show without having to do a lot of thinking. Radio was also an important source of news and entertainment and could be used for background noise. Today, we often use radio (or music in our headphones) in the same way.

Television became common in people's homes in the mid-twentieth century, and at first simply borrowed its content from the radio programs that existed earlier. Shows like *Amos'N'Andy* were lifted from their radio format and presented on television. But soon, the medium changed the content, and shows were created to take advantage of television's specific characteristics. For instance, television is well suited for close-up shots of people's faces so interview shows were a natural for TV. See Table 8.2 for a timeline of the turning points in mass media history.

TABLE 8.2 Turning Points in Mass Media

1446	Invention of moveable type by Gutenberg
1455	Gutenberg prints the first Bible
1500	Printing presses in every European city
1640	Cambridge Press publishes first book in the North American colonies
1690	Ben Harris publishes the first newspaper in the North American colonies
1741	First two magazines published in the North American colonies by Andrew Bradford and Benjamin Franklin and weekly newspapers were being published in the larger cities of the colonies
1837	Charles Babbage creates the Analytical Engine, the precursor to the modern computer
1838	Samuel Morse demonstrated the first telegraph
1877	Thomas Edison invented a phonograph that could record and play back sound
1888	William Dickson invented the motion picture camera
1895	The first radio transmission accomplished by Guglielmo Marconi
1925	Radios became common in US homes
1927	Philo Farnsworth discovered technology enabling television transmission
1930-1939	The Golden Age of cinema in the USA
1950	Televisions became common in US homes

Media Representations

A key issue for consumers and researchers concerns how media represent women and members of minority communities such as people of color, and LGBT people. You may remember the #OscarsSoWhite movement in the United States in 2015 and 2016, drawing attention to the fact that in 86 years (as of 2015) of Oscar awards for outstanding achievement in Hollywood films, only 37 awards (out of 2,900) went to people of color. That changed somewhat in 2017, which was called a landmark year for diversity (Nolfi, 2017), because actors of color, Mahershala Ali (*Moonlight*) and Viola Davis (*Fences*), both won supporting actor awards. The greater number of awards to people of color and films focusing on people of color was explained in part by an effort made by the Academy of Motion Pictures Arts and Sciences (AMPAS) to diversify its membership. The members of AMPAS are the voters for Oscar winners.

Brennan Williams, Christopher Rosen, and Irina Dvalidze (2015) wrote in the *Huffington Post* about why it mattered that films had so few people of color recognized at the Oscars. They noted that, "people want to see themselves reflected in films and on television" (para. 24). And, they also assert that when people do not see their own reflection in the media, that means their voices and their life experiences matter less than those whose reflections do appear. When Sterling K. Brown, of *This is Us*, accepted the Golden Globe in 2018, for best actor in a television series drama, he echoed this belief. Brown thanked series creator and writer Dan Fogelman for writing a role that could only be played by a black actor, and stated that this made it harder to dismiss him or anyone who looked like him in the future. This response generalizes well to all groups of people underrepresented in the media.

In addition to underrepresentation, media critics have noted that the media misrepresent or provide only one-dimensional representation of some groups. This problem is apparent when we see Middle Eastern characters consistently presented as villains or terrorists. It also exists when we frequently see young African American men playing the role of gang members, or when women of any ethnicity are represented as sex objects. A great deal of the research on the representation of women (and some research investigating how men are portrayed) in the media focuses on this type of one-dimensional focus.

For example, some research examining how women are presented in advertising concludes that gender stereotypes still power the images of women in print and television ads, projecting unrealistic perceptions of beauty, perfection, and sexuality (Jhally, Kilbourne, & Rabinovitz, 2010). While some companies exhibit pushback in their campaigns (e.g., the Dove soap campaign, www.youtube.com/watch? v = XpaOjMXyJGk) these gendered stereotypes persist, according to the research. Other research noted that magazines targeted toward young girls represent the same stereotypes of feminine beauty and objectification now that were present 50 years ago (e.g. Hata, 2014). Daniel Beck (2017) found that televised sports present women in stereotypical ways, and sports commentators speak about women and men differently following gendered norms. A large body of research has examined how women politicians are represented in the media in the USA, concluding that gendered stereotypes inhibit women's political advancement (e.g., Carlin & Winfrey, 2009; Isaacs, 2016).

Some studies have also addressed women's media representation in a variety of countries (even those where women hold high political office) and have found gendered stereotypes still exist (e.g., Lachover, 2017).

Much less research focuses on the representation of LGBT people in the media, and most of it concentrates on televisual portrayals. A 2016 survey from GLAAD (Gay & Lesbian Alliance Against Defamation) reports that the percentage of LGBT series regulars on broadcast TV is the highest it's been since the organization began tracking the numbers in 2004 (Gonzalez, 2016). The survey showed that 43 of 895 series regulars (or 4.8 percent) identified as LGBT. This increased visibility on US television is undoubtedly a positive thing because two studies demonstrate that the more young people watch depictions of LGBT characters on television, the more likely they are to support gay rights and equality (Bond & Compton, 2015; Garretson, 2015).

However, Sandra Gonzalez (2016) warns that numbers don't tell the complete story because television shows killed off 25 lesbian characters across all platforms (streaming, broadcast, and cable) in 2016. Gonzalez quotes Sarah Kate Ellis, the president and CEO of GLAAD, as commenting that these deaths were generally in service of furthering the narrative of a heteronormative character in the cast.

Theoretical Insight in Mass Media: Agenda-Setting Theory (McCombs & Shaw)

We review **Agenda-Setting Theory** by Maxwell McCombs and Donald Shaw. It shows audience members as active even though they're influenced by what they see and hear in mass media.

The theory was built on several concepts that preceded the formal theory itself. These concepts include:

- gatekeeping
- surveillance
- correlation

Gatekeeping, a term coined by Robert Park (1922), means that powerful people in media (like newspaper editors) can suppress some stories and advance others. Thus, what editors deem important will be what gets into the newspaper, and what they think is irrelevant will not. In this way, editors manage the public's access to news, as well as influence what the public believes is newsworthy. Of course, editors are not all-powerful and they are beholden to the owners and publishers of newspapers. So, sometimes their judgment of what makes it into the paper is colored by the political, financial, and social concerns of their bosses.

Surveillance, as defined by Harold Lasswell (1948), is the process of scanning the environment and deciding which events to concentrate on in reporting the news. Lasswell echoes the notion of gatekeeping here, but focuses more on how reporters have myriad stories that they could write about. Through surveillance they decide which stories they'll deploy their energies toward. At the same time, Lasswell also discussed the concept of **correlation**, meaning that the media direct the public's and policymakers' attention to the same things at the same time. The media, the public, and policymakers thus experience a "correlation of attention" (Dearing & Rogers, 1996, p. 11) to specific events (e.g., natural disasters, the Super Bowl, or President Trump's tweets).

These three concepts – gatekeeping, surveillance, and correlation – came together when Maxwell McCombs and Donald Shaw (1972) published an empirical test of the hypothesis that the media agenda becomes the public agenda over time. They interviewed undecided voters just before the 1968 presidential election, asking what they thought were the most pressing issues at the time. According to the respondents, the top five issues were foreign policy, law and order, fiscal policy, public welfare, and civil rights – it's interesting to think about how much or little has changed in the intervening years. McCombs and Shaw said those formed the public agenda.

They measured the media agenda by examining the number of news stories that had been published or broadcast in the nine main mass media outlets serving the areas where the people they'd questioned lived. They found an almost perfect correlation between what the media had been communicating and what the undecided voters reported as their top five issues. McCombs and Shaw induced the Agenda-Setting Theory from this study.

Agenda-Setting Theory takes the approach of an active public, and although the media set the agenda, the public was free to think whatever it wished about it. This led to the often noted aphorism that media tell the public what to think *about*, not what to *think*. However, some researchers (e.g., Guo & Vargo, 2015) suggest that the media do indeed influence more than simply the overall public agenda. For example, Beth, from our chapter-opening story, seemed to be thinking about Chinese people in a particular way based on movies and news reports. She didn't exactly form her own independent opinions. This is addressed in the theory by identifying two levels of the media's agenda setting function.

The first iteration of the theory only focused on the **first level of agenda setting**; creating a sense of the important issues of the day. As the theory developed, a second level, sometimes called **attribute agenda setting**, was added. This level focuses on what attributes, or parts, of the issues are most important. For instance, Beth thinks that China is suspect and a poor ally for the USA because of the way the news has presented the information to her. The topic of China made it to the media agenda (first level) and the way the topic is presented constrains how Beth thinks about China (second level). The second level refers to the process known as **media framing**, or the way that the presentation of a story shapes a receiver's response to it. It doesn't mean that the audience has no choice, and certainly many people hear the same story and form different opinions (think about controversies around topics like climate change, immigration, or abortion, for instance). Framing means media exert an influence on a receiver's response by the way they present stories.

A process related to framing is **priming** (Clawson & Oxley, 2017) which emphasizes the media's power to influence what people think, at least temporarily. For instance, if you read, heard, or watched news reports in the *New York Times* and the *Washington Post* about Donald Trump, Jr.'s meeting with a Russian attorney, you might be primed to believe that President Trump's campaign did collude with the Russians in an effort to win the US presidential election in 2016. If you hadn't paid attention to those reports, or if you consulted a source like *Breitbart News* with different priming, you might conclude that no collusion existed.

You've probably noticed that Park coined the term gatekeeping in 1922, the terms surveillance, and correlation surfaced in 1948, and McCombs and Shaw first introduced their theory in 1972. Certainly, as we've discussed, social media applications and technological innovations have altered the definitions of technology, public, and professionals in the twenty-first century. You might be thinking that Agenda-Setting is a rather dated theory, despite the more recent innovations regarding levels of agenda setting and framing and priming. However, most researchers believe Agenda-Setting Theory remains a viable explanation for mass communication-audience interaction, and the theory has adjusted to changes in mediated communication over time.

McCombs, Shaw, and David Weaver (2014) published an essay reflecting on past insights and future directions for the theory as it neared its 50th anniversary. Other researchers (e.g., Yang, Chen, Maity, & Ferrara, 2016; Moeller, Trilling, Helberger, Irion, & DeVreese, 2016) continue applying Agenda Setting in contemporary media settings with useful results. Do you think Agenda-Setting Theory provides a satisfactory explanation for how you use media today?

Fundamental Issues in Social Media

It's difficult to explain social media in one short section of a single chapter; but we know you're quite familiar with social media already. Here we offer a definition of social media and discuss some important effects of using social media. Later, in the skill application section, we'll focus on another critical topic for social media users: civility.

Interpreting and Understanding Social Media

In some ways, it's easier to define **social media** than mass media because they are a more recent innovation, and perhaps not as diffuse as mass media. But in other ways, there may be confusion around the definition because social media are new and quickly evolving. As a starting point, we'll use the definition found in the online Merriam-Webster dictionary. Social media are:

> forms of electronic communication (such as websites for social networking and micro-blogging) through which users create online communities to share information, ideas, personal messages, and other content (such as videos) (*www.merriam-webster.com /dictionary/social%20media*).

This definition encompasses a plethora of applications such as Facebook, Twitter, Instagram, Snapchat, and so forth. Some scholars (e.g., Bradley, 2010; Weber & Pelfrey, 2014) distinguish between specific *social technologies* (such as texting, YouTube, and instant messaging) and *social media* (which include all technologies focused on forming a potentially massive, collaborative community).

Social media may also be interpreted in terms of their contrast with mass media. If we examine our three key definitional terms for mass media (technology, professional communicators, and the public) through the prism of social media, we can draw some interesting insights.

First, the technology for social media has to be digital as the definition above suggests: websites, blogs, apps, and so forth. Computer technology was needed for the development of social media. And, as digital technology evolves, we can see the evolution of social media as well. Table 8.3 shows the timeline for social media's evolution. Although the timeline for social media is shorter than the one for mass media (see Table 8.2), that's only because digital technology is relatively new. Undoubtedly, students 400 years from now will be learning about a timeline for social media that rivals the length of the one we currently have for mass media given the pace of innovation in digital technology.

Perhaps where social media deviates the most from mass media is in the concept of a professional communicator. A person doesn't have to study or adhere to a code of ethics as journalists typically do in order to post something on social media. We are all "journalists," and "authors" as we post on our Facebook pages and our blogs. We didn't need to study literary criticism to post a critique of a book we've recently read. It's not necessary to study journalism or be particularly knowledgeable about restaurants to post a review on Yelp. We're all able to post our thoughts and opinions easily if we have access to a computer. One downside of this is the fact that what we produce on social media never really goes away. Sometimes an ill-advised post can come back to haunt its author. Have you ever had that experience?

TABLE 8.3 Turning Points in Social Media

1942	John Atanasoff and Cliff Berry invent the first digital computer
1953	IBM produces its first computer
1968	Hewlett-Packard provides the first mass marketed desktop computer
1976	Apple debuts its first computer
1990	Tim Berners-Lee invents the World Wide Web
1992	IBM introduces the Simon, the first smart phone
2004	Mark Zuckerberg and his colleagues launch Facebook (then called the Facebook)
2010	Kevin Systrom and Mike Kruger found Instagram
2013	Evan Spiegal and Bobby Murphy launch Snapchat

Everyday Talk: How Social Media Affected Dr. Chu's Employment

In 2017, Christine Hauser reported about a case where the use of social media affected a dean at Yale University (www.nytimes.com/2017/06/21/us/yale-dean-yelp-white-trash.html?smprod=nytcore-iphone&smid=nytcore-iphone-share&_r=0).   According to Hauser, Dr. June Chu, the dean of Pierson Residential College at Yale, posted a series of reviews on Yelp dating back to 2015, about restaurants and movie theaters in New Haven, Connecticut, where Yale is located. In her reviews, Dr. Chu used derogatory and racist language. Hauser quotes the following from Dr. Chu's Yelp reviews, the first about a local Japanese restaurant and the second about a local movie theater's concession workers:

> *"If you are white trash, this is the perfect night out for you!"*
>
> *"So what they have is barely educated morons trying to manage snack orders for the obese and also trying to add $7 plus $7."*

In her review of the Japanese restaurant, Chu goes on to say that the restaurant is "perfect for those low class folks who believe this is a real night out." Hauser reports that these reviews came to the attention of university officials, and Dr. Chu was initially put on leave and then fired. Dr. Chu emailed an apology to the members of the residential college saying in part:

"I have learned a lot this semester about the power of words and about the account-ability that we owe one another. My remarks were wrong. There are no two ways about it. Not only were they insensitive in matters related to class and race; they demean the values to which I hold myself and which I offer as a member of this community."

But her firing stood, and Hauser reports that Yale was looking for Dr. Chu's replacement.

1. Do you think Dr. Chu's words warranted her dismissal? Hauser reports that Dr. Chu deleted her Yelp reviews. Do you think that makes any difference in the case?
2. How do you think the fact that the reviews were on social media impacted the workplace decision? If Dr. Chu had told a few friends the same things about the restaurant and the concession workers do you think she would have been fired?
3. How might Dr. Chu have acted if she utilized the three questions (does she have a good reason to communicate, is she being honest, and is she putting herself in the others' place and empathizing with them?) we suggest for increasing civility online on p. 211?

Social media serves a democratizing function in allowing everyone to have a voice, but some scholars and writers have concerns about this. Vyacheslav Polonski (2016) observes that internet voices played a large role in Britain's departure from the European Union, which he regards as a grave political mistake. Polonski argues that amusing visuals and simple messages communicated over the internet substituted for statistics and rigorous expert opinions, leading the British people to vote to leave the EU.

William Brady and his colleagues (2017) make a similar argument with regard to Twitter and the US presidential campaign of 2016. Brady, Julian Wills, John Jost, Joshua Tucker, and Jay Van Bavel conducted a study showing how the use of emotion-laden words in a tweet causes others to retweet it. The researchers argue that statistics and expert opinions are no match for emotion in encouraging retweeting, or the spread of an idea. They also found that retweeting does follow an "echo-chamber" effect; conservatives were more likely to retweet conservative messages to other conservatives and the same for liberals who retweeted liberal messages to other liberals. The researchers' most important conclusion with reference to our point here is that anyone can get others to retweet their words if they use emotion-laden language; no professional training is required.

Finally, social media seems to lack the concept of public as advanced in our definition of mass communication. Yet, it's true that ideas spread throughout the greater culture on social media even if not everyone is watching the same TV program at the same time, as they were in the 1950s–1990s. Do you and your friends watch the same television programs? Listen to the same music? If you do, do you think that makes you all part of a public? How does that change the meaning of public for you?

It's also the case that social media users have several ways to share ideas with one another across platforms and geography. Some of these methods include:

- hashtags (like #BLM)
- gifs (small video clips often simply used to make a group of people engage emotionally, usually with laughter e.g. http://i.giphy.com/2AilMg2L8rTAA.gif)
- memes (cultural ideas and symbols that spread virally usually with the goal of making people laugh or making fun of others, e.g., the "Be like Bill" meme that was popular in 2015–2016, www.smh.com.au/content/dam/images/g/m/c/h/n/j/image.imgtype .articleLeadwide.620x0.png/1453507631732.jpg)

These connections allow people to partake in a collective culture in a different way than the traditional notion of public, but the results are similar. However, hashtags, gifs, and memes are usually smaller in size and more targeted, and generally more homogeneous, than the public definition of mass communication.

The Effects of Social Media

Our definition of social media points toward several of its effects. Social media serve to both connect and divide people. Social media leave an electronic footprint that could be regrettable, and social media allow individuals who might previously have been silenced to have a voice. We'll explore a few of the most discussed effects of social media next.

Jean Twenge has been studying generational differences for over 25 years and in 2017, she summarized some of her findings in *The Atlantic* online (Twenge, 2017). She noted that the generation born between 1995 and 2012 (that she calls *iGen*) is in many ways radically different than any other generation she's studied. Twenge attributes this to the fact that *iGen* is "a generation shaped by the smartphone and by the concomitant rise of social media" (para. 7). This immersion in social media has, according to Twenge, affected virtually every aspect of the lives of members of *iGen* both positively and negatively.

On the positive side, Twenge cited data showing that *iGen* adolescents were physically safer than previous generations. They were less likely to be in car accidents (because they drive less), less likely to participate in unhealthy drinking behaviors (because they don't drink alcohol as much), and less likely to be sexually active and experience teen pregnancies. Twenge notes that teen birth rates hit an all-time low in 2016 when they decreased 67% from their peak in 1991. Further, Sherry Turkle (2015) observes that social media creates online community, expands and intensifies friendship groups, and soothes anxieties for users.

However, high social media use in teens is correlated with many negative outcomes as well, according to Twenge (2017): poor sleep habits, higher rates of depression, and more suicides and suicide attempts. She cites a survey showing that heavy use of Facebook correlates with self-reported loneliness and depression. Twenge speculates that this could be the case because, although adolescents are not always with others in person, they are able to see the activities of a vast number of others on Facebook. They see evidence of parties that they weren't invited to, for instance, and this engenders feelings of being left out. Cyberbullying is another negative effect of social media, especially for girls, who are most often the victims of this behavior (Rivers, Chesney, & Coyne, 2011).

Although teens told Twenge (2017) that social media use soothed their anxiety because it gave them more time to compose their contributions in conversations, others have found that frequent social media use correlates with anxiety. This is especially the case when people fail to respond to you quickly after you've texted them (Beck, 2018; Turkle, 2015). According to Julie Beck (citing a 2007–2008 survey by Baron), people feel controlled by their phones, and their feelings of obligation to respond to texts and other messages were unpleasant. Beck concludes that we're becoming accustomed to only asking for and giving others "slivers of . . . distracted time" rather than full attention. Both Beck and Sherry Turkle conclude that this is a disturbing trend prompted by social media.

Theoretical Insight in Social Media: Social Information Processing Theory (Walther)

In this section we review Joseph Walther's **Social Information Processing Theory**. This theory explains how people form and maintain relationships online.

Joseph Walther devised Social Information Processing Theory (SIP) in part as a reaction against assertions that relational ties on social media are inferior to those created in face-to-face encounters. Walther was struck by how intense and poignant online communication could be for those engaging in it. As he researched online communication to develop his theory, Walther found that far from feeling estranged from their partners when they communicated with them online, participants claimed online communication was more powerful and important to them than was their face-to-face communication (Walther, 1996; 2011). The feeling of closeness and effectiveness that participants said they experienced online Walther called the **hyperpersonal perspective**. One attribute of the hyperpersonal perspective is the ability to take your time and think about your responses. Further, you may do this in a **synchronous** manner (e.g., the participants engage together in real time like on FaceTime), or you can give yourself even more time by responding in an **asynchronous** fashion (e.g., the participants are not necessarily online at the same time and engage whenever they have the time to do so as in Facebook).

In SIP, Walther examined three components of communication from the early models of communication we discussed in Chapter 1:

- senders
- receivers
- feedback

According to SIP, senders have the ability to present themselves in highly strategic ways in order to appear in the most positive light possible (Tong & Walther, 2015; Walther, 1996). **Affinity seeking**, or providing information online that a sender thinks will cause another to like them and what they post, underlies the hyperpersonal perspective advanced in SIP. Think about our chapter opening. Although Beth and Chao aren't beginning their relationship online, they are able to engage in affinity seeking by eliminating some of the issues that irritate them when they're together. When on Skype neither one of them is bothered by the differing standards they hold for neatness, for example, and they're free to focus on more agreeable things.

You might question Walther's position that senders wish to have others like them when you think about the negativity that sometimes occurs online, including serious cases of cyberbullying. Walther acknowledges that negative behaviors such as deception do occur online (Walther & Parks, 2002). SIP accounts for online deception in some measure through a concept we discuss a bit later.

The second component of the communication process is the receiver, and the hyperpersonal perspective is grounded in how receivers interpret messages from senders. When we interact with others on social media, we're making judgments about those others and their behaviors. Think about how you react if a friend waits a couple of days to text you back, or fails to respond as you'd expected to a meme you sent them. Those judgments you draw are called **attributions** and they consist of the motives or characteristics you ascribe to another (or yourself) based on their (or your) behaviors. You may remember this term from our discussion in Chapter 3 about Attribution Theory. If Callie sees that her boyfriend has replied to a joke she texted him by writing LOL, she may think he's a nerd or not really amused by her joke, because LOL was overused online and it's so 2015. Thinking he's a nerd, is Callie's attribution.

When receivers make the attribution that others are trying to manipulate or deceive them online, they engage in warranting. Walther defined **warranting** as "the perceived legitimacy and validity of information about another person that one may receive or observe online" (Walther, 2011, p. 466). In other words, the receiver wants to check the accuracy of what the sender has shown or told them. When receivers engage in warranting they usually try to connect with the sender's off-line network or eventually they may seek to meet the sender in a face-to-face setting to test the truth of what they've presented online.

Do the Right Thing: Should You Act Based on Social Media Information?

You have a friend, Alexander, with whom you were very close in college. Now that you've both graduated and no longer live in the same town, you keep up with one another using social media. Alexander has been posting a lot of selfies on Facebook and Instagram. When you first met him, Alexander was a pretty big guy; he'd played football in high school and college, and he probably weighed at least 300 pounds. After graduation, some of his friends had told him he should probably lose a little weight for his health. You hadn't joined in with these comments because you didn't think it was your business, and Alex hadn't asked for your advice. But now you notice that he seems to be getting progressively thinner in each selfie. You know men are sometimes subject to anorexia even though people usually just hear about women experiencing it. As you look over Alex's recent Facebook posts, you become concerned; he has definitely lost weight. It's probably healthy for him to weigh less than 300 pounds, but as you examine the posts, he seems far less than that. Alex is a tall guy, so he could easily weigh 200 pounds and not damage his health, in your opinion. But he might weigh around 150 pounds in the selfies you're looking at. You try to decide if you should reach out to him. You want him to know you're concerned and supportive, but you don't want him to think you're butting in where you don't belong. You wish you had a chance to see him in person to check whether he's really as thin as he looks in the pictures before you decided whether to say anything. Your work commitments probably make a trip unlikely for several months though.

1. If you used the categorical imperative as your ethical system, how would you proceed?
2. If you used utilitarianism as your ethical system, how would you proceed?
3. If you used the ethic of care as your ethical system, how would you proceed?
4. Specifically, if you had to write out a script for a conversation with Alex, what would you say to him?

The third component that Walther addressed was **feedback**, which he defined as a "reciprocal influence that partners exert" (1996, p. 27). When you're interacting online, feedback is more restricted than it is in person because you don't have access to all the same nonverbal cues. This makes the feedback you do have more important, leading some researchers to note that when people interact online they have "heightened expectations and idealized impressions" (Ramierz & Wang, 2008, p. 34). However, Walther didn't believe that made the online experience impoverished. Actually, he argued that there were a great many things that people could do online to provide feedback and express themselves, such as varying the size of the font, using capital letters or refusing to use them, utilizing italics, and, of course, using emojis and emoticons.

Figure 8.1 Social Media Provide People with a Way to Connect with Each Other Across the Globe

The three components, sender, receiver, and feedback, indicate that SIP reflects the communication process as it's captured online. Walther (2010) states that SIP is a process theory because communication is an ongoing and dynamic process. Online communication and relationship development accumulate over time. The theory illustrates that online communication is just as rich and valid as communication occurring face-to-face (see Figure 8.1).

Enhancing Your Skills

In this section, we briefly discuss two sets of skills to improve our abilities as users and consumers of media. First, we explore how developing media literacy helps us when we consume mass media. Then we attend to how engaging in civil discourse is a critical skill in using and producing social media.

Developing *Media Literacy* as a Media Consumer

Researchers suggest that media consumers should know what different forms of media and different media techniques communicate, and how they exert effects. For example, we should be aware of how the film version of *Spiderman* is different from the comic book version. And, we should know how political advertisements are constructed to create positive feelings about one candidate and negative feelings about the opposing candidate. When we know these things, we possess **media literacy**, or the ability to assess the messages sent through mediated formats. Media literacy is an umbrella term (Vivian, 2017) encompassing:

- linguistic literacy
- visual literacy
- film literacy
- internet literacy

Initially, mediated messages were very word-centric, and communication via text or email continues to be word-centric. Thus, linguistic literacy requires us to have vocabulary, grammar, reading, and composing skills.

As media history progressed, mass media became more visual. John Debes, who coined the term *visual literacy* in 1969 (Vivian, 2017), defined it as the ways in which a person is able to make sense of visual images, and "read" the meaning that's communicated by them. Visual literacy interacts with linguistic literacy and allows us to develop a critical perspective toward mediated messages. In this way we can decide whether we'll be influenced by a persuasive appeal that we see on television, for instance, or whether we'll reject it as overly emotional.

Film literacy means that we are conversant in the techniques that are specific to filmmaking such as close-ups, flashbacks, dissolves, and use of color. As we become critical consumers, we understand these techniques and again, can decide whether we wish to be persuaded by them. When you watch a film, do you ever think about the techniques the filmmaker has used to manipulate your emotions and draw you in to the story?

Nicholas Carr (2011) wrote in his book *The Shallows*, that the Internet has changed our brains, and not in a good way. Carr argued that the nonlinear aspects of surfing the web, gathering bits and pieces of information, changes brain functioning making it more shallow and fragmentary, and reducing our ability to being considerate.

Applying *Civil Discourse* Online

It has almost become a cliché to talk about how we need more civil discourse on social media, but it's quite true. Probably the most extreme example of incivility online involves cyberbullying. Sarah Holder (2017) reports in *Politico* that communities are diminished when their members are cyberbullied, and cyberbullying can only be stopped through community efforts. Holder observes:

A bully's power has everything to do with social status. If a community—a school, a Congress, a country—accepts and tolerates a bully's actions, those actions usually continue. It's only through social rejection that they are incentivized to stop. (para. 17)

Further, Holder cites Emily Bazelon, the author of a book about bullying, saying:

"It's not up to the victim of bullying to stop it or fight back," explains Bazelon, drawing on her research about adolescent bullies and their victims. "It's up to the community to make it clear to the bully that bullying is unacceptable. It's on all of us." (para. 18)

Do you agree with these assertions? What do you think Holder means by social rejection of a bully's actions? How do you think a community can organize to stop cyberbullying (or any type of bullying behavior)?

Cyberbullying is an extreme example of incivility online, but by no means is it the only example. You might read a post on Facebook that degenerates into name-calling and using obscene language. You might get a text from a friend that contains hurtful words. You might dash off a brusque and curt email that makes the recipient upset. There are myriad examples of incivility online. But, being civil online doesn't have to be difficult, and it is much like being civil face-to-face. David Brooks (2017) noted that civility is harmed when people forget to think about others in small ways. Brooks writes that we're living in "the golden age of bailing," and by that he means that social media make it easy to bail on social obligations. So you might agree on Monday that you'll meet a friend for coffee on Thursday, but when Thursday comes, you don't feel like meeting your friend after all. A quick text and you can bail. Have you ever bailed on a commitment using social media? Have you ever had someone bail on you?

Sometimes it's perfectly legitimate to cancel an appointment, but perhaps technology makes bailing too easy; Brooks (2017) comments that "technology wants to make everything smooth, but friendship is about being adhesive. As technology pushes us toward efficiency, we should probably introduce social rules that create friction" (para. 12). He then suggests some social rules that would make it harder to bail and could be generalized to make communication online more civil overall.

Brooks' social rules boil down to the following three questions:

- Do you have good reasons for doing what you propose to do? Think about the "reasonable person" standard; would most reasonable people agree that you have justification for doing what you plan to do online?
- How effective have you been in your communication: have you been honest, clear, and thoughtful?

- How will your actions affect the other? This requires that you practice empathy as we discussed that skill in Chapter 6.

Now, we'll illustrate how you can apply this approach in two specific communication situations.

Applying *Online Civil Discourse* in the Family

Every time Ella opened her email account she saw a message from her sister-in-law, Bethany, advising her how to save herself by finding the Lord. Somehow she had gotten on Bethany's mailing list and now received a lot of unwelcome religious messages. Ella was a private person and she felt her religious beliefs and spiritual life were nobody else's business. Also, lately Bethany had been sending messages about how bad abortion was; Ella found this offensive because she was strongly pro-choice and had even marched in many pro-choice rallies. Often Bethany copied long articles into the email espousing political positions that Ella disagreed with. She wanted to get off Bethany's mailing list, but her husband, Drew, whose brother was married to Bethany, didn't want her to make waves and possibly upset his brother. Whenever Ella brought up the subject with Drew he just shrugged and said, "Just let it go, Ella, it's not a big deal to delete an email." Ella got that, but she was struggling to explain that after she read those emails, she was jumpy and upset for hours, and she was finding it tough to "let it go."

Bethany is her sister-in-law, so it's difficult for Ella to completely ignore her; and she probably doesn't want to do that. So, she does have a good reason to communicate with Bethany. If she is honest and empathic, she can probably send her an email telling her that she respects her opinions though she doesn't share them. She could ask to be taken off the email list or she might suggest that they meet for coffee so they can talk about this in person. Knowing Bethany should help Ella to craft an email response that takes her feelings into consideration.

Applying *Online Civil Discourse* with Friends

Zora heard her phone ping and opened her texts to see a message from her friend Talia. Talia's text is about a celebrity couple who's divorcing. Talia wrote "OMG, can you believe those two broke up? I mean they have kids!" "Well Talia", Zora responded, "celebrities divorce all the time, I don't get why we need to talk about it." Zora isn't a fan of tabloids, but Talia is an avid consumer of pop culture and celebrity news, and she continues texting all the juicy details of the couple's divorce as explained in the media. Zora begins to ignore the texts as she thinks about what's happening in the world that Talia doesn't seem to care about. Many of Zora's relatives live in Serbia, and she's been keeping up with the stories from there. Hundreds in her parents' hometown have been killed by bombs, but Talia keeps going on about a celebrity divorce. Zora fantasizes texting "Hey Talia? Would you read your magazine if they had an article about war or refugees? Could you think about something important for a change!" And then imagining her squirm.

Zora might simply decide to cease being friends with Talia, or at least cut back on texting with her, because they have such differing concerns. But, she might think that Talia needs an explanation that Zora could prepare in an honest and empathic way. A nasty text is best kept in the fantasy zone. However, there's nothing wrong with being honest and telling Talia how she feels; just not how she thinks Talia should feel or behave. Zora should think about Talia receiving her message and avoid saying anything indicating that she thinks Talia is petty or focused on unimportant concerns. However, Zora is within her rights to let Talia know that she, herself, would rather talk about other things.

Communication Response: Beth Wilder and Chao Li

In our Communication Encounter, Beth Wilder begins a relationship with Chao Li without knowing much about Chinese Americans except what she's seen and read in the media. Chao has more knowledge of Beth's culture from personal experience and doesn't have to rely on mediated representations. Then Beth and Chao utilize social media to keep in touch after Chao moves away for graduate school. After thinking about the material in this chapter, answer the following questions:

1. How might Beth and Chao have difficulties in communication based on Beth's stereo-types about Chinese people that came from the media?
2. In what ways do you think Chao also might have been influenced by media in his responses to Beth, even though he grew up among European Americans like her in his hometown?
3. Both Beth and Chao are apprehensive about their first face-to-face meeting after their separation. Why do you think that is? What would Social Interaction Processing Theory predict for their future?

Questions for Understanding

1. Define mass communication explaining the important concepts of technology, professional communicators, and public.
2. Define social media and discuss how social media change the notions of professional communicators and public that are key to understanding mass communication.
3. Explain Agenda-Setting Theory. Discuss how it adds to our understanding of mass communication.
4 Explain Social Information Processing Theory. Discuss how it adds to our understanding of communication using social media.

Questions for Analysis

1. Construct an argument for or against the notion of a single public for mass communication. Explain your reasoning.
2. What do you think should be done to change the problems with the ways that women, people of color, and LGBTQ people are represented in mainstream media? Create a plan for better representation.
3. Suggest ways to ensure that online conversations are conducted with civility. What do you think can and should be done to elevate the level of discourse found online?

Suggestions for Further Reading

Critical studies of media (blog). https://investigatemedia.wordpress.com/page/2/

Katz, E., Hass, H., & Gurevitch, M. (1973). On the use of the mass media for important things. *American Sociological Review, 38*, 164–181.

McDougall, J. (2012). *Media studies: The basics*. New York: Routledge.

Shuter, R., & Chattopadhyay, S. (2010). Emerging interpersonal norms of text messaging in India and the United States. *Journal of Intercultural Communication Research, 39*, 121–145.

Turkle, S. (2015). *Reclaiming conversation: The power of talk in a digital age*. New York: Penguin.

9 Preparing and Composing Your Speech

CHAPTER OUTLINE

CHAPTER GOALS

At the completion of this chapter, you will be able to:

- Explain why presentations and public speaking are so prevalent in societies across the globe.

- Articulate the important contributions of Aristotle to presentational speaking.

- Differentiate between informative and persuasive public speaking.

- Describe ways of selecting and narrowing a speech topic.
- Provide strategies for researching a topic.

- Articulate the various components and patterns related to speech organization.

COMMUNICATION ENCOUNTER: VICTORIA BRUNO

Among her other tasks at the National Speaking Effectiveness Foundation (NSEF), Victoria Bruno is a professional trainer. Although her primary responsibilities are related to marketing, she is also an excellent public speaker and the NSEF Executive Director and Governing Board members are keenly aware of her speaking talents. They often send her out when the foundation is solicited by organizations interested in training their employees to be more effective in their communication skills. This time, however, things were just a tad different. Despite her 11 years of corporate training, Victoria was busy preparing for what would become a very challenging audience for her: medical interns at Rockton Hospital. There were a wide range of topics to facilitate, but Victoria decided to take a "case study" approach and outline her presentation within this context.

The interns clearly were not in a mood for any "Brown Bag Lunch" training on "Communicating with Difficult Patients and their Families." But they had no choice since the training was mandated. Ironically, most interns, according to the Director of Medical Intern Education, felt they knew how to handle the "tough job" of talking to patients. Victoria told them otherwise. She began her speech with a case study and asked one intern how he'd respond to that circumstance. After a rather lengthy explanation, she began to highlight the most recent national survey showing that 65% of patients find their doctor's communication skills either "poor" or "very poor." She started out her presentation with a story about Glynnis, a Somali immigrant who, because she never asked a doctor for clarification, gave her husband too many pills and he ended up in the emergency room. She then proceeded to explain the importance of speaking with clarity. She next overviewed her presentation by first acknowledging that a wide variety of subjects on public speaking exist, but that she was more interested in focusing on the importance of nonverbal communication during a physician–patient conversation. And, as if on cue, Victoria glanced around the lecture hall and couldn't help but notice the nonverbal communication of her audience; they were clearly not interested in being there.

Speaking with a group of friends or individuals whom we know well is normally not a nerve-racking experience. In fact, most of us are quite comfortable talking about some of our most personal feelings in front of people with whom we hang out on a regular basis. Yet, it seems this level of comfort dissipates once some people are asked to speak in front of many people whom they do not know. In fact, Sheri Ledbetter of the Chapman University Survey of American Fears (2017) notes that in addition to terrorism, bio-warfare, and identity theft, *speaking before a group of people* is ranked among the top fears that US citizens identify. Perhaps comedian Jerry Seinfeld underscored this best: "According to most studies, people's number one fear is public speaking. Number two is death. Death is number two. Does that sound right? This means to the average person, if you go to a funeral, you're better off in the casket than doing the eulogy."

For many, public or presentational speaking is no laughing matter. Scores of people – even some of you – have fear, anxiety, uncertainty, and just general unease speaking before a group of people. Chris Anderson (2016), the head of the global organization TED Talks (TED refers to the convergence of Technology, Entertainment, and Design), states that all kinds of people – from Leonardo da Vinci to Jackie Kennedy to Elon Musk – have found themselves in a public speaking situation with which they were not fully comfortable. Yet, Anderson believes that "anyone who has an idea worth sharing is capable of giving a powerful talk" (p. 12). Being "capable," however, is different from being "willing".

Some of you may be perfectionists and if every issue is not "in place" before and during the speech, you may be fraught with frustration. Others of you may be anxious about fumbling your words and simultaneously becoming humiliated. Still others of you may simply be uncomfortable trying to create meaning with people with whom you have no prior life experience. (We address these sorts of speaking uncertainties in Chapter 10.) Are you in one of these categories? Another one?

Background

This chapter provides you an important foundation related to public speaking. We divide this topic into two chapters (Chapters 9 and 10) in order to illustrate the preparation, organization, and delivery of a presentation. We realize that many of you have either enrolled in, or will enroll in, a course on presentational or public speaking; for some of you, it's an elective and for others it's a requirement. Here, however, we provide you only with a glimpse into the world of presentational communication to continue our goal of introducing you to the communication field. Over the next two chapters, we focus on a number of different areas so you will leave this course with several themes and skills that you can draw upon as you encounter public speaking opportunities. We begin with a brief historical note on public speaking and then we examine the prevalence of presentational speaking today. We move on to an overview of two important types of public speaking and then elaborate on several important themes related to researching and organizing a speech. We conclude with a few skills to consider related to many of these topics.

Aristotle: One Philosopher's Major Influence

In Chapter 1, we mentioned that the communication field traces its earliest roots to ancient Greece. Most cultures across the globe rely upon one's ability to speak effectively (Boromisza-Habashi, Hughes, & Malkowski, 2016). This notion can be traced back over 2,400 years ago when the philosopher Aristotle talked about rhetoric, or as we noted in Chapter 1, the available means of persuasion. Let's take a brief journey together to understand the rhetorical framework related to public speaking. Honoring public speaking's legacy is often neglected, but it provides us some historical sense of how things got started.

To begin, it's important to point out that Aristotle was not solely concerned with improving speaking skills. To be sure, he was preoccupied with the belief that rhetoric should produce enlightened citizens (Kuypers & King, 2001), a goal that is not on the minds of most public speakers today. In addition, although Aristotle felt that rhetoric's application to speaking was of primary importance, he simultaneously viewed rhetoric as a way of life. For instance, using the available means of persuasion was viewed as a "civilized substitute for harsh authority and ruthless force" (Oliver, 1950, p. 1). R.T. Oliver further noted that rhetoric was related to the daily choices people made in their lives and being able to articulate those choices effectively to others was of paramount importance. Today, scholars who study rhetoric take a comprehensive approach and are interested in how a host of messages, including mediated images, books, films, and so forth, influence us.

Aristotle believed that the speaker has a responsibility to his or her audience, a topic we will delve into in Chapter 10. After all, one essential goal of a speaker is to meet the needs of the audience. He subsequently developed the *Rhetoric*, which is considered by some to be one of the most influential pieces of writing in the Western world (Di Blasi, 2017). He later articulated several tenets and issues related to rhetoric, many of which we provide a bit later in the chapter.

Everyday Talk: Persuasive Charisma in the Workplace

In an interesting essay published in the Harvard Business Review (https://hbr.org/2012/06/learning-charisma-2), John Antonakis, Marika Fenley, and Sue Liechti conclude that a speaker's charisma, interestingly enough, includes attention to the basic rhetorical modes that influence the persuasiveness of a presentation. The authors assert that charisma is "rooted in values and feelings." They further contend that while the term is generally associated with an inspiring speech or presenter, the logos, pathos, and ethos also need to be acknowledged as equally influential on perceptions of speaker charisma. Antonakis and his colleagues believe that charisma is born out of an amalgam of these three Aristotelian principles and that if a speaker (or leader) can effectively address all three, "he or she can then tap into the hopes and ideals of followers (audiences), give them a sense of purpose, and inspire them to achieve great things." Finally, the authors propose that organizing or "mapping out a speech" is instrumental if one is to be effective in their presentations and that this competency will carry over into daily conversations as well. In the end, being "charismatic" will help a speaker develop an "emotional connection" with others.

1. Other than employing Aristotle's thinking, what other ways can you demonstrate your speaking charisma?
2. Discuss any cautions that you believe exist when trying to attend to logos, pathos, and ethos in speechmaking.
3. What responsibilities do audience members have to ensure that a speaker is successful in their presentation?

Our Presentational Society

Today, although we are not expected to have the speaking responsibilities that people in Aristotle's time did, we still have the expectation of being effective in public communication skills. For instance, the National Association of Colleges and Employers consistently asserts that communication skills are essential for job advancement and job security. Further, many professions, including nursing, law, nutrition, psychology, and medicine, rely on effective oral communication skills. In addition, given that societies as diverse as Brazil, New Zealand, and the USA tend to embrace deliberation and debate (e.g., political campaigns, family arguments, parliament, etc.), being able to deliver a cogent argument is instrumental and even expected. Moreover, presentations are now required – from middle school to college, and even those jobs that do not require a college degree (McDonald's manager, for instance) necessitate speaking to audiences at times.

Finally, think, too, about the importance and pervasiveness of social media as we discuss public speaking. The speech you deliver in Montana or Malta, for example, can now simultaneously be viewed in India and later be available on *YouTube*. Consider Shinjini Das, a writer for *Levo* (a magazine dedicated to millennials in the workplace). She points out that without her understanding of the components of speechmaking, she would not have acquired self-confidence, which, in turn, resulted in her getting one job promotion after another. In sum, we are all part of an era that requires us to know how to communicate a message thoughtfully and with ethical conviction. Although cultural variations exist, public speaking remains one of the most important skills around the globe.

Types of Presentations

We already understand that oral communication skills are paramount in presentation-centered societies across the globe. Public dialogue is everywhere and understanding the various forms of this dialogue will allow you to be prepared when speaking opportunities arise for you. Standing before an audience and delivering a speech can take many forms. The next part of this chapter to two predominant presentational types: informative and persuasive speeches. Again, our collective effort here is to overview the communication field. And, although much more can be included, our goal is to survey various presentational communication features. These two areas are among the most discussed and embraced.

The Speech to Inform

Presenting information on a topic or issue is an informative speech. This sort of presentational type is abundant. The **speech to inform** has audience learning as its primary goal. That is, the speaker is interested in providing information to a listener and in doing so, the listener will leave the speech with a better awareness and understanding of the topic. For the most part, informative speeches do not typically incite dissension or anger. Still, some information you share may emotionally arouse audience members.

Informative speaking can be as simple as demonstrating how to plant a Japanese Maple tree or speaking about the life of Muhammad Ali. Or, this speech type can be as complex as explaining the various monetary systems around the world. What remains important is that you keep in mind that audiences will likely view you as the "expert" and one of your primary goals is to communicate that expertise effectively.

The primary types of informative speeches, as we alluded to previously, are related to demonstrating and defining/describing. In both speech types, you need to make clear why the audience should listen to you. In other words, ensure a rationale for the speech, so that your listeners will stay tuned in throughout the speech.

The steps related to a **demonstration speech** should be of concern since you are showing the audience how to complete or perform a process or task. You should make efforts to explain the steps clearly, provide relevant mediated or non-mediated visual illustration of the steps, and be sure to reiterate the demonstration process. If, for example, you demonstrate how to register to vote, you may want to start by talking about the value of a citizen-democracy. You may want to provide details related to the state, province, or country you are in (each level registers voters differently). Next, it may be appropriate to download and complete the registration form in front of the audience via a large projection screen. Integrating a printed version of the form that you can distribute to the audience may also be important.

The **defining or describing speech** is a second way to inform an audience. Victoria Bruno from our opening is asked to deliver this sort of informative presentation. In this type of speech, you are explaining a topic (person, place, object, event) to a group of listeners who are either unfamiliar or not fully familiar with your subject. This approach requires the speaker to use words or create images that audiences can envision. Think about, for instance, an informative speech describing a new way retailers catch identity thieves. You may describe the process by talking about restaurant wait staff who have handheld skimmers and who steal your credit card data via the magnetic strip on the card. In doing so, to make the informative speech more compelling for the audience, you could provide a real-life example of a former thief, now turned Secret Service informant. What other sorts of speech topics can you think of that relate to what's going on at your campus or in your community right now?

As a college student, you've had numerous informal informative speaking experiences – you just may not realize it. Perhaps because your native country is not large and relatively unknown, you were asked to describe your country's political system. Your boss may have told you to write up a committee's report and explain it to a company's team. Or, suppose you're an avid crowdfunding user and a friend asks you how to raise money for an event. Or, perhaps you're a caregiver to an aging family member and a work colleague asks you about the various challenges and joys related to caregiving. Even entire careers rely upon informative speaking competency, including those related to nature conservancy, event planning, insurance, medicine, construction, and of course, teaching/education. As you can tell, not every informative episode involves large audiences attending a formal occasion, but they do illustrate that speaking to inform is a part of everyone's life.

The Speech to Persuade

Our lives are not solely reliant upon informing others. In fact, as Aristotle believed, we are inundated with both occasions and opportunities to persuade others. We do this both formally and informally. Being persuasive is a fact of everyday life, whether we're with a co-worker, roommate, or family member. We define **persuasion** as a process whereby a speaker attempts to convince others to change their behaviors or attitudes regarding an issue. A persuasive message is conveyed nonverbally and/or verbally. In a very general sense, being able to persuade another in your speech is to employ influence upon another. After all, you're putting words together that you hope will affect another person's belief and/or behavioral system. In a **speech to persuade**, you are trying to get others to not only think about a particular topic, but to have them consider your point of view and your suggestions/recommendations. There may be times when someone may not have a strong opinion regarding your topic. In fact, speaking before an audience member who is neutral or uninformed about a topic may be the most opportunistic time for you to be persuasive (O'Keefe, 2015). Moreover, these sorts of speeches usually relate to questions of facts, values, or policies that you wish to modify or reconsider.

It's important that the persuasive speech be organized appropriately. Although we identify the importance of organization a bit later in the chapter, let's present two prominent organizational patterns in persuasion. First, the **Problem-Solution Format** includes identifying a particular problem or challenge and then proposing one or more solutions to the problem. The problem may be one that you believe exists, yet some of your listeners may have a different impression. So, your goal is to provide evidence that a problem exists. Further, you need to identify a solution (or solutions) that is (are) reasonable and doable. A second pattern is the **Motivated Sequence**, which is a five-step approach to developing a persuasive argument. The steps include: gaining attention (securing immediate audience awareness), establishing a need (rationale for topic/problem), satisfying the need (introducing solution to problem), visualizing the future (a vision of the results of your solution), and cultivating action (providing a plan of specific things for the audience to do after the speech).

Which pattern is best? Clearly, it's not a "one size fits all" mentality. You need to consider your topic, purpose, audience, knowledge and resources. Again, we will get into much more detail regarding organization a little later in the chapter.

Embedded in the persuasive speaking process is an informative process as well. That is, you cannot begin to persuade another person without informing the person about your topic. In doing so, you will have a much easier time influencing a person as you present the "background" to your topic. As a current college student, suppose your former high school guidance counselor asks you to return to school to deliver a speech to rising juniors about the value of a college education. You will likely inform your audience of the size of college (e.g., large, small), types of colleges (e.g., liberal arts, research-based), course format options (e.g., face-to-face, online), types of majors and degrees available (e.g., science and technology, art history), financial aid opportunities (e.g., grants, scholarships), among many others. To make the greatest impact, you could first inform your audience about the job prospects for high school graduates compared to those with college degrees. You could then provide salary differences between jobs for those with a high school diploma and those not requiring a college degree. Although all of these claims and data fall under the "information" portion of your speech, they are also subtly persuasive (who doesn't want to be employed and make more money?). However, an ethical communicator will also provide information on other less appealing features, including college loan debt, refuting them as necessary.

Do the Right Thing: Trying to Make it Right for Another

You work as an assistant store manager for a tie company in the mall, you have been approached by Alan, an executive and regular customer who wants you to speak to his employees at his company's retreat. As a customer, Alan has been impressed by your ability to persuade him to buy ties, even though he did not necessarily need them! He felt that if you had that ability one-on-one, then you're able talk about your strategies to his 40-member sales force . . . and get paid for it! You, however, simply don't understand it. You work on commission – as Alan knows – and it's simply part of your job to get customers to buy ties. Further, you're following a customer service manual that requires you to say certain things, something that Alan doesn't know. You don't see yourself as having any special skills in speaking, but then again, if Alan is willing to pay you a stipend, why should you tell him about the company's policies and procedures. What will you do?

1. If you used the categorical imperative as your ethical system, how would you proceed?
2. If you used utilitarianism as your ethical system, how would you proceed?
3. If you used the ethic of care as your ethical system, how would you proceed?
4. If you wrote up a script for talking with Alan, what would it say?

Fundamental Issues

Thus far in this chapter, we have explained the influence of Aristotle's thinking on our public speaking. We've introduced you to the value, prevalence, and importance of public speaking in contemporary society. Further, we have reviewed two primary types of presentations: informative and persuasive. To continue our overview of presentational communication, we now turn our attention to a few central issues related to the speaking process: topic selection, research support, and outlining/organization.

Selecting and Narrowing a Topic

Unless you're assigned a specific topic to speak on, determining what you speak about is of critical importance in the steps pertaining to the speaking process. After all, if you don't know what you're talking about, the audience will lose interest, resulting in both personal embarrassment and the loss of meaning. To help avoid both, we identify several efforts that you can consider when developing a speech topic.

 First, you have to determine the purpose of the speech. That is, why are you presenting? Is it, as we identified earlier, to inform? To persuade? A combination? Or is there another reason, say, for example, to eulogize a close friend or give a toast at a wedding? Purpose, however, also includes being specific. You may be asked to give a eulogy, but is the purpose to celebrate or mourn the deceased? Being specific means providing even more

TABLE 9.1 Questions to Ask When Narrowing Your Topic

> ✓ **Does the topic interest me and will it interest my audience?**
> ✓ **Is there a time allocation pertaining to your speech?**
> ✓ **If the speech begins to fall apart (e.g., lose my notes, forget important points, etc.), is it a topic that I know well enough to avoid a disaster?**
> ✓ **What is the occasion or setting?**
> ✓ **What (print and/or non-print) resources will I need to develop the speech content areas?**

clarity. So, if your general purpose is to inform a group of senior citizens about phone scams, your specific purpose may be to provide what specific kinds of scams exist. To exemplify these purposes, a speaker constructs a **thesis statement**, or a simple and brief declarative sentence that communicates to the audience the essence of your speech. Let us use the example above.

General Purpose:	To inform
Specific Purpose:	To inform seniors (my audience) about the various phone scams that relate to health care, grandchildren, cemetery plots, and obituary next-of-kin.
Thesis Statement:	Phone scammers target senior citizens and these calls are responsible for the loss of millions of dollars a year as well as the integrity of our most vulnerable citizens.

For many of you, you may have discovered a speech topic simply by **brainstorming**, or generating as many topics as possible without evaluation. Yet, you're learning that this is an insufficient process. Examining the purpose is essential.

Once the all-important purpose has been determined, then think about several subordinate issues (Table 9.1). First, find a topic that interests you, but that also will interest your audience. What do you know about a topic, not know, or want to learn? You might find motorcycle gas mileage interesting, but really: Will your audience? Second, is there a time limit pertaining to your speech? Discussing the history of the US or British Academy Awards may seem interesting, but if you have only six minutes to speak, the topic makes little sense. Next, think about a topic that if everything goes awry, you could still keep on speaking. If you were to have a speaking mishap (e.g., notecards drop, overwhelming sense of nerves, etc.), can you retain your composure or would the speech simply stop? A fourth consideration relates to the situation. In other words, as we suggested earlier, what is the occasion or setting? An anniversary? Bar mitzvah? Funeral? Fifth, a speaker should not ignore the resources available to develop the speech content. Scan all available databases for key words or relevant phrases for innovative or unknown areas. If you wanted to speak on marriage equality, for example, instead of discussing the legal efforts related to the topic, you might research the extent to which same sex couples stay together or break up. These preceding five recommendations will help you in finding a topic that will resonate both with you (speaker) and your listeners (audience) (Table 9.1).

Researching and Supporting Your Presentation

In addition to establishing a speech purpose, all presentations must be supported by outside (re)sources. Beginning speakers often mistakenly believe that their personal beliefs and opinions are sufficient to bolster their speaking claims. Sometimes, personal knowledge is useful, such as talking about baking tips if you work at a bakery. But the more skilled communicator understands that research and supporting details enrich the quality, integrity, and execution of a presentation. Therefore, we devote this section to the importance of integrating research and other materials into your speech.

Any decision to incorporate research into a presentation must first be based on the presentation's purpose. If your goal is to entertain an audience, then research seems less important. If your goal is to inform an audience, then research is imperative. Victoria, from our chapter's opening, plans on incorporating research into her presentation (e.g., the use of a survey, research on physician–patient communication skills, and so forth), especially because an audience with medical credentials ultimately expects that.

Like a speech topic, research comes in all forms. There is research found on the internet, in academic journals, in popular magazines, from experts, and from (social) media. It's impossible to explain fully the various cautionary tales related to each because there are too many unique situations. However, let's provide a number of different suggestions to consider when deciding the use of research and supporting materials:

- develop a research plan
- use research to support your thesis
- appropriately integrate research into a speech
- ensure that your research is relevant
- critically evaluate the research beforehand

Develop a Research Plan. Don't make the mistake of simply waiting until the speech is completed and then incorporate research as necessary. College students have reported that they spend about 21 percent of their entire speech preparation time on research (Pearson, Child, & Kahl, 2006), clearly a significant portion of time. Before any speech is written, a **research plan** must be established and at a minimum, include: (a) thinking about the goal(s) of the presentation (e.g., inform, persuade, etc.), (b) a consideration of the topic and what type of research (scientific, historical, survey, etc.) is necessary, and (c) budgeting sufficient time for the research process.

A well-developed research plan should include:

- thoughts about the speech's goal
- consideration of the topic and the research needed
- attention to the time to conduct the necessary research

Use Research to Support Your Thesis. At times, relying on your arguments or ideas is insufficient. In most cases, incorporating research into your presentation will help advance your thesis. For instance, think about Mindy as she tries to persuade her audience to avoid texting while driving (TWD). If she incorporates statistics on the number of car accidents that happened when people TWD, her speech will have more persuasive power. Incorporating the data will add more value to her speech.

Appropriately Integrate Research into a Speech. Most novice speakers either use too little or too much research. But, a measured and moderate approach to research integration is best. Mindy may be tempted to provide statistics on several aspects of TWD, including state-by-state regulations on distracted driving, a demographic breakdown of those who were injured or who died, the number of people who talk on the phone while driving, the penalties related to TWD, among other areas. Although this research may be valuable, listeners will be inundated with too many details, usually forgetting or ignoring her central points. The goal is to be judicious in research, making sure that your thesis is not lost because of the research citations.

Ensure that your Research is Relevant. Too often, speakers will prepare a presentation and insert research or supporting materials that have little relevancy to the topic. This can result in a less-than-compelling speech. Imagine if Mindy included research on the various types of cell phones available and the most popular brands used by her audience. Although this information can be interesting, it's irrelevant to her thesis and it will have little persuasive appeal.

Critically Evaluate the Research Beforehand. Simply because something is published in a journal, newspaper, or online does not mean that it has value nor that it is of importance. In fact, today, more than ever, it's quite easy to develop a website or write a blog from which others can quote. Online media may be especially problematic unless the research is shared by a user that an individual knows and/or respects (Media Insight Project, 2017)(see Agrawal, 2016). Critically examining the sponsor of a website or blog, augmenting an online reference with published respectable research, and ensuring that you've spent enough time exploring online content for errors are expectations of a presenter who's about to face a skeptical audience. Among the most likely sources consulted is Wikipedia, although this online collaborative encyclopedia is filled with source omission, misinformation, profitability obsession, and biased opinions (Greenstein & Devereux, 2017). In the end, public speaking scholars generally agree that the college library, fortunately for you, is still considered the most appropriate "one-stop shop" to find individual expertise, books, online databases, reports, and reference compendia that are difficult to find on the internet.

Organizing and Outlining

Virtually none of what we have discussed thus far is useful unless your presentation is clearly organized. An organized speech allows both you and your audience to establish a connection or relationship, underscoring the transactional communication process. An organized speech is easier to remember, more captivating, and facilitates the audience's acceptance of the speech's purpose. It was once said that "the best way to find a needle in a haystack is to sit down." What this means is that instead of frustrating yourself and finding yourself without direction, take a moment and develop a strategy. The same can be said about speechmaking. Without a clearly organized speech, you and your audience will grow increasingly confused and anxious.

Speech Organizational Structure and Patterns

The most effective speeches adhere to an organizational pattern that is as fluent and detailed as necessary. The most basic of organizational approaches is the **simplified organizational pattern** consisting of an introduction, body, and conclusion. This is somewhat of a generic speech approach in that it can be used for nearly every speaking occasion. The *introduction* is an effort at capturing the attention of the audience. It establishes topic significance, establishes speaker credibility, and previews the main points. The *body* reflects a speaker's main and minor points, accompanied by examples. Finally, the *conclusion* will necessarily sum up the main speaking points, reiterate the thesis, and leave the audience with a lasting impression. Going back to our chapter opening on training medical interns, Victoria worked toward gaining her audience's attention by providing an example of an immigrant family member who never asked the physician for clarification. Her speech might contain major points, such as (1) the number of mistakes that occur in hospitals because of poor communication,

(2) the financial and personal "costs" of these mistakes, and (3) what various hospitals around the globe are doing to combat poor communication between physicians and patients. She may conclude her speech by reiterating her thesis and by referring back to her introduction. This is a "simplified" organizational structure, but make no mistake: It can be rather complex in detail.

Organizational templates are like blueprints; we need a design plan in our speech in order for us to "build" our ideas and arguments with a solid foundation. Any speech template brings together the various elements in a speech (e.g., introduction, body, conclusion) and provides audiences with **signposts** or transitions to different speaking points. We've already addressed one general (simplified) and two specific (Problem-Solution and Motivated Sequence Formats) patterns. Let's address a few others that you will find yourself thinking about for different speaking opportunities: the chronological, the sequential, and the topical patterns.

When speakers adhere to a speech that follows a particular order or time pattern, they are following a **chronological pattern**. This organizational approach is usually related to presenting information about an historical event or biography. This progression pattern can be used when a speaker is addressing time – either forward or backward. For example, historians and archivists are often asked to give a speech on the background of an important figure, event, or location. An architect, for example, may be asked to present a speech to members of an historical society on various home architectural styles such as Log Homes, Victorian, Mission, Queen Anne, Ranch, among others. The architect will be following a chronological speaking pattern if they decide to begin by talking about classical architecture during early Greek and Roman times and subsequently move to contemporary home design.

As we already know, speakers are called upon to explain a process or demonstrate a process. The most utilized organizational pattern in this sort of presentation is the **sequential pattern**, which is organizing using a step-by-step sequence. The sequential pattern is undertaken when there is a process-centered topic, meaning that there are stages to understanding. For example, think about an expert on wines, an individual who's often called a sommelier. The speaker may be invited to a wine tasting gathering and asked to talk about how wine is made. Despite the audience preference, it's likely that the speech will not begin with how to taste wine! Rather, the sommelier will begin with how grapes become wine, focusing first on the harvesting of the grape, then on the crushing and pressing of the grapes, followed by the clarification process, and concluding with the aging and bottling process. This is a sequential process. But, imagine if the speaker chose, at random, to speak about grapes and then proceeded to discuss the types of wine and then on to the cost of wine; the audience members will rightfully be confused. Instead, the sequential pattern allows for a clear approach to a potentially confusing topic.

In addition to the chronological and sequential patterns, presenters may also consider using the topical pattern. The **topical organizational pattern** refers to dividing a speech topic into various divisions and subdivisions. If Marianne, the HR Director of a financial planning firm, is asked to speak about the company's human resources department at the "Newcomer's Orientation," she will use a topical pattern. She may divide her speech into four general categories; Personnel, Finances, Policy, and Benefits. Within each of those areas, she will discuss a number of other topics, including safety, recruitment, compliance, and recognition.

These are just a few of the many types of prevalent patterns that speakers can draw from when considering their speech topics. There are others that are not as popular, including a **gimmick organizational pattern** that relies on a particular memory device such as a mnemonic device (see our discussion of PACT in Chapter 5 on listening). This pattern provides for a memorable and creative effort in speech organization. In addition, a **pro-con organizational pattern** is chosen when an argument or issue can be divided into two sides. For example, think about some of the more controversial issues taking place around the globe, including marriage equality, abortion rights, climate change, or immigration reform. If you're adopting a pro-con strategy, you will balance out your arguments based on this dichotomy. You can see that this works well with informative speaking more so than persuasive speaking. In sum, the need to consider an organizational pattern in your presentation should be the second step in the speechmaking process (preceded only by the topic selection). Once this pattern is understood, it's now time to outline the speech.

Speech Outlining

The outlining process is an extension of the organizational pattern you choose in your speech. The **outline** is the skeleton of your speech. Think, too, of the outline as the engine of your speech; everything relies upon a clear delineation of your points and like a vehicle, without a working engine, you're not going anywhere! There are many aspects to outlining and it's clearly a presentational imperative that shows you are committed to co-creating meaning with your audience.

An often-quoted maxim regarding public speaking is: "tell 'em what you are going to tell 'em, tell 'em, and then tell 'em what you told 'em" (Safire, 1999, p. 31). A more sophisticated interpretation of this suggests that any speech should contain an outline of what you are about to present to your audience. As speakers, we are called upon to be credible sources of information and of course, the speech purpose will often determine the details of an outline. Regardless of speech intent, however, every speech should follow a content outline plan that contains a main heading of each central point and subordinate headings that exemplify or explain the main points. Finally, all outlines include the thesis statement, a subject we addressed

```
I.   First main heading follows a Roman numeral I.
     A.   Subordinate headings follow capital letters.
          1.   Minor points support the subordinate point.
          2.   A second minor point must accompany the first point.
          3.   Indent each appropriately.
     B.   A second subordinate heading must accompany the first point
          1.   You may or may not have a minor point under this Subordinate heading.
          2.   If you do, again, a second minor point must accompany the first minor point.

II.  Second main heading follows Roman numeral II.
     A.   You may or may not have a subordinate heading under this main heading.
     B.   If you do, a second subordinate heading must accompany the first subordinate point.
```

Figure 9.1 Example of Outlining Protocol

earlier in this chapter. Let's spend some time discussing the primary components of speech outlining.

The **main heading** of an outline refers to the primary points of your speech. These are the central ideas comprising the speech and these should be complete sentences to demonstrate complete thoughts. Depending upon the time limits, there may be as few as two main headings. Although there is no magic number, most speeches generally have about three to four main headings. The **subordinate headings** pertain to the expansion of the main headings. Subordinate headings explain or otherwise clarify the central points of your speech. The subordinate points answer the following question: What will you tell the audience to support your main points? Perhaps you will have further details or examples.

We offer two more points on outlining that are subsumed under one claim: follow a symbolic standard. First, as a speaker, you need to follow an equal and consistent coordination of points. Main heading "A" should not be referenced for several minutes while you speak about main heading "B" for only 30 seconds. Each main heading should be allocated in a balanced manner; avoid being lopsided in time allotment. Second, employ an outline approach that is recognizable and easily retrieved. Many of you may be able to recall in your early grades the alternating letters and numbers approach to *hierarchical* outlining (for every **I**, you'll need a **II**, for every **A**, you'll need a **B**, and for every **1**, you'll need a **2**, etc.) (Figure 9.1). And, make sure that you do your best to allocate equal subordinate detail for each main heading.

We've presented you a foundation to consider when deciding how to outline a presentation. Let's close this section with an example so you can see how outlining functions. Suppose that Johnette was asked to speak to a group of philanthropists to persuade them to fund her project, "Art-I-Can," an art therapy collaborative dedicated to helping young refugees cope with trauma they experienced in their homeland. Although her speech outline will be much more detailed, let's take a look at one template Johnette might think about:

I. <u>Introduction</u> (personal story of 16-year-old artist in Lebanon)
  A. Thesis: *Using art therapy will assist the most troubled young people around the globe and help them cope with their emotional suffering.*
  B. Preview of Main Points

II. <u>Main Point #1</u> (*Refugees arrive in countries with all kinds of emotional, psychological, and physical difficulties*)
  A. Stages of the resettlement process
  B. The "welcoming protocol" of countries with large refugee populations (e.g., Turkey, Pakistan, etc.)

III. <u>Main Point #2</u> (*Art therapy is an empowering experience*)
  A. What is art therapy?
  B. Example of art therapy across the globe

IV. <u>Main Point #3</u> (*From the camera to the canvas, art is helping others and you, too, can help Art-I-Can*)
  A. Success stories
  B. Why and how you should contribute

V. <u>Conclusion</u>
  A. Summarize main points
  B. Reinforcement of the thesis
  C. Return to opening story

Clearly, creating an outline in a standard form with connecting points and subordinate details will provide both you and the audience more clarity and organization. Further, demonstrating the relationship between and among points by indentation and by a progression of numbers (1, 2, 3 or I, II, III) and letters (A, B, C) reflects a speaker who is well on the way to being prepared for any speaking engagement.

Much more can be undertaken regarding these three areas of speechmaking. Yet, presenting this preliminary foundation related to topic selection, research support, and organization/outlining shows you that a presentation is filled with an ongoing commitment to rigor and oversight.

Theoretical Insight: The *Rhetoric* (Aristotle)

As we alluded to earlier, public speaking has its roots in ancient Greece. Aristotle was, as we discussed, critical in identifying specific theoretical issues (see Figure 9.2). His

Figure 9.2 Aristotle, the "Father" of Modern Speechmaking

thinking has application across the broadest array of topics and yet, most scholars agree that his work related to speechmaking remains most informative. We now present an overview of Rhetorical Theory.

Earlier in our chapter, we noted the major contribution of Aristotle from the *Rhetoric*, his pioneering collection of essays from the fourth century BC. His book, from which Rhetorical Theory is derived, was not really a formal piece of writing, but rather a collection of his lecture notes and random thoughts about issues that he had written. Over the years, rhetorical scholars have done their best to try to understand the various levels of complexities related to the treatise.

The *Rhetoric* is composed of three books and it provides the "how to" related to being a public speaker. Although his thinking was rather complex and his writing packed with equivocation, what Aristotle did offer was a template of audience appeals to consider before, during, and after the speaking process. He called these appeals logos, pathos, and ethos.

Let's briefly examine these audience appeals. **Logos** relates to the logic of the speech. In this situation, logic is broadly defined and goes beyond the rationale a person makes in a speech. Think about the importance of evidence and research, for instance, in a speech on teenage pregnancy. Victoria Bruno, in our opening, uses surveys

TABLE 9.2 Types of Oratorical Speaking

Branch of Oratory	Primary Purpose	Topics/Subject Areas
Judicial	Defend, Indict, Win	Justice, Injustice
Deliberative	Motivate	War, Peace, National Defense
Epideictic	Commemorate, Blame	Death, Retirement

and other data as she constructs her main points and she'll be appealing to the logical minds of the interns. **Pathos** refers to the emotional aspects of speechmaking. That is, what does the speaker do to draw out and stir the emotions of his or her listeners? In a speech on driving while drunk, it's likely that any speaker who has had a family member impacted by a drunk driver will elicit quite a bit of audience emotion. In our opening Communication Encounter, the trainer shared a story about a Somali immigrant in order to integrate an emotional component into the presentation. Finally, **ethos** pertains to the credibility of the speaker or their trustworthiness. It's worthwhile to note that credibility varies across cultures. In some African cultures, for instance, credibility is defined by wealth and how much you use your wealth to help others (Neville Miller, 2002). And, in some tribal nations in Native American communities, speakers with more credibility as those who are considered the "elders" (Grande, 2015). Victoria Bruno was asked to speak because of her communication expertise and because of the ethos she brings to the situation.

Aristotle felt that these three appeals are essential in speaking. He further felt that the effective public speaker should make an effort to ensure that each is present in every speech. Let's now delve a bit further and articulate another significant element in the theory: oratory.

Aristotle contended that formalized public speaking, or **oratory**, could be divided into three areas: judicial, deliberative, and epideictic (Herrick, 2017). Table 9.2 illustrates these oratory styles.

The first branch of oratory – judicial – will likely be found in courts of law. **Judicial oratory**, also called **forensic oratory**, has as its primary aim to distinguish between justice and injustice. For instance, think about the number of judicial statements made in a courtroom that require courtroom observers and participants to determine guilt or innocence. Ian Worthington (2010) writes that Aristotle wrote about "moral goodness" and this had particular value in courtroom cases. If you've ever served as a juror, a skilled attorney may have persuaded you with judicial rhetoric.

Deliberative oratory, the second strand of oratory, involves public debate on issues and actions undertaken by legislators who are viewed as deliberative assemblies. When speakers use deliberative oratory, the tactics they use to persuade a group are the same that they use to persuade an individual. The value of deliberative speaking has been discussed for over a century. In fact, over 200 years ago, John Quincy Adams (1810) commented on the pragmatic value of deliberative oratory: "Whoever in the course of human affairs is called to give advice, or to ask a favor of another, must apply to the same principles of action, as those, which the deliberative orator must address" (p. 258). Ralph Curtis Ringwalt (1898) later wrote that "deliberative oratory has had a record of singular power and service. It lighted the fires which burned into the Revolution. The Constitution is its product" (pp. 10–11). Using deliberative oratory, then, resulted in one of the most important documents ever written in US history.

In addition to judicial and deliberative oratory, Aristotle also investigated **epideictic oratory**. This type or speaking is sometimes called ceremonial speaking. The word "epideictic" comes from the word *epideixis*, which means "a show or display."

Connections: Speech Preparation and Culture

Culture and presentational communication are linked in a number of ways. Looking specifically at persuasive speaking, for instance, it's impossible to attain speaking effectiveness without understanding not only the cultural backgrounds of the audience, but in the following situation, the challenge of incorporating the speaker's cultural background into a speech:

As he prepared for his speech on why people should donate to the United Nations Refugee Agency, Khaled wanted to try a unique approach. Instead of telling people the tragedies related to worldwide refugees, he felt that making it more personally relevant would elicit more generosity in spirit and donations. So, he considered all of his own cultural components, focusing on age, family background, physical ability, and socio-economic status. He was a poor Afghan refugee with a single parent, but was unsure of how to weave these facts into his speech without it becoming too personal. His partial blindness was clearly a disability, but again, he didn't want his audience to be too disengaged because of this disclosure. Khaled kept focusing on the goal of soliciting new volunteers and donations, but he was in a bind determining the appropriate balance between his personal cultural background and the audience.

Describe Khaled's circumstance as it relates to the connection between presentational communication and culture. Explain why incorporating too many cultural components into his speech may result in an unintended result. What would you propose to Khaled in order for him to achieve his speaking purpose?

In contemporary epideictic speaking, the speaker may be presenting a speech that aims to demonstrate community. For instance, let's think about some of the world's most horrific tragedies: the shooting at Sandy Hook Elementary School in Newtown, Connecticut; the bombing at a concert in Manchester, England, consecutive bomb blasts on commuter trains in Spain and the Orlando, Florida shooting at a LGBT nightclub. In each of these circumstances, the country's Prime Ministers and Presidents aimed to bring various communities together with an epideictic speech. Each speech was clearly aimed to express the country's grief and communicate the nation's support during a very difficult time in history.

Rhetorical theory dates back centuries and it's impossible to capture all of the nuances related to Aristotle's thinking in this brief review. Yet, even this brief discussion provides you with information to draw upon as you consider how the most timeless of all theories in communication studies applies to effective presentational speaking.

Enhancing Your Skills

In this introductory communication text, our ongoing goal is to present to you a snapshot of the communication field. We know very well that we could never eloquently capture the comprehensive nature of presentational speaking. Although we dedicate two chapters to this vital communication context, we certainly recognize how limited our discussion is. Nonetheless, this chapter focused on the organization of your speech, and throughout we have presented several secondary skills to practice in speechmaking. We now provide two primary skill recommendations: establish and maintain clarity and conduct a *personal inventory of speaking experiences*. We conclude how the latter skill functions with friends.

It may seem obvious, but establishing and maintaining clear preparation processes are essential to having any speaking ethos. Your ethos is always at stake the minute you walk in front of a group of listeners. Some in your audience may be hostile to your speaking topic. Others may simply tune you out if they disagree with some of your points. Still other audience members will be highly critical because of a particular affiliation of yours. Regardless of audience reaction, you need to do your best to prepare and organize with clarity. For instance, the following preparation "strategies" are especially detrimental:

*Determine your organizational pattern one day ahead of the event
*Rely on a few loosely-connected points to support your thesis
*Forget to include your thesis statement

*Fail to include an attention-getting introduction

These and a host of other behaviors characterize those speakers who fail to keep a clear and concise speaking plan. The idea of clarity is not something that should be taken for granted. Recall that Aristotle believed that all speakers must be concerned with their audiences. If an audience doesn't understand the speaker's intent or purpose because the speaker is unorganized or unclear, then how is a speaker to be informative or influential?

In addition to clarity, a second skill we suggest relates to a personal assessment. In particular, we recommend that you create a personal inventory of speaking experiences prior to accepting and/or engaging in any speaking opportunity. We often look at others to help us in public speaking preparation; just reading this chapter is verification of that. Yet, we usually fail to conduct a personal examination of our own speaking abilities. Such intrapersonal communication will help us to focus on what messages were effective and which ones failed to connect with audience members. Further, a personal inventory of speaking allows for us to be candid about ourselves.

Chances are, as you read this chapter, you were thinking about your own speaking abilities. Several questions are relevant for such a personal assessment. How many speaking occasions have you participated in? Were they successful? If so, how did you determine success? Did you have speaking regrets? If so, what were they? Did audience reactions affect you? Why or why not? What did you do to prepare for the speech and how did you organize (or not organize) your speech? If you have little to no speaking experiences, what excites you about speaking in front of others? What frightens you? These and several other questions should be explored to provide you a foundation as you contemplate your next presentation.

These two skills – coupled with several others we articulated in this chapter – illustrate that the speaking process includes more than just words. How you prepare and organize those words for an audience will determine your effectiveness. Let's take a closer look at one of these skills – establishing a personal inventory of speaking – as we explore one circumstance between two friends who also happen to be roommates.

Applying *Establishing a Personal Inventory of Speaking* with Friends

Soledad was busy in her dorm room texting her boyfriend about a party on Friday. Her roommate, Alexis, came in the room with a surprised look on her face: "What are you doing? Isn't your speech outline due tomorrow in your Speech class? What's the topic?" Soledad looked up: "It's our first one so we can talk about ourselves. But I don't know where to start. Anyway, I want to be a screenwriter and let's face it: I'm behind the camera and won't be giving speeches so . . . " Alexis cut her off: "Look. You're like 20 years old; what do you know about any job you'll have years from now? And, you should think about what it'll look like on your transcripts if you get a C or D in a *communication* class!"

Soledad shot up from bed and wanted to disagree, but she knew that her roommate was right. The real problem, she thought, was where to begin.

Perhaps you can identify with Soledad. But, perhaps her real challenge is/was not about *where* to begin, but *when* to begin. The speech should have been organized and outlined weeks ago, but it's "crunch time" now – not the best time for any graded assignment! First, of course, she needs to dig in and determine the assignment requirements. Next, since her first speech is rather general, she should immediately undergo a personal examination of the issues that have made her passionate over the past few years. Was she involved in any civic issue? Is she doing any extra-curricular activity that she could talk about? In addition, Soledad should also think about what speaking experiences have made her the most comfortable. Given that she's a sorority officer, her speeches to pledges and other "sisters" may be something to consider. These are important beginnings as Soledad works toward refining her speech topic and preparing for her presentation.

Communication Response: Victoria Bruno

The opening story of Victoria, a trainer with over a decade of experience, is rooted in the speaker–audience relationship. Recall that she was asked by a hospital to facilitate training related to communicating with difficult patients and their family members. Despite her best efforts in organizing her speech and outlining it appropriately to the occasion, Victoria encountered an audience that was less than interested in what she had to say. After reading and thinking about the material in this chapter, respond to the following questions:

1. What sort of information did Victoria plan to use to gain the attention of the audience?
2. Identify which components of her speech will be informative and which will be persuasive.
3. Should Victoria abandon her approach and organizational speaking plan based on her audience feedback? Why or why not?
4. What advice would you give Victoria if she encountered an overtly hostile audience member?

Questions for Understanding

1. Define *rhetoric* and provide a contemporary example of its use.
2. Differentiate between an informative speech and a persuasive speech by describing each and providing an example of each.
3. List and exemplify the various persuasive speaking organizational patterns.
4. Explain why an outline should be requisite, regardless of speaking occasion.

Questions for Analysis

1. Some people believe that organizing a speech that will only last a few minutes is simply wasted time; it'd be better to focus on how to make the speech more compelling for the audience. What is your reaction to this claim?
2. If Aristotle was alive today and you could have dinner with him, describe the kind of dialogue you'd enjoy having with him.
3. Explore the following statement: "Ethos is the most critical of all the rhetorical strategies."
4. What would be the most useful organizational pattern(s) to use in a speech on (a) the political triumphs of Abraham Lincoln, (b) how to change a car's oil, and (c) the dangers of texting and walking on the street?

Suggestions for Further Reading

Aristotle, & Roberts, W. Rhys (2015). *Rhetoric*. Montgomery, AL: Mockingbird Book Classics.

Boromisza-Habashi, D., Hughes, J. M., & Malkowski, J. A. (2016). Public speaking as cultural ideal: Internationalizing the public speaking curriculum. *Journal of International and Intercultural Communication, 9,* 20–34.

Frymier, A.B. (2017). *Persuasion: Integrating theory, research, and practice*. Dubuque, IA.

Obama, B. (2014). Transcript: President Obama's speech outlining strategy to defeat Islamic State. *Washington Post, 10.*

10 Audience Analysis and Speech Delivery

CHAPTER GOALS

At the completion of this chapter, you will be able to:

- Identify the complexity of the speaker–audience relationship.

- Describe how audience analysis functions in speaking.

- Interpret communication apprehension and identify at least one way to manage it.

- Summarize the intersection between technology and speaking.
- List the various methods of delivering a speech.

- Distinguish among the various speaking delivery components.

COMMUNICATION ENCOUNTER: DEXTER WARD

For nearly five years, Dexter Ward has served as the Chief Information Officer (CIO) at GoingMyWay, a Memphis-based startup dedicated to luxury travel. As CIO, Ward has attended dozens of company meetings over the years and has never had any trouble speaking up or speaking out about tech issues in the company. But, now he's nervous. For the first time, Dexter has been asked to speak at a joint meeting of travel startups in Memphis. He already knows that more than 1000 people from around the city will be in attendance and in addition to his startup colleagues, many of them are important political and society leaders. He has to speak on "IT Viruses: The Future in Travel" and although he knows his material and clearly has the credentials, he is terrified about getting behind a lectern to speak to such a large gathering.

As he prepares his 15–20 minute presentation, Dexter keeps wondering about the most effective way to capture and keep the audience's attention. After all, he thought, this is a technology topic and most people's eyes glaze over whenever he talks about software updates or password protection. He thought about where to move in his speech, what words to emphasize, and even thought about the reactions that some of his audience members might have to his presentation. He also struggled with whether or not to write out the entire speech or simply have a detailed outline and try to sound spontaneous. The 41-year-old kept thinking about some of his favorite public speakers and watched YouTube videos of them over and over again, trying to mimic their communication style. All of these thoughts were doing nothing but adding more anxiety to his speech preparation process.

After nearly two weeks of preparation, presentation day arrived. He was scheduled to be the second speaker and as he sat on the stage thinking about how effective he was going to be, he couldn't help but also think that he could bomb the speech and leave the stage in humiliation. Just as he concluded this thought, the moderator began to introduce him.

The speechmaking process is a complicated one because we have to worry about what takes place before, during, and after a presentation. In Chapter 9, we discussed the preparation and organization that is needed when you are asked to deliver a speech.

We know that planning a speech is just as crucial to speaking effectiveness as the speech itself. The various organizational options available to speakers are vast and choosing the right one will influence your effect upon your audience.

But, as we stated, planning is but one part of being a credible speaker. Being able to deliver a speech that has impact is a critical second part. Further, the delivery of your speech influences your audience members in the same way that audience members influence your speaking delivery. This symbiotic relationship between the speaker's delivery and the audience has been talked about for centuries, as we know, and so let's address a variety of themes embedded in how a person presents a speech and the role of the audience in that presentation.

Background

When we present a speech to other people, we are trying to establish relationships among the speaker, audience, and topic. The preparation of a speech is already difficult enough. But, it can (and usually does) get much more challenging when you couple that preparation with a concern for your audience and a concern for how you're delivering your speech to that audience. As we explore the numerous subjects in this chapter, keep in mind – as always – that a great deal of the research related to these topics are framed with a Westernized lens. We will, when possible, provide you cultural caveats along the way.

The Audience–Speaker Relationship

Speakers who wish to make a difference in their speeches make sure that they are tuned into their audience, focusing on audience needs, willingness to listen, motivation to change, among other areas. In addition, great speakers make an effort to understand the fields of experience of audience members and whether or not, for instance, they have access to technology to watch their speech via a smart phone, tablet, or other electronic devices. Moreover, an effective speaker is considerate of the time that an audience member has to listen to their speech in addition to the real and virtual environments in which a speech is delivered (see Figure 10.1).

Presenting with Substance

Speech delivery is a significant component in speechmaking. Let's be clear: Without employing quality, relevant, and effective nonverbal behaviors in your speech, you will not achieve your purpose in speaking. Or worse, you will fail miserably in effectiveness. Although it's vital that you refine your speech's organization prior to speaking, it's also essential that you work toward delivering a meaningful speech. Attending to your voice (including your rate, pitch, volume) and your body movements (including your gestures and eye contact) can be

Figure 10.1 Think About the Audience as You Strive to Deliver an Effective Speech

the difference between a forgotten speech and a memorable speech. The way you communicate your message to your listeners will determine how well your speech is received.

We already know that presentations can be fraught with unpredictable events. But, you can improve your chances of speaking with confidence and competency by making sure that you do your best to understand your audience and work toward enhancing your delivery skills. We now unpack these and other themes in this chapter devoted to the audience and your speech delivery.

Fundamental Issues

There is no "magic list" of the issues that you should attend to if you are asked to deliver a speech. However, in Chapter 9, as well as in this chapter, we delineate a number of central concerns that should be of high priority for you. Regardless of whether someone is presenting at a sales meeting, a retirement party, a student organizational meeting, a workplace retreat, an anniversary celebration, or at a town council meeting, numerous concerns arise when individuals are asked to speak before an audience. We explore four of the most important: audience analysis, communication apprehension and technology, and delivery.

Audience Analysis

Consider the dilemma that speakers like Dexter face. He may spend a great deal of time preparing his speech. He will spend time practicing his speech, maybe even in front of his friends, his colleagues, or his mirror. He will dedicate time editing and reediting his speech to accommodate for things such as word usage and overly complex ideas. What he won't be able to anticipate, however, is the reaction of his listeners. Dexter may expect supportive reactions, but he can't confidently guarantee how the audience will react or whether or not they will even listen to his speech. Some of his audience members may be apathetic, uninformed, resistant, or divided. His challenge is what public speaking experts call "audience analysis" and being audience-centered is essential to becoming an effective public speaker.

For our purposes, **audience analysis** occurs when a speaker examines and evaluates information about his or her listeners and the setting in which a speech occurs. The speaker is asking the following question while undergoing audience analysis: *How can I construct and prepare my speech to accommodate the interests, knowledge level, and engagement of my audience?* Aristotle commented upon the value of the audience in speechmaking: "Of the three elements in [speechmaking]—speaker, subject, and person addressed," he argued, it is the listener who "determines the speech's end and object" (cited by Roberts, p. 102). Think of a speaker trying to adapt to an audience prior to the speech itself. Ideally, a speaker will be able to adjust their speech based on various kinds of information that is demographic (e.g., age, educational level, etc.), attitudinal (e.g., perceptions and experiences with topic, etc.), and environmental (e.g., seating arrangement, room size, etc.). Having this knowledge beforehand is "ideal"; in practice, however, it's difficult to get this sort of information without having a questionnaire, for instance, and distributing it to audience members prior to a speech and/or knowing the precise number of attendees. And, of course, even with a questionnaire, listeners may not be inclined to (accurately) complete them. Remember, not every speaking opportunity will be as advantageous to you as it is for Dexter. He does, after all, know the topic well and the audience will likely be interested. Still, whether or not you have prior knowledge or experience with a topic, you will still have to undergo some audience analysis. Let's now briefly examine three types of audience analysis.

A **demographic audience analysis** occurs when you examine the classifications and various characteristics of your listeners. Having information about the number of women and men (biological sex) in your audience may influence the examples you use. Whether or not your audience members have college degrees (educational level) may affect the way you demonstrate a process, or knowing the various income levels (socio-economic information) of your audience prior to a speech will probably allow you to determine the extent to which you can persuade them to purchase a product, for instance.

Many speakers analyze their audience using a very common demographic category: age. Invoking age, however, is not always easy. Various generations of listeners (e.g., baby boomers, millennials, etc.) have been raised with different values. For example, although one generation may value face-to-face communication, another generation may see technological communication as a viable substitute, and perhaps an even better vehicle for "conversation". It's already true that millennials use social media such as Facebook in vastly different ways than baby boomers (Towner & Lego Munoz, 2016). Each generation has different goals and has lived through unique historical periods. Knowing the age cohort of your audience, then, may help you tailor your message appropriately, but approach this with caution.

One caution regarding demographic analyses seems apt. Although knowing about your audience is helpful, you will run into trouble if you assume that there is a "typical" woman, a "predictable" college graduate, or a "classic" wealthy person. For instance, if you're presenting a persuasive speech supporting the legalization of marijuana, you need to caution yourself in analyzing a "conservative Republican" audience as being unreceptive to your thesis. Some national surveys show that the majority of conservatives support its use. See our comments on stereotyping in Chapter 3 for the pitfalls related to fixed impressions of (co)-cultural groups.

Thinking about an audience's demographic profile, without engaging in overt stereotyping, can help you tremendously in the preparation and execution of your speech. We are not suggesting that you simply adjust your content because you have a certain demographic listening to your speech. Rather, we believe that being insensitive and ignorant of the variations in demographic groups can jeopardize your ethos.

In addition to a demographic analysis, a speaker should consider undertaking an **attitudinal or psychographic analysis** that requires assessing perceptions, beliefs, and values of listeners. Unlike demographic analyses, examining an audience's attitudes on your topic is a lot more difficult. It requires, among other things, the ability to survey your audience prior to your speech so you have some insight regarding how and where they stand on a topic or issue. For instance, imagine that Miranda, a 34-year-old mother of two, was asked to speak to other women in her daughter's parent-teacher association about the stresses related to work-home balance. She would clearly draw from her life experiences, but would also be interested in knowing how others reduce the stress of balancing home and work expectations. This sort of attitudinal analysis will ultimately help Miranda in her speech as she constructs her ideas and examples.

How would you endeavor to make the topic of retirement planning relevant to a younger audience? Suggesting that an audience member has unwavering attitudes, beliefs, or values is rather naïve. Think, for example, about a 20-year-old's perception of retirement compared to the perception of a 60-year-old. Clearly, the younger person would likely find 401k rates to be rather unimportant, but that person will likely find it to be quite significant three decades later. Just think about how your perceptions have changed even from a few years ago. Let's suppose that you found yourself as an audience member listening to a speech on career success. It's probable that if you heard this speech when you were a high school sophomore, you would find it less impressive than you would if you heard it just before your college graduation. Our point here is that perceptual profiles change over time. Being aware of how your audience adapts to these changes is paramount as you prepare and deliver your presentation. We realize that undergoing a survey of audience members is not always feasible or appropriate. But, their effective speakers try to imagine the mindsets of an audience and shape a speaking approach appropriately.

Demographic and psychographic audience analyses are often complemented with an **environmental analysis**. This type of analysis is quite different than the previous two in that it requires you as a speaker to survey the physical surroundings and make adjustments as necessary. If you are speaking in front of a large group in a hotel ballroom, for instance, you will likely have a microphone and a lectern or stand on a podium. You won't able to move too much and yet your gestures, if any, will have to be bold enough so that the back row will be able to see them – with or without a projection screen. You may speak in a relatively formal tone in this setting. But, what if you're asked to speak to a class of 20 students? That sort of physical environment is amenable to a more conversational tone, and listeners will be able to attend to your nonverbal displays (e.g., eye contact, distance between speaker and audience, etc.) more clearly than if you're presenting in a large room.

Analyzing the physical environment is more than looking at the size of the room and its set up. Think about, for example, the time of the day that you are presenting your speech. Chronemics (a topic we explored in Chapter 4), or the use of time, not only affects the speaker but the audience members as well. Are you presenting your speech in the early morning when some of your audience members may be tired? Is your speech delivered during a luncheon? If so, are you prepared for silverware to drop or water glasses to clink? What if you're speaking at a charitable event before a meal, and you are the only thing standing between the audience members and their dinner? And, what happens if on the day of your speech, a major cultural event occurs (e.g. hurricane, death of a celebrity, etc.)? Do you incorporate the event into your speech? Even if it just occurred a bit earlier than your speech? In 2018, at the Golden Globes Awards, nearly every entertainer wore black, demonstrating symbolic support for the #MeToo movement, a social movement created just weeks earlier to denounce sexual assault and harassment. In 2016, James Corden, the Tony Awards host, spoke about the Orlando, Florida nightclub shooting of 49 people. This tragedy occurred a little more than 20 hours prior to the Tony broadcast, and many of the speakers referenced it in one way or another.

What if you're Dexter Ward? Should a celebrity death, or other current events, get integrated into a speech on computer viruses? The time of day when you present your speech and the events in the community occurring at the time of your speech are instrumental environmental features to acknowledge in your audience analysis.

Conducting an audience analysis is critical in presentational speaking, but it's often ignored or devalued. Such an audit, however, will provide you important information so you can be viewed as both credible and effective. The more you know about an audience's background and their needs, the more you can plan your message and speech. Audience analysis can be undertaken formally (survey) or informally (casual conversation with a small group on the topic). A truly skilled presenter can even modify their speech while they're delivering it as they observe audience reactions. As we learned earlier, when you are a speaker, every effort should be made to connect with your audience. We now turn our attention to a second significant issue in speechmaking: communication apprehension.

Communication Apprehension

It may seem odd to think about a CIO like Dexter Ward from our Communication Encounter being concerned about his effectiveness as a speaker. He has been with the company for several years, and he's going to speak on a topic he knows well. Yet, as we noted in Chapter 9, many people rank public speaking as one of their worst fears. There are so many things to worry about when delivering a speech: Will your hands tremble or shake, will your mind go blank, will your words not make sense to audience members? So, Dexter's fear and concern are understandable, and he is not alone. Celebrities including Rihanna, Mel Gibson, Barbra Streisand, Carly Simon, and Adele have all admitted to feeling very nervous, even intimidated, while speaking in public. And these people are *paid* to communicate in public venues!

People experience uncertainty or anxiety in public speaking for a variety of reasons, namely because of (a) speaking abilities ("I won't be able to project my voice"), (b) audience response/evaluation ("They're going to be bored"), (c) relevancy and content of topic ("I'm not sure if it'll be new information"), (d) the speech setting ("Will they be too busy eating to care?"), and (e) possible breakdown in technology ("What if my PowerPoint doesn't work?"). You may know people who worry about public speaking. Are you one of these people?

Communication researchers have termed this nervousness communication apprehension. **Communication apprehension** (CA) refers to a level of either real or perceived fear and anxiety related to speaking before a group of people. This fear can affect job success and prevent you from even getting a job or becoming an effective leader (Blume, Baldwin, & Ryan, 2013). Although some researchers associate CA with everything from speaking to a parent to speaking to a small group of friends, most writers contend that CA pertains to the apprehension one feels in front of a large group. In other words, CA is a public speaking phenomenon and it deals with how a person *feels* about communication and not about *how* a person communicates (Richmond, Wrench, & McCroskey, 2012). CA has also been

TABLE 10.1 Symptoms of Communication
Apprehension

Symptoms of Communication Apprehension
• Nauseous Stomach
• Dizziness
• Sweaty Hands
• Excessive Perspiration
• Fast Heartbeat
• Wobbly Legs
• Stumbling over Words
• Losing Speech Fluency
• Forgetting Parts of Speech
• Use of Irreverent Speech

called performance anxiety, stage fright, and even "the hidden communication disorder" (Horwitz, 2002, p. 1).

The symptoms of presentational anxiety are vast. They can range from the subtle to the obvious (see Table 10.1). Some speakers have sweaty hands, shortness of breath, fast heartbeat, and an upset stomach. More profound symptoms include flushed face, excessive perspiration, wobbly legs, and dizziness. Sometimes the nervousness can take the form of forgetting or losing your train of thought, flubbing up word usage, and even using profanity because of your lack of speaking fluency. Most people experience mild cases of CA and like most areas we have discussed in this book, the cultural background of the communicator influences the frequency and intensity of the apprehension (Neuliep, 2017).

Research shows that people are generally nervous about a few elements of the speaking process, not the entire process itself. There are some topics that may make us more anxious than others (e.g., a nonprofit executive talking about an impending bankruptcy). In addition, when all eyes are on us, we may become self-conscious and worried, causing us to be more apprehensive. Some research exists (e.g., Witt, Brown, Roberts, et al., 2006, p. 89) illustrating the following **A-CAR pattern** of stress during speechmaking:

Anticipation (The minute prior to starting the speech)
Confrontation (the first minute of the speech)
Adaptation (the last minute of the speech)
Release (the minute immediately following the end of the speech)

At first glance, you may think that those who experience CA must simply "deal with it". At times, nerves can be a source of positive energy if appropriately placed within a speech. And, there are those who approach a public speaking opportunity and forge ahead, modifying and handling the challenges as they arise. Yet, there are those for whom "dealing with it" is problematic, and they must undergo more formal strategies to head off CA. Among the most common is **systematic desensitization**. This process entails having an individual recognize the various tensions in muscle groups and trying to relax those tensions. Once that's achieved, the individual is exposed to environmental conditions that prompt incremental increases in tension. Before moving to the next level of tension, the person must have effectively managed the previous tension. Imagine this process and how it relates to speaking anxiety. The key points are to build confidence and sustain attention.

In addition to systematic desensitization, speakers who are anxious have other opportunities to reduce their apprehension. First, speakers can *restructure personal fears*, knowing that they are not alone in their apprehension. Sometimes it helps to know others are having the same feelings you are! In addition, speakers might consider using *positive self-talk,* which includes envisioning a successful speaking experience rather than failure. Finally, when possible, speakers may be able to feel more comfortable if they are familiar with their surroundings. Therefore, they might try to *create speaking conditions* that mimic the actual speaking environment. That is, if you're speaking to a class, try finding a room similar in size and space. Can you think of additional techniques that have helped you and that you would recommend to a friend or classmate to reduce CA?

Audience analysis and communication apprehension are two fundamental issues related to the speechmaking process. They require speakers to understand the complexities of presentational speaking and each issue varies from one speaking occasion to the next. We next turn to a third issue that has gained more prominence lately: technology.

Technology

We are aware that many of you may have already fused together technology and public speaking. You may have delivered a speech online, presented a speech to a virtual audience, or used technology as a supplement to your face-to-face presentation. Your speech may be archived on YouTube or you may have posted pictures of your presentation on Facebook. Maybe some of you put a small video of a speech on Instagram. Or, perhaps some of your speaking lines have been tweeted. Although we believe technology has forever altered the presentational landscape, we appreciate the words of the late Steve Jobs, the founder of Apple: "I would trade all my technology for an afternoon with

Socrates." For Jobs and others, thinking about ideas and having a conversation about those ideas are as important as, if not more important than, the ability to use technology.

Still, we are a tech-driven world these days. Therefore, we address a few themes related to the intersection of technology and public speaking. First, we discuss the format of speaking vis-à-vis an online presentation and second, we address the use of technological support during your presentation.

More and more professions are requiring their employees to conduct online presentations and many of these require both informative and persuasive skills (Agrawal, 2016). One of the great advantages of the internet is that it allows us to present material online. This usually takes the format of a webinar. Although some could consider this format a lecture or seminar, the reality is that it requires us to consider our topic, the audience, the organization of our presentation, and any supporting details. In other words, the webinar is tantamount to a speech with a clear technological anchor.

If, in your job, you are asked to develop a webinar, keep in mind that the preparation of a webinar is similar to that of a speech in a more traditional setting. In most cases, you will be the facilitator/speaker at the webinar (some may have some additional facilitators requiring different tasks) and you will be the go-to person for content and follow up questions and answers. With this one-speaker format, you will likely be responsible for deciding audience invitations, determining the content, demonstrating/informing/persuading the listeners, and then spending some time responding to queries. Remember that all of this is done online, making it even more important to employ visual support (photographs, charts, etc.). Further, in a webinar, your audience may take a coffee break, run to the restroom, answer a phone, or other behaviors that are unlikely in face-to-face circumstances. Although you're not likely aware of these behaviors, they often interfere with the clarity of message being delivered in the speech.

In addition, whereas the channel of communication in an ordinary public speaking occasion is person-to-person, the webinar may be streamed live or taped. The audience for a webinar is required to dial-in their participation. In other words, audience members have *chosen* to be included in this speaking platform. Finally, just as you would do in an informative or persuasive speech, speaking "at" a webinar requires you to be organized. You can't "wing it", if for any other reason, webinar fees may be charged to the company or employee. People are not pleased if they have paid for a shoddy presentation. Therefore, stick to your outline or agenda, especially because it may be difficult to assess audience reaction to your words, one aspect that makes webinars different from face-to-face presentations.

In addition to online presentations, a second technological issue relates to how a traditional public speaker enhances or extends their presentation with technology. In other words, how can technology be integrated into an informative or persuasive speech to make it more appealing? Clearly, like the internet itself, technology can be both a blessing and a curse. Consider the words of Denise Graveline (2013): "The chance to look and sound effortless or more polished may be a problem for speakers if technology smooths out rough edges at the expense of a real connection" (p. 25). And yet, technical advancements have made speeches more compelling and in many cases, listeners may be more inclined to pay attention to the speaker's message when technology is incorporated into a speech.

What sorts of technological support can make a speech more effective? Let's talk about three examples. First, in a demonstration speech, you can use a Wiki to provide a follow up to the demonstration you undertook. For instance, suppose you presented a speech on "How to 'Green' Your Home/Apartment". After securing audience contact information, you might set up a Wiki following your speech. This Wiki could serve as an outlet whereby audience members further contribute to your ideas by informing others about their "greening" home processes (e.g., receiving tax breaks for energy-efficient windows, saving water and saving money, recycling, sustainability efforts, etc.). In an informative speech, instead of talking about books or essays that audience members might consider, you might find appropriate YouTube channels for further audience reference. Think about a topic such as the life of suffragist Susan B. Anthony. After this speech, should audience members want to learn more, directing them to channels on women's rights activists may prove quite valuable. Finally, your persuasive speech might be enhanced by offering blog opportunities to your listeners. As is always the case, maintaining professional decorum would be expected in each post, a challenge for even the most attentive tech person (think of this as technological ethics).

Extending a speech's impact through technology is, as we noted above, potentially difficult. It may erode the speaker-audience relationship. Still, when appropriately integrated, technology can be valuable and add to a speaker's ethos.

We have focused most of our chapter on the preparation and content of a presentation. But, as we've reiterated in this chapter, unless a speech is delivered effectively, the message and its meaning will be lost. Therefore, we turn our attention to the delivery component of speechmaking, one of the most central themes of any discussion related to speechmaking.

Delivering a Presentation

As early as 1918 – about the time of World War I – the communication discipline was talking about the power of public speaking. Glenn Merry (1918), for example, then a member of the National Association of Public Speaking Teachers (now the National Communication Association), published an open letter about the importance of speech teachers enlisting in the "war effort". He proposed that the association develop a memo of understanding that would communicate support for national defense. A "campaign of public speaking" (p. 58) was undertaken by the government and Merry (and many others) urged the association members to provide their expertise in this effort.

This historical footnote serves as a backdrop to the belief that people can make a difference with their speeches and that speeches can make a difference in society. As Merry contended, it would behoove all educated citizens to have a repertoire of "the best speeches delivered" for future generations.

Delivery that is natural, respectful, animated when appropriate, and that establishes an audience connection will result in a speech that others will find compelling. And, delivery effectiveness is essential in various professions. In the legal arena, for instance, the Hon. Dennis Saylor and Daniel Small (2017) advise attorneys this way: "Your delivery, no less than the content, should persuade the jury." In medicine, doctors are advised to deliver bad news with silence (to acknowledge sadness), brevity, clarity, empathy, and with appropriate pausing for patient input (Reddy, 2015). For those in politics, speaking delivery should be filled with passion, in a conversational tone, and responsive to the occasion (campaign speech, policy speech, call-to-action speech, and so forth) (Perloff, 2013). We now discuss a few important aspects related to speech delivery, hoping that you may perform a speech with lasting impact.

Delivery Formats

To begin, we briefly note that delivery can take a number of forms and depends greatly upon the occasion and time allocation. Think about these four different scenarios:

- A political candidate delivering a speech on universal health care
- A mother delivering a speech at her son's 50th birthday party
- A best man at a wedding delivering a toast to the guests
- A college student delivering a presentation on social media addiction

Each of these situations will dictate one of four different delivery options (Table 10.2). The **manuscript delivery format** is a word for word speech that a speaker reads to an audience. This type of speech likely appears in future published records (e.g., conference proceedings, community records, etc.). A **memorized delivery format** occurs when a manuscript speech is committed to memory and recited to an audience. This approach is best for short speeches. When you are asked to deliver a speech during a large gathering such as an anniversary, you are usually unprepared and present your speech in a spontaneous fashion. This spontaneous or **impromptu delivery format** is an unprepared and unrehearsed speech that is undertaken with little or no notice. Finally, an **extemporaneous delivery format** pertains to a carefully prepared and rehearsed

TABLE 10.2 Methods of Delivering a Speech

Methods of Delivering a Speech
Manuscript – a speech that is written out word for word and read to an audience
Memorized – a speech that is committed to memory and delivered to an audience
Impromptu – a speech that is delivered to an audience with little or no preparation
Extemporaneous – a speech that is thoughtfully prepared and delivered to an audience with a limited set of notes

speaking approach that contains a pre-chosen organizational structure and is delivered in a conversational style. This is often the most preferred form of delivery since it appears more conversational than a rigidly memorized or manuscript form of delivery. Each delivery option may also be influenced by the technology available. Now that you have an overview of the various formats, which option is best suited to the examples above?

Delivery Components

A speaker's delivery format and delivery behaviors can have a profound influence upon the audience's perceptions of speaker credibility and speech effectiveness. Delivery also communicates a speaker's confidence and preparedness. Some delivery components are tangible while others are intangible. We encourage you to **P-R-E-V-I-E-W** your delivery with several considerations:

Pauses
Rate
Eye contact
Volume
Intonation
Energy
Wildcard

Regardless of whether you read your speech (manuscript method), memorize it, or use notes in your delivery, PREVIEWing your speech is paramount.

Pauses allow you to collect your thoughts and consider your next point. Pausing can help you manage unexpected lapses in memory or allow you to regroup following a flub.

In addition, pauses give your speech variety, and allow time for the audience to think about an important point you have just made. Many novice speakers avoid pausing because they erroneously believe it's a sign of confusion or lack of knowledge. In addition, because cultures such as the USA believe that silence is an uncomfortable state, pausing is often not recommended. More seasoned speakers understand, however, that a pause allows audiences to reflect upon the speaker's words, can be used for dramatic effect, and can serve as a transition between points. As Mozart claimed: "The music is not *in* the notes but in the silence *between* them." Honor the pause in presentational speaking.

Second, a speaker's **rate** is the pacing or speed of speaking. Research continually shows that most listeners in most nations with English as their native language can process up to 400 words per minute. But, most speakers average about 125–150 words per minute. The Japanese and Spanish speak much more quickly, with Mandarin being among the slowest of all speaking rates (Kluger, 2011). Simply increasing the speed of your delivery to ensure audience attention is not the goal. Rather, being flexible in your rate throughout your speech is essential. Think, for instance, about Dexter from our chapter opening. When he discusses computer viruses, he may want to slow down during some of the more complex content; he may want to speed up while summing up various sections. Speaking at various rates during a speech will enhance audience engagement.

Perhaps no delivery quality has received more attention by public speaking scholars than **eye contact**, a third consideration in presentational delivery. Eye contact ability is a behavior that can vary tremendously from one person to another and from one culture to another. Still, creating and maintaining eye contact with an audience is critical in many cultures. Eye contact assists us in showing a connection or bond with our listeners, enhancing trustworthiness. As a speaker, making eye contact invites the audience members into a conversation. Conversely, limited or no eye contact generally means audience members will perceive you as less confident, in the USA and most Western European cultures. When possible, eye contact begets eye contact; when we look at an audience, they, in turn, will generally look at us. In many cases throughout the speech, speakers and audience members should strive toward a mutual gaze.

Finally, regardless of what some so-called public speaking "experts" state, never, ever look above the heads of your audience members. First, when we speak to someone, we usually don't do that. Second, if you want to speak to walls or windows, why are people even in the same room with you as a speaker?! Third, when you connect with an audience through eye contact, you can receive feedback that will help you see if people seem to be following your points. Finally, the credibility of a speaker is seriously jeopardized with "wall looking".

As you consider your rate, use of pausing, and eye contact, you should also be concerned with appropriate **volume**, the fourth delivery area. First, let's clearly note that listeners need to hear what you are saying. If there are competing noises either inside or outside of the room, then adjust your volume. Close appropriate windows or doors, if convenient. If you have a microphone, you know not to yell or raise your volume too much. Sometimes audience members may privately converse with one another. Speaking over this sort of chatter may not boost your credibility so do your best to provide some caveat prior to your speech ("I'd be happy to answer questions or respond to comments after my speech"). Sometimes checking in with the audience is important, too ("Can you hear me?"). Finally, volume can be varied to make your points more compelling. If, for instance, Margarita is trying to persuade a group of teenagers not to smoke, and she shares a story of a family member who was a heavy smoker who died of lung cancer, she may want to lower her volume for effect. When she suggests ways to quit smoking, she wants to show more passion and so she increases her volume.

A fifth delivery aspect in speaking is intonation of your speech. **Intonation** is pitch, tone, and sound attribute levels employed in speech delivery. We've all heard speakers who speak in a monotone with no range in vocal delivery. In fact, in the classic movie, *Ferris Bueller's Day Off*, Ferris's economics teacher becomes known as "the monotone and hypnotic teacher" because of his vocal droning.

But, think about speakers who explore the full range of their voices. Pitch can convey a number of different speech issues, namely emphasis, surprise, or indicating whether you are asking a question, posing a statement, or expressing shock. These sorts of meanings are important signals for the audience as you aim for speaking effectiveness.

Earlier we mentioned that delivery is both tangible (concrete) and intangible (unquantifiable). We can actually measure a speaker's eye contact, for instance (tangible). But, our sixth area for review, enthusiasm, is intangible. **Enthusiasm** shows passion for your topic. Enthusiasm is difficult to measure but as audience members, we tend to know it when we see it. To a large extent, enthusiasm involves all of the delivery elements, including how you use your voice, your eye contact, and the words you use in your speech. Your enthusiasm should communicate authenticity; don't fake enthusiasm, as your audience will figure that out quickly.

Our final area related to speech delivery collapses several different considerations into one. We term it the delivery *wildcard*. Several areas constitute the wildcard in speech delivery. First, *gestures* and other forms of appropriate body movement are essential in a speech. If you are not required to stand on a podium or behind a lectern, learning to use gestures can enhance effectiveness. *Rehearsing* your speech prior to delivery is another feature of the delivery wildcard. Practicing will result in clarity that will inevitably result in audience members understanding your points more clearly.

Another area to think about is your *physical appearance*. This area alone could elicit pages of discussion. But for our purposes, we offer the following. You may think, for example, that dressing casually will result in you being more comfortable while speaking. How you look and how you dress impacts perceptions of your credibility (Dorai & Webster, 2015). It's not all about your comfort with respect to your appearance, but rather the occasion should dictate your appearance. If you're speaking to a group of peers or close co-workers, being casual usually makes sense. If you're presenting to audience members with whom you've had no prior experience, wearing clothing that is appropriate for the situation, topic, and audience should be your goal. However, it isn't a good idea to wear something that makes you feel uncomfortable because it doesn't fit well or is too provocative or has some other problem. You should feel good in the clothes you choose, and you should make them appropriate for the occasion. Checking out your appearance in front of a mirror before entering the speech setting is also an apt last-minute suggestion. Finally, don't forget to approach the speaking environment with dignity. That includes walking with professional posture and a stride of confidence. We believe that your speaking experience begins the moment you rise to deliver your presentation. Each of these very different areas – gestures, rehearsing, and physical appearance – should be given attention since if they're executed poorly, they could jeopardize your presentational integrity.

Do the Right Thing: Will You Lose Your Job for Being Thoughtful?

In order to help pay for college, you need to juggle several jobs. One of your jobs is working in the evening, stocking shelves at a local discount store. Although the job pays the bills, your new supervisor, Carla, is really making it very uncomfortable for you. During some of the conversations and presentations to the team, she uses words and phrases that are clearly out-of-date, including "black sheep of the family", "sold down the river", and "gyp". Lately, as she presents new information to you and others, her language is becoming even more bothersome because she uses words like "Oriental" and on one occasion, used a phrase that clearly made you very upset: "Look alive! You crackers need to move faster!" Nearly all of your co-workers are also offended by her ongoing use of insulting words, regardless of whether they're used in a formal speech to the team or in her dialogues with others. Yet, it seems no one wants to talk to her or they fear that if they do, she'll retaliate in some way. The Human Resources department is located in another city and it seems like it'd be useless to talk to HR. You know the job pays decently and you don't want to get into any drama, but you simply can't imagine keeping calm any further because you find the situation quite distressing. What is your response, if any, to this challenging workplace?

1. Articulate how categorical imperative is present in this situation.
2. Discuss utilitarianism in this scenario.
3. How might you arrive at an ethic of care?
4. Specifically, if you had to write out a script for a conversation with Carla, what would you say to her?

Theoretical Insight: Contagion Theory (Nuttin)

You already know that the field of communication has its roots in ancient Greece. Over the years, theoretical developments have been multidisciplinary, that is, many disciplines have influenced the development of communication theory. Similar to other theories we spotlight in this book, Contagion Theory has been the subject of much research – including from those who study presentational speaking. We examine this theory below and its relevancy to communication apprehension in particular.

The notion of contagion was originally framed in cognitive psychology (Nuttin, 1975), but the communication field found it quite relevant and applicable to dialogues, listeners, and audience members. **Contagion Theory** generally refers to how feelings, emotional states, and other nonverbal cues are "caught" by those who surround an individual. Contagion is mostly an emotional state, which means that those who are affected by it will "mimic the expressions, voice, gestures, and postures of an individual" (Behnke, Sawyer, & King, 1994, p. 247) who is undergoing a feeling of arousal. In its simplest form, contagion occurs when a person experiences an emotion and a listener adopts or integrates that emotion. Within groups, research (Barsade, 2002) shows that positive emotional states communicated by a speaker to listeners resulted in positive mood shifts by these listeners. In addition, these same listeners were more inclined to be cooperative in group decision making, less prone to interpersonal conflict, and more confident in the outcome of discussions with others. But how does contagion work in presentations?

Components of Contagion Theory have been extensively studied with public speaking. In particular, researchers have found contagion to be ever-present in episodes involving speakers with communication apprehension. Whether a speaker reported anxiety or whether audience members perceived the anxiety, the contagion effect takes place. Let's examine this notion of contagion as it relates to speaking and speaker anxiety.

We already know that Dexter, in our chapter opening, is quite nervous about speaking to the large group, even though he is informed about his topic. If he manifests this nervousness in front of others, through stammering, fidgeting, and using "gap fillers" including "um" in his speech, contagion will likely happen. According to Ralph Behnke and his team, if a second speaker follows Dexter, that person will have a difficult time since "speakers who follow anxious speakers are at a competitive disadvantage" (p. 250). Conversely, other research (Berg, Söderlund, & Lindström, 2015) discovered that when positive behaviors such as smiling and displays of joy are employed, audience members respond in kind. Some writers (Doherty, 1997) call this **emotional contagion**, which is a tendency to imitate sensory, motor, physiological, and affective states of other people. Emotional contagion results in someone "catching" the emotions of another person. Thus, the word "contagious" remains the term to describe this phenomenon.

At its core, Contagion Theory is a model that has **synchronization** as its primary vehicle. In conversations – as well as in presentations – listeners and other speakers will unconsciously align, or synchronize, themselves with what behavior precedes them. As we now know, if a presenter experiences high levels of communication apprehension, the audience will recognize this anxiety and, regardless of effectiveness, a second presenter will not be perceived as effective. However, if a presenter comes across as engaged, articulate, and poised, the audience will view a subsequent speaker as effective.

Enhancing Your Skills

In this chapter, we have collapsed a great deal of information – information that dates back thousands of years – into one, relatively brief, chapter. Along the way, we have offered several ideas to consider as you think about your own opportunities in public speaking. We close our chapter with two additional, but more general, skills as they relate to presentations and then apply one particular skill to the work environment.

Everyday Talk: The Reach of Snapchat

Dara Fontein (2015) discusses on Hootsuite (https://blog.hootsuite.com/how-snapchats-impact-is-felt-in-three-different-industries), the value of Snapchat in various industries, including fashion, film, and travel. She notes that the platform users have risen to over 100 million each day, which require various businesses not only to understand its value but also embrace it. Fontein believes the 10-second fragment has grown in influence particularly with the 13- to 34-year-old cohort and this can be especially valuable for companies as they seek to connect with young consumers.

Fontein identifies Snapchat's value in fashion by allowing viewers an opportunity to see posts from "front rows" at fashion shows, something that without Snapchat would likely be difficult. She quotes a Vice-President from one fashion house: "Snapchat allows you to experience something that feels exclusive and inaccessible in a really accessible way." In a similar vein, Fontein explains that film, too, has achieved success with Snapchat. She reports research that indicates when Snapchatters view a film promotion on the platform, they were 60 percent more likely to go to the movie than non-Snapchat users. Finally, the travel and tourism industry has been branded by Snapchat use. The Marriott Hotel chain, in particular, says Fontein, is credited with being the first major hotel group to use Snapchat to market its brand. In fact, Marriott has a Snapchat channel, according to Fontein. In sum, Snapchat has allowed various kinds of industries to prosper and to cultivate an important demographic.

1. Are platforms such as Snapchat a "passing fad" or do you believe they're here to stay?
2. What additional examples in business and industry might benefit from Snapchat and other mobile messaging types?
3. What drawbacks exist for companies who rely on social media for branding and other promotional purposes?

The audience, as we now know, is of utmost importance in your speech. With respect to delivering a speech in particular, if you are ineffective, your audience will be the first to let you know. They may fidget, avoid eye contact, or simply leave your presentation. We know that you have various options to deliver your speech, but one thing should always be forefront in your mind: be audience-centered. What this means is that you not only undergo the audience analyses that we articulated earlier in this chapter, but that you also adapt to your audience *during* your speech when necessary. You've already learned that audience members bring with them various expectations about the topic, speaker, and even the occasion. Consequently, you will have to determine when to modify your speaking delivery. Your speech practice sessions are very different from the real speaking circumstance; sometimes your rate will change, your pitch level will be altered, and your gestures will be more grand. Sensing audience reaction throughout your speech and adapting appropriately is difficult, but necessary.

A second general skill is *sustaining professionalism* throughout your speech. This may seem too obvious, but consider the fact that each speaking situation results in very different circumstances. What if the stage or room lights go out during your speech and you're unable to read your notes? What happens if an audience member suddenly becomes openly hostile to the ideas you're expressing? Suppose you were allocated 15 minutes for a presentation and then you are asked to "hurry it up" and conclude faster because another group needs the room. Let's say that you're using the internet to demonstrate something and Wi-Fi shuts down. These are real-life events that will require you to maintain your self-control and self-confidence. Indeed, these types of experiences have happened to nearly all seasoned public speakers.

Let's now discuss how *sustaining professionalism* relates to a specific situation in the work environment.

Applying *Sustaining Professionalism* at Work

Leeann is the CFO of BankPlus, a large institution with several hundred employees across four southeastern states. As a financial expert, she is customarily asked to speak to large groups of people in the banking industry and is normally not nervous to speak at all. Yet, her comfort level changed recently when she was asked to speak to a community group about how to purchase a home during difficult financial times. During her speech, she was greeted by a group of audience members who shouted "You rip off poor people!" and held up signs saying things like "Stop your $$$ polluting!" Leeann is clearly unsure about how to proceed in her speech with these disruptions. She knows that she simply can't walk off the platform, and she also knows that she needs to deal with this situation . . . now.

Clearly, Leeann is not accustomed to such a hostile audience. Because it's likely the protestors will not abandon their passion with a simple request, Leeann may simply have to rely on either security removing the rowdy audience members or she could continue on as if nothing is occurring. Certainly removing the audience members would likely silence the protestors, but ignoring their outbursts would not be the best recommendation. She could welcome the verbal protest, suggesting that she is a firm believer in First Amendment rights whereby speech is protected. Or, she could acknowledge that there are some banks that do "rip off" consumers, but BankPlus is not one such bank. And, if she were truly proactive, Leeann could have some planned professional responses prior to her speech in case such hostile reactions occurred. Regardless of her decision, Leeann should not engage in a conflict in front of others. She should remain dignified but not shout back that the audience outbursts are ridiculous, or even dismiss the audience members as "unstable". She can acknowledge the concerns of the audience protestors while continuing with her presentation.

Connections: Speech Delivery and Verbal Communication

To many audience members, how you present your speech is as, if not more, important as the content of the speech. Yet, the words we choose in our speeches can resonate in both predictable and unpredictable ways. Examine the following speaking scenario as you also think about the intersection between the words we use and the speeches we present:

Shoshanna was quite accustomed to getting up in front of audiences. She is a sought-after speaker with a compelling personal message of triumph. As an assault survivor, she has spoken on college campuses across the globe, using her life experience as a foundation to discuss the prevalence of sexual harassment and assault. Yet, it was her presentation to a group of sorority and fraternity members that surprised this speaker with nearly 50 presentations behind her.

As she began to speak to the group about that January evening when a man broke into her apartment, Shoshanna continued: " . . . So I sat in the chair . . ..looking at this man, this pig, no . . . this animal! I had no idea what he was about to do, but I just sat there. Motionless. Frozen like the ground outside. I tried to talk to him, tried to humanize this beast in front of me. I asked him about . . . " Just then, one guy yelled out: "So why did you talk to him? You should've run out of your apartment!" Anyone sitting in the hall at the time could hear the audience audibly gasp. Shoshanna turned to the left side of the room where the shout came from. There were a few "boos" heard and at least one woman yelled, "Shut the hell up!" Clapping ensued. At that moment, Shoshanna – a speaker with an extensive speaking background – looked at her notes sitting on the lectern. She knew that she had never experienced this sort of audience chaos, and wasn't sure if she was pleased with the spontaneous nature of it or simply mortified by its development.

Comment upon the interplay between Shoshanna's speech delivery and the words in her narrative. Was there a way for her to avoid this audience reaction? Should she acknowledge the outbreak or simply move on to the next part of her speech? If you were Shoshanna, what sort of preparation, if any, would you have undertaken either to prevent or control the fraternity member's reaction? Are there other words that could have/should have been used?

Communication Response: Dexter Ward

Our Communication Encounter saw Dexter Ward being asked to address the topic of IT viruses to audience members who are experienced in start-ups. Although Dexter has expertise with the topic, he has a level of communication apprehension that has caused him to question his effectiveness. He prepared for his speech but on the day of his presentation, Dexter clearly could not shake off his anxiety. As he listened for his name to be called to speak, his jitters became more pronounced. Should Dexter admit to the audience that he is nervous? Or, should he avoid mentioning it? What if he does, indeed, show high levels of apprehension? After reading this chapter on presentational speaking, answer the following questions:

1. Imagine the various verbal and nonverbal anxieties that Dexter is likely to experience.
2. What suggestions do you have for Dexter to manage his apprehension?
3. Does it make a difference whether or not Dexter is informing or persuading his audience members? If not, why not? If so, why?

Questions for Understanding

1. Discuss the value of undergoing audience analysis prior to a presentation.
2. What is communication apprehension and how can it affect your speech?
3. Define A-CAR and provide an example of each term.
4. Is the delivery of a speech the same as, more important than, or less important than the preparation of a speech? Explain with examples.

Questions for Analysis

1. Look up www.ted.com/talks and review any "talk" on public speaking. What speech did you choose? Why? What did you learn from this presentation that is relevant to this chapter?
2. Explain how culture influences the delivery process in speechmaking.
3. Communication apprehension is viewed as a real and serious threat to public speaking. What happens if a speaker breaks down during a speech? What would you suggest to a speaker on how to handle this potential calamity?
4. Think about a speaker who you felt had effective delivery. What made this presentation so compelling?

Suggestions for Further Reading

Aristotle, & Roberts, W. Rhys (2015). *Rhetoric*. Montgomery, AL: Mockingbird Book Classics.

Blume, B. D., Baldwin, T. T., & Ryan, K. C. (2013). Communication apprehension: A barrier to students' leadership, adaptability, and multicultural appreciation. *Learning & Education*, *12*, 158–172.

Cicero, M. T. (2016). *How to win an argument: An ancient guide to the art of persuasion*. Princeton, NJ: Princeton University Press.

www.disabilityhorizons.com/ 19192015/08/disability-and-public-speaking-overcoming-the-fear/. Disability and public speaking: Overcoming the fear.

www.youtube.com/watch?v = AHY2UzOonig. The King's Speech.

Jones, K. T. (2015). Teaching audience analysis with presidential "victory" speeches. *Communication Teacher*, *29*, 1–5.

Appendix A Careers in Communication

Program Coordinator/Facilitator

A program coordinator/facilitator leads workshops in a variety of venues focused on topics such as breaking down barriers between people and creating understanding, community, and compassion while empowering individuals. Program coordinators/facilitators lead discussions and facilitate understanding on a given topic or goal (such as helping high school students to increase empathy, for instance).

Regulatory Communications Coordinator

Regulatory Communications Coordinators are responsible for the timely reporting and investigation of stakeholder complaints at a specific company. For example, at a company specializing in the development of minimally invasive medical devices, a person in this position would manage sensitive information and assess situations to determine effective forms of communication. The job requires a person to be informed of current regulatory laws and safety practices and also to present information to diverse audiences, including both corporate and government officials.

Communication Specialist

A communication specialist helps develop communication strategies and plans and helps coordinate media campaigns, creates trade show displays, manages social media and visual communication, and develops content for special events including workshops, conferences, and competitions.

Public Relations Assistant

Entering the public relations field as a PR assistant is a great job choice for communications degree graduates. This job requires first-rate writing ability, great organizational skills and a personable demeanor: all skills that a communication degree develops.

Advertising Copywriter

Copywriters write the ad copy for all kinds of things, from corporate brochures to product packaging. A communication degree is very useful for developing the language skills, creativity, and knowledge of advertising that this job requires.

Marketing Assistant

A job as a marketing assistant is an ideal position for communication graduates. This job involves many duties including maintaining contact with clients, sending out marketing emails, and assisting in the conception and organization of marketing campaigns.

Editorial Assistant

Editorial assistants sort and read incoming manuscripts, coordinate contact with authors and agents and help in the editing of manuscripts. A communication degree is a good background for this job.

Account Executive

In this position, a person facilitates many aspects of a company including fundraising and marketing functions. The job also includes consultations with clients on strategies and tools for reaching their growth and development goals.

Human Resources Assistant

Human resources assistants will help out with anything from recruiting new employees to leading seminars for current employees. You will also need solid interpersonal and public speaking skills.

Hospitality Communications

People in hospitality may work on cruise lines, in restaurant chains or hotels. Roles are diverse: responsibilities may vary from addressing customer complaints to promoting the organization through work in the marketing department.

Social Media Manager/Digital Marketing Strategist

A social media manager and digital marketing strategist oversees the influencer capabilities of a company, working to identify and create relationships with influencers to enhance awareness and engagement of the company's products through organic social media. In this job, people develop creative global social media programs that lead to increased awareness, use, and engagement.

Political Campaign Coordinator

Political candidates need campaign coordinators who are well spoken, able to think on their feet, and excellent writers. A communication degree qualifies you for this career path.

Grant Writer

Many nonprofits need skilled writers and communicators to help secure grants. Grant writers need to think of creative ways to present an organization's needs and need to familiarize themselves with the rules and standards of a variety of granting agencies.

Community Organizer

Community organizers use their communication skills to talk to members of a community to partner with them to make sure their needs are met. Communication graduates will find that this is a rewarding way to gain experience in politics and community service.

College/University Admissions Representative

College/university admissions representatives market a college or university's programs to prospective students. In this job, efficient communicators speak to and recruit incoming freshmen, and may also write press materials for the college/university.

Customer Service Representative

Customer service representatives help customers and make them feel valued. This job involves problem solving and empathy skills as well as good listening abilities.

Communication Associate

A communication associate contributes to building a company's brand, as well as supporting its fundraising and the expansion of the impact of its work. In this position a person develops and manages the execution of the company's strategic communications plan, designs, creates and manages messaging and materials for external audiences and internal use, as well as managing communications projects and supervises consultants.

Executive Vice President of Communications

In this role, a person develops and implements integrated communication strategies, writes and curates content, and provides counsel based on best practices in the field. In this position, a person needs outstanding organizational skills and attention to detail, as well as excellent written and oral communication skills.

Communication Consultant

Either working freelance or with a company, a person who is a communication consultant helps others develop the important communication skills such as clarity, conciseness, and nonverbal behaviors that help them become effective in their specific businesses.

Appendix B Professional Communication Associations

American Communication Association (ACA) (www.americancomm.org/)

The ACA is a not-for-profit virtual professional association with actual presence in the world of communication scholars and practitioners. ACA is committed to enabling the effective use of new and evolving technologies to facilitate communication instruction, research and criticism, and to offering a technologically supportive venue for all who study the ways in which humans communicate. While the Association is based in the United States, it is a virtual organization that welcomes participation from academics and professionals throughout the world. [Association Mission Statement]

Association for Education in Journalism and Mass Communication (AEJMC) (http://aejmc.org/)

The Association for Education in Journalism and Mass Communication (AEJMC) is a nonprofit, educational association of journalism and mass communication educators, students and media professionals. The Association's mission is to promote the highest possible standards for journalism and mass communication education, to cultivate the widest possible range of communication research, to encourage the implementation of a multi-cultural society in the classroom and curriculum, and to defend and maintain freedom of communication in an effort to achieve better professional practice and a better informed public. [From the Association's website]

Association for Women in Communications (AWC) (www.womcom.org/)

The Association for Women in Communications is the one organization that recognizes the complex relationships that exist across communications disciplines. Modern communicators must demonstrate competence in varied disciplines and be able to network and make career moves across the broad spectrum of communications fields. Disciplines represented within the association include print and broadcast journalism, television and radio production, film, advertising, public relations, marketing, graphic design, multimedia design, and photography. The list is continually growing as the profession expands into the newer media. [From the Association's website]

Central States Communication Association (CSCA) (www.csca-net.org/)

The mission of Central States Communication Association is to unite and educate people with both an affinity to the central region of the United States and a scholarly interest in all areas of communication for promotion of their mutual goals and advancement of their field. Central States Communication Association is an academic organization of communication professionals including college and university professors, students, and K-12 educators. CSCA was founded in 1931 to promote the communication discipline in educational, scholarly, and professional endeavors. The association, which consists of the 13 Midwestern states of North Dakota, South Dakota, Nebraska, Kansas, Oklahoma, Missouri, Illinois, Iowa, Wisconsin, Minnesota, Michigan, Indiana, and Ohio, is governed by an Executive Committee and is legislated by its constitution and bylaws. [From the Association's website]

Eastern Communication Association (ECA) (www.ecasite.org/)

The Eastern Communication Association was initially established in 1910 and continues as the oldest professional communication association in the United States. As a distinguished service-oriented organization with a history of achievement in research, criticism, communication theory, and excellence in teaching, the association welcomes members who share the goals and objectives of a membership dedicated to participation in state, regional, and national activity. [From the Association's website]

International Association of Business Communicators (IABC) (www.iabc.com/)

Setting a standard of excellence since 1970, the International Association of Business Communicators is a vibrant global membership association with thousands of members from around the world, representing many of the Global Fortune 500 companies. IABC serves professionals in the field of business communication, bringing together the profession's collective disciplines. We deliver on the Global Standard in communication through our educational offerings, certification, awards program, resource library, online magazine and annual World Conference. We support our community of business communication professionals with innovative thinking, shared best practices, in-depth learning and career guidance. [From the Association's website]

International Communication Association (ICA) (www.icahdq.org)

The International Communication Association aims to advance the scholarly study of human communication by encouraging and facilitating excellence in academic research worldwide. The purposes of the Association are (1) to provide an international forum to enable the development, conduct, and critical evaluation of communication research; (2) to sustain a program of high quality scholarly publication and knowledge exchange; (3) to facilitate inclusiveness and debate among scholars from diverse national and cultural backgrounds and from multi-disciplinary perspectives on communication-related issues; and (4) to promote a wider public interest in, and visibility of, the theories, methods, findings and applications generated by research in communication and allied fields. [Association Mission Statement]

National Communication Association (NCA) (www.natcom.org/)

The National Communication Association advances Communication as the discipline that studies all forms, modes, media, and consequences of communication through humanistic, social scientific, and aesthetic inquiry. NCA serves the scholars, teachers, and practitioners who are its members by enabling and supporting their professional interests in research and teaching. Dedicated to fostering and promoting free and ethical communication, NCA promotes the widespread appreciation of the importance of communication in public and private life, the application of competent communication to improve the quality of human life and relationships, and the use of knowledge about communication to solve human problems. [Association Mission Statement]

Organization for the Study of Communication, Language, and Gender (OSCLG) (http://osclg.org)

OSCLG – the Organization for the Study of Communication, Language and Gender – has grown from a series of interdisciplinary conferences that began at Bowling Green State University in 1978. Since that time, it has sought to provide a forum for professional discussion, presentation of research and demonstration of creative projects in the areas of communication, language and gender, and to promote recognition of those doing work in this area.

Members of OSCLG believe that interaction across a wide spectrum of disciplines is needed to foster more insightful discussion of the issues of language, gender and communication. Similarly, OSCLG seeks to include contributions from teachers, consultants and practitioners as well as researchers . . . The mission of Women and Language is to provide a feminist forum for those interested in communication, language and gender. [From the Association's website]

Public Relations Student Society of America (PRSA) (www.prsa.org/)

The Public Relations Society of America is the nation's largest professional organization serving the communications community with a mission to "make communications professionals smarter, better prepared and more connected through all stages of their career." Our membership collectively represents more than 30,000 members composed of communications professionals spanning every industry sector nationwide and college and university students who encompass the Public Relations Student Society of America (PRSSA). [From the Association's website]

Religious Communication Association (RCA) (www.relcomm.org/)

RCA is an academic society founded in 1973 for scholars, teachers, students, clergy, journalists, and others who share an interest in religious speech, rhetoric, media, and performance. The association is nonsectarian and provides a setting for professionals of various faiths, or no faith, to study problems of communication and religion. Through its annual conferences and quarterly journal, the association fosters significant scholarship and respectful dialogue that reflects the diverse beliefs, subject matter concerns, methodologies, and professions of RCA members. [From the Association's website]

Southern States Communication Association (SSCA) (www.ssca.net/)

Southern States Communication Association's purpose is to promote the study, criticism, research, teaching, and application of the artistic, humanistic, and scientific principles of communication. SSCA, a not-for-profit organization, exists for educational, scientific, and literary purposes only. [From the Association's website]

The Broadcast Education Association (BEA) (www.beaweb.org/)

The Broadcast Education Association (BEA) is the premiere international academic media organization, driving insights, excellence in media production, and career advancement for educators, students, and professionals. The association's publications, annual convention, web-based programs, and regional district activities provide opportunities for juried production competition and presentation of current scholarly research related to aspects of the electronic media. These areas include media audiences, economics, law and policy, regulation, news, management, aesthetics, social effects, history, and criticism, among others. BEA is concerned with electronic media curricula, placing an emphasis on interactions among the purposes, developments, and practices of the industry and imparting this information to future professionals. BEA serves as a forum for exposition, analysis and debate of issues of social importance to develop members' awareness and sensitivity to these issues and to their ramifications, which will ultimately help students develop as more thoughtful practitioners. [Association Mission Statement]

Western States Communication Association (WSCA) (www.westcomm.org)

The purpose of this Association, a not-for-profit organization, shall be to unite those persons of the Western States who have an academic, lay, or professional interest in communication and who want to promote their mutual educational interests. This organization does not contemplate pecuniary gain or profit to the members thereof and is organized for nonprofit purposes. [From the Association's Constitution]

Glossary

abstract – symbols that represent a non-tangible concept or idea like *hate*.

A-CAR pattern – a model of speaking stress that includes Anticipation, Confrontation, Adaptation, and Release.

action-centered listeners – want messages to be highly organized, concise, and error free.

active listening – transactional process in which a listener reinforces the message of the speaker.

advisory groups – the same as formal groups but their task is a short-term one.

affectionate communication – the behaviors individuals overtly use to express caring, closeness, and fondness to each other and consists of three dimensions: verbal statements, nonverbal gestures, and social support behaviors.

affinity seeking – providing information online that a sender thinks will cause another to like them and what they are saying.

Agenda-Setting Theory – a theory explaining the relationship between the audience and the mass media. The theory states that the media set the agenda but the audience is active and decides what to think about the issues on that agenda.

ambushing – an obstacle to listening when a communicator accumulates the words of another and saves them for an attack.

arrangement – organizing the ideas in the most effective manner for persuasion.

asynchronous – engaging with others on social media on your own time when everyone isn't online at the same time.

attitudinal or psychographic analysis – an assessment that includes assessing perceptions, beliefs, and values of listeners.

attraction – a motivation to act positively toward another person.

attribute agenda setting – the media's role in directing consumers to what attributes, or parts, of the issues are most important.

attributions – motives or characteristics you ascribe to another (or yourself) based on their (or your) behaviors.

audience analysis – an assessment that occurs when a speaker examines and evaluates information about his or her listeners and the setting in which a speech occurs.

autonomy and connection dialectic – a part of Relational Dialectics Theory, it represents our desire to be independent or autonomous while simultaneously wanting to feel a connection with our partner.

avoiding stage – a stage in relational development when two people try to stay away from each other.

behavioral interdependence – the behaviors of the people involved in a relationship affect one another.

behavioral symbols – an element of Organizational Culture Theory, it includes things like traditions within the organization such as the annual family picnic, the holiday party, and gifts that are given to people upon their retirement.

biphobic language – verbal symbols demeaning bisexuals.

body artifacts – a type of kinesics, referring to how things such as clothing, jewelry, uniforms, body piercings, tattoos, hair color, make-up, and so forth communicate to others.

bonding stage – a stage in relational development when two people make a public commitment concerning their relational ties.

boundary spanning – when members of the organization speak to others in a different company, or to those served by the organization.

brainstorming – the process of generating as many topics as possible without evaluation.

castes – historical classifications of social standing in India.

categorical imperative – Immanuel Kant's idea that acting ethically refers to following moral absolutes.

CCO approach – the idea that communication constitutes organizations.

central executive – a component of Working Memory Theory; prompts the memory to attend to relevant information while ignoring or suppressing irrelevant information.

channel – the pathway for the message.

chronemics – how we think about and use time.

chronological pattern – an organizational structure in speechmaking that adheres to a particular order.

circumscribing stage – a stage in relational development when two people establish topics that they wish to avoid talking about for fear of conflict.

cisgender – people who are consistent among sex, gender, and sexual/affectional preferences (e.g., a biological male who's masculine and heterosexual).

close relationships – a relationship that has behavioral interdependence, mutual influence as well as a strong sense of attachment and irreplaceability; in close relationships partners develop unique communication patterns.

Co-cultural Theory – a theoretical tradition that suggests societies are hierarchical and that those at the top of the hierarchy are afforded power, privilege, and position.

cohesion – a measure of how much group members like one another.

collective rationalization – a symptom of groupthink occurring when group members ignore information that's contrary to their beliefs.

collectivism – a value that places the group's norms, values, and beliefs over the individual.

communication – a transactional process using symbols to create (shared) meaning.

communication apprehension – a level of either real or perceived fear and anxiety related to speaking before a group of people.

competency – the part of a field of experience representing how much a person knows about the subject of a communication encounter.

complex cyclic path – a group beginning one approach to problem solving only to abandon it and take up another.

concrete – symbols that represent a tangible event or object like *desk*.

conflict stage – one stage in Fisher's model of group decision making; it focuses on members engaging in discussions about the feasibility of a variety of solutions.

connotative meaning – meaning derived from people's personal and subjective experiences with something.

consensus – the degree to which other people behave the same way in similar situations; high consensus means a person's behavior is similar to that of others in the same situation.

consistency – the stability of the behavior across time; high consistency means the person behaves this way all the time.

Contagion Theory – refers to how feelings, emotional states, and other nonverbal cues are "caught" by those who surround an individual.

content-centered listeners – focus on the facts and details of a message.

content conflicts – conflicts centered on a specific subject, involving questions of fact and opinion.

context – a component of the holistic model, it focuses on the environment in which a message is sent, and has three dimensions.

correlation – the media direct the public's and policymakers' attention to the same things at the same time.

Covariation Model of Attribution – a theory explaining how people make judgments about the causes of their own and others' behaviors by thinking about how the information they have from various sources works together.

cultural context – a dimension of the context emphasizing the rules, roles, norms, and patterns of communication that are unique to the particular culture where the communication takes place.

cultural empathy – a learned process of learning about the cultural experiences of another and conveying that understanding responsively.

culture – learned system of life experiences of a group who have a common set of values, beliefs, norms, and traditions.

culture clashes – disagreements and conflicts over cultural expectations.

cyclic alternation – a part of Relational Dialectics Theory, it is a coping strategy for managing dialectical tensions by featuring each opposition at alternating times.

defensive listening – a type of listening that occurs when a listener listens to words that a speaker communicates as personal attacks or hostile expressions.

defining or describing speech – a type of informative speech which includes the speaker explaining a topic to a group of listeners who are unfamiliar with the topic.

deliberative oratory – a branch of oratory that involves public debate on issues and actions undertaken by legislators.

delivery – using a pleasing voice and significant gestures in giving a speech.

demographic audience analysis – an assessment that includes examining the classifications and various characteristics of a speaker's listeners.

demonstration speech – a type of speech that shows an audience how to complete a process or task.

denotative meaning – the literal, conventional meaning that is found in a dictionary.

destructive side of communication – negative communication exchanged between people or negative effects that result from communication encounters.

diaspora – the movement of a group of people from their native country.

differentiating stage – a stage in relational development when two people begin talking about the ways they are not alike; begins the Coming Apart phase of the relationship.

disqualifying – a part of Relational Dialectics Theory, it is a form of the integration coping strategy for managing dialectical tensions; it allows people to cope with tensions by exempting certain issues from the general pattern.

distinctiveness – the extent to which a person's behavior is unique to the situation; high distinctiveness means the behavior only occurs in this situation.

downward communication – messages coming from a higher power individual in the organization sent to those with less power.

dyadic effect – disclosing something that matches our partner's disclosure in intimacy level.

dyads – groups of two people where interpersonal and relational communication often takes place.

effect – a component of the holistic model showing that a result always comes from a communication encounter.

elocution movement – a movement focused on elevating the canon of delivery.

emergence stage – one stage in Fisher's model of group decision making; it focuses on when the group closes in on a solution.

emotional contagion – a tendency to imitate sensory, motor, physiological, and affective states of other people.

empathy – the ablity to understand or feel what another person is experiencing from their frame of reference.

enculturation – the process of identifying with a particular culture and its various customs, values, and patterns of interaction.

enthusiasm – the passion employed in a speech to influence speaking effectiveness.

environmental analysis – an assessment that includes surveying the physical surroundings and making adjustments as necessary.

epideictic oratory – a branch of oratory that involves acknowledgement, praise, or blame and involves a ceremony/event of some sort.

ethic of care – Carol Gilligan's idea that ethical decisions should be based on relational connection.

ethics – the perceived rightness or wrongness of an action or behavior, involving moral decision making.

ethnocentrism – when we place our own beliefs above others, when we believe that the cultural group to which we belong is somehow superior to others, and/or if we view ourselves as morally above others.

ethos – the credibility of the speaker and their trustworthiness.

Expectancy Violations Theory – a theory that helps us understand why we feel uncomfortable when someone invades our personal space, and why we sometimes allow this invasion to occur.

experimenting stage – a stage in relational development when two people engage in interactions that are relaxed, pleasant, uncritical, and casual.

extemporaneous delivery format – a carefully prepared and rehearsed speaking approach that contains a pre-chosen organizational structure and delivered in a conversational style.

external attribution – an explanation for why people do something that is found in factors outside a person's control.

external feedback – responses to your messages received from other people.

eye contact – the use of eye behavior to influence speaking effectiveness.

face – the image of ourselves that we present to others; our public self.

facework – to act in cooperation with others to preserve two types of face: positive and negative.

fact – a verifiable claim.

familiazation – cultures where the state government takes over some of the burdens of caring for working families.

feedback – a component of the interactional model of communication consisting of responses to a sender's message; the reciprocal influence that partners exert.

feminine cultures – cultures that emphasize equality, quality of life, and caring for others.

field of experience – a component of the holistic model, representing a person's culture, past experiences, personal history, competency, skills, and heredity.

first level of agenda setting – the media's role in creating a sense of the important issues of the day.

five canons of rhetoric – Cicero's idea that rhetoric was divided into five parts: invention, style, arrangement, memory, and delivery.

formal groups – groups that have a long-term task, or a series of tasks, are structured in a formal way, and have restricted membership.

fundamental attribution error – when we attribute the cause for our behaviors to external factors and the cause for others' behaviors to internal traits.

gatekeeping – the idea that people who have power over the media (like editors of newspapers) have the power to suppress some stories and to advance others.

gimmick organizational pattern – an organizational structure that relies on a particular memory device.

grammar – a set of rules dictating how words should be combined to make a meaningful message.

group – a collection of more than two people sharing the following social characteristics: a shared purpose, interdependence, interpersonal interactions, perception of membership, structured relations, and individual motivation.

Groupthink – a theory explaining how poor group decisions result when group members become more concerned with consensus than with critically assessing all options for solutions to the problem or problems they are considering.

haptics – communication through touch.

hearing – physical process of letting in auditory stimuli without trying to understand those stimuli.

historical context – a dimension of the context clarifying that messages are understood in relationship to the historical period in which they were exchanged.

holistic model of communication – a picture of communication in the transactional mode that provides five more components to capture the complexity of the process.

homogeneity – a perceptual bias where we assume that others are similar to us.

homophobic language – verbal symbols demeaning gays and lesbians.

horizontal communication – interactions between co-workers or peers on the same power level in the organization.

hyperpersonal perspective – the feeling of closeness and effectiveness that people feel during online communication.

Hypodermic Needle Theory – the belief that powerful media "inject" ideas into the mind of a compliant public.

illusion of invulnerability – a symptom of groupthink occurring when group members believe that they are special and they know more than most other people; they begin to think they can't make a mistake.

illusion of unanimity – a symptom of groupthink occurring when silence is interpreted as agreement.

image conflicts – conflicts occurring over differing perceptions about self-images.

impression management – the attempts we make, consciously or unconsciously, to influence others' perceptions of us.

impromptu delivery format – an unprepared and unrehearsed speech that is undertaken with little or no notice.

individualism – a value whereby a culture prefers the individual over the group.

inference – an interpretation of a factual claim.

in-group – a group to which a person feels he or she belongs.

initiating stage – a stage in relational development when two people indicate to each other that they are interested in making contact; begins the Coming Together phase of the relationship.

integrating stage – a stage in relational development when two people form a clear identity as a couple; they talk about themselves as a unit.

integration – a part of Relational Dialectics Theory, it is a coping strategy for managing dialectical tensions by making an effort to combine the oppositions more fully than the three previous strategies; it takes three different forms.

intensifying stage – a stage in relational development when two people develop a deepening intimacy.

intentionality – whether or not a communicator means to send a particular message.

interactional model of communication – a picture of communication emphasizing how both people in the interaction are senders and receivers, just not simultaneously.

internal attribution – an explanation for why people do something that's rooted in personality traits.

internal feedback – when you think of an assessment of your own communication.

interpersonal communication – the process of message transaction between two people to create and sustain shared meaning.

interpersonal conflict – the interaction of interdependent people who perceive incompatible goals and interference from each other in achieving those goals.

interpersonal relationship – seeing a person regularly and having both behavioral interdependence and mutual influence in the relationship; in interpersonal relationships, your interactions become more unique.

interpreting – the third stage of perception; it involves assigning meaning to our perceptions.

interpretive communities – groups of media audiences constituted by demographics, social roles, and by ways of thinking about reality, or the interpretive frames, that they use in making sense of mediated messages.

intimate distance – one of Hall's categories of personal space, it covers the distance that extends from you to around 18 inches from you.

intonation – the use of pitch, tone, and sound to influence speaking effectiveness.

invention – discovering evidence about a topic and deciding what to say about it.

judicial oratory (forensic oratory) – a branch of oratory that distinguishes between justice and injustice.

kinesics – the study of communication through gestures, posture, and other bodily motions.

lexical gap – when concepts remain unnamed in a language.

linear model of communication – a picture of communication emphasizing the transmission of a message to a destination. Based on five components: sender, receiver, message, channel, and noise.

Linguistic Determinism/Relativity Theory – a theory explaining how the words we use determine (or influence) our ability to perceive and think.

listening – transactional activity that requires us to receive, respond, recall, and rate stimuli and/or messages.

listening style – preferred approach to the messages we hear.

logos – the integration of logic and evidence in a speech.

long-term orientation cultures – cultures that focus on the future, embracing the excitement and unpredictability of change.

main heading – the primary point in a speech.

manuscript delivery format – a word for word speech that a speaker reads to an audience.

masculine cultures – cultures that emphasize assertiveness, competition, self-centeredness, power, and strength.

masculinity-femininity – the extent to which a culture represents masculine or feminine traits; a dimension of national culture.

mass media – using technological means for professional communicators to communicate with many people (the public) at the same time over large distances.

meaning – what people make out of a message; can refer to the content level or the relationship level.

media framing – the way that the presentation of a story shapes a receiver's response to it.

media literacy – the ability to assess the messages sent through mediated formats.

melting pot – the blending of cultures into one national culture.

memorized delivery format – occurs when a manuscript speech is committed to memory and recited to an audience.

memory – concentrating on remembering the material for the speech.

message – how the source encodes the idea or thought.

meta-conflicts – conflicts about a conflict, or a way of conducting conflict.

mindful listening – type of listening that includes both being aware of one's internal thoughts and reactions as well as suspending judgments and criticisms of another's words.

mindfulness – behavior that requires us to pay close attention to an incoming message.

mindguards – a symptom of groupthink occurring when some group members (usually self-appointed) actively work to keep contrary information from the rest of the group.

model of communication – a visual representation of the complex process of communication.

monochronic culture – a culture where expectations are that one thing is done at a time.

Motivated Sequence – a persuasive speech organizational pattern that includes gaining audience attention, establishing a need/rationale, satisfying the need through a solution, visualizing the future, and cultivating action.

multiple necessary causes – when we can come up with a lot of reasons for a certain behavior.

multiple sufficient causes – when we observe a behavior and can think of one satisfying explanation, and that's all we need to make the attribution.

mutual influence – the people in the relationship affect each other emotionally or socially.

naïve psychologist – when a person tries to make sense of their social interactions following the same patterns that researchers use, without applying them as rigorously as professionals do.

negativity bias – a perceptual bias involving the tendency to give more credence to bad information than to good.

negative face – feeling free to act as we wish.

neutralizing – a part of Relational Dialectics Theory, it is a form of the integration coping strategy for managing dialectical tensions; it involves compromising between the two oppositions.

noise – anything that interferes with the message; consists of four types.

nonverbal codes – all behaviors – other than spoken words – that communicate messages.

nonverbal communication – the process of exchanging non-linguistic cues.

novelty and predictability dialectic – a part of Relational Dialectics Theory, it represents our simultaneous desires for unpredictability and stability.

omnipotent listening – a type of listening that occurs when a receiver tries to complete the message of a speaker, even before that speaker has sent a message.

openness and protection dialectic – a part of Relational Dialectics Theory, it represents our desire to self-disclose our innermost secrets to a friend, but we also want to protect ourselves from the chance that we'll be vulnerable to that friend after we self-disclose.

opinion – a personal assessment on evolution.

oratory – formalized public speaking.

Organizational Culture Theory – theory explaining how organizations construct a unique culture through their practices, especially their communication practices.

organizations – groups of groups working together with the following essential characteristics: interdependence, differentiation of tasks and functions, a goal orientation, control, and repeated communication practices.

organizing – the second stage in perception, it refers to placing potentially confusing pieces of stimuli into an understandable, accessible, and orderly pattern.

orientation stage – one stage in Fisher's model of group decision making; it focuses on when members get to know one another and figure out their goal and adopt some role behaviors that they might maintain for subsequent meetings.

out-group – a group to which a person feels he or she does not belong.

out-group stereotypes – a symptom of groupthink occurring when group members characterize those outside the group in rigid and often negative ways.

outline – the skeleton of your speech.

paralanguage – nonverbal behaviors such as pitch, rate, volume, inflection, tempo, pronunciation, disfluencies, and silence that accompany verbal communication but are not words.

pathos – the emotional aspects of speechmaking.

pauses – strategic interruptions to influence speaking effectiveness.

people-centered listeners – concerned with other people's feelings or emotions.

perception – a social process, in four stages, using our senses to assign meaning and respond to stimuli in our environment.

personal distance – one of Hall's categories of personal space, it ranges from 18 inches to 4 feet from you and is the space most people use during conversations.

personal space – the distance we put between ourselves and others; according to Hall there are four categories of personal space.

persuasion – a process whereby a speaker attempts to convince others to change their behaviors or attitudes regarding an issue.

phonological loop – a component of Working Memory Theory; refers to the auditory nature of a message, including both the physical sound as well as how that sound is being received.

phubbing – snubbing a partner who's in your presence by concentrating on your phone.

physical environment – the attributes of where you study, sleep, socialize, exercise, play music, worship, and so forth.

physical noise – one type of noise, also called external noise; involves stimuli outside of the receiver that make the message difficult to hear.

physical symbol – an element of Organizational Culture Theory, it includes things like logos, building architecture and décor, and material objects around the office.

physiological noise – one type of noise that refers to biological interferences on message reception.

polychronic cultures – cultures where many things are expected to take place at the same time.

positive face – our ability to think highly of our competence in a social encounter.

power distance – the degree to which the less powerful expect and accept that power is distributed unequally.

pregendered – the belief that some nonverbal behaviors are masculine or feminine; for example, crying is seen as a feminine nonverbal in the USA.

prejudice – a loathing toward a particular group.

pressure applied to dissenters – a symptom of groupthink occurring when dissenters are asked to leave the group or are made to feel so uncomfortable that they resign. Sometimes members provide verbal and nonverbal feedback to convince dissenters that they should conform to the rest of the group's will.

priming – how the media influence what people think, at least temporarily.

private information – consists of evaluations, both good and bad, that we have made about ourselves as it reflects our self-concept.

private language – idiosyncratic words and phrases based on past experiences developed in the intensifying stage of relational development.

Problem-Solution Format – a persuasive speech organizational pattern identifying a particular problem or challenge and then proposing one or more solutions to the problem.

process – an ongoing, unending activity that is always changing.

pro-con organizational pattern – an organizational structure that divides an argument or issue into two sides.

productivity – the output of the task work a group does.

professional communicators – people who study to become producers of messages.

proxemics – the study of how communication is influenced by space and distance.

psychological noise – the third type of noise, also referred to as internal noise, refers to a communicator's biases, prejudices, and feelings toward a person or a message.

public – a mass audience that tunes in to the same radio and television programs and reads the same books.

public distance – one of Hall's categories of personal space, it occurs at 12 or more feet from you and allows the entire person to be seen.

public information – facts that we make a part of our public image—the parts of ourselves that we present to others.

racist language – verbal symbols and practices demeaning people based on ethnicity.

rate – the pacing or speed of speaking.

rating – evaluating or assessing a message.

re-appropriation – when a group gives a positive meaning to a word that has been used by others to denigrate their group. The word then can be used by the group members as a way of establishing group cohesion.

recalling – storing a message for future encounters and remembering it later.

receiver – the intended target of the message.

receiving – attending to a message and focusing attention on it.

Reception Theory of Mass Communication – a theory advocating that different audience members will have different responses to the same mediated messages based on their differing backgrounds.

reciprocal – behavior that mirrors another's; self-disclosures are usually reciprocal.

reframing – a part of Relational Dialectics Theory, it is a form of the integration coping strategy for managing dialectical tensions; it involves rethinking the poles so that they no longer form an opposition.

reinforcement stage – one stage in Fisher's model of group decision making; it focuses on when the group congratulates itself on finding a solution and begins to praise their work.

relational communication – communication occurring within the context of a developed relationship.

relational conflicts – conflicts focused on what's wrong with a relationship, disagreements about the relationship definition, or clashes about the way a relationship is being conducted.

Relational Dialectics Theory – a theory that explains relational life as a series of tensions resulting from people's desire to have two opposing things simultaneously, and notes that everything we say in a relationship is in dialogue with all the past things that have been said in that relationship.

relational history – prior interactions shared by the communicators.

relational rules – the rules established to govern a relationship.

relational schema – an aid in the interpreting stage, it provides us with frames that guide our expectations and understanding of relationships.

relational uniqueness – how much a given relationship differs from others that you have.

research plan – the approach employed to undertake the speechmaking process.

responding – providing appropriate feedback to another communicator.

retrieving – the final stage of perception, it requires us to recall information stored in our memories.

rhetoric – using all available means to convince others.

role relationships – relationships that allow people to accomplish a certain task.

schema – part of the organizing stage of perception, it is a mental framework or memory structure that people rely on to understand their experiences.

segmentation – a part of Relational Dialectics Theory, it is a coping strategy for managing dialectical tensions by allowing people to isolate separate places, rather than times, for the oppositions.

selection – a part of Relational Dialectics Theory, it is a coping strategy for managing dialectical tensions by simply choosing one of the opposites while ignoring the other.

selective attention – the first stage in perception, it requires us to make the choice to pay attention to some things.

selective listening (spot listening) – a type of listening that involves filtering out bits of a message while disregarding other parts.

selective retrieval – remembering information that agrees with our perceptions and selectively "forgetting" information that does not.

self-censorship – a symptom of groupthink occurring when group members have dissenting ideas but stop themselves from expressing them to the group.

self-concept – the relatively stable set of perceptions we hold about ourselves.

self-disclosure – personal information, shared intentionally, that another person would have trouble finding out without being told.

self-esteem – the part of self-concept that is composed of how we evaluate our performance in the roles we play in life.

self-image – the part of self-concept that is composed of the roles that we play in life.

self-monitor – a part of the skill of focusing on your audience, it requires you to reflect on your own behaviors and how they affect others.

self-serving bias – a perceptual bias existing when we focus on information in a way that places us in a favorable light.

semantic noise – one type of noise, referring to interference caused by various meanings attributed by senders and receivers to the words the sender uses.

sender – source of an idea or thought.

sequential pattern – an organizational structure that uses a step-by-step sequence.

serial conflicts – conflicts that occur repeatedly over time in the same pattern, almost as though the partners were reading from a script.

sexist language – language that demeans or excludes one sex.

sexting – the practice of sending sexually explicit texts, within the context of relationships.

short-term orientation cultures – cultures that emphasize the present and the past and which embrace tradition.

signposts – transitions used between different speaking points.

silent listening – a type of listening that requires us to stay attentive and respond nonverbally when another is speaking.

simplicity bias – a perceptual bias involving the belief that people can express themselves thoughtfully and listen effectively without education in these practices.

simplified organizational pattern – an organizational pattern in speechmaking that includes an *introduction*, *body*, and *conclusion*.

situational approach to leadership – an approach to understanding leadership by focusing on how certain leadership behaviors might work better in some situations than others.

situational context – a dimension of the context focusing on the tangible environment in which communication occurs.

skills – the part of the field of experience representing a person's communicative abilities.

small talk – gossip, comments about work and school, sports, or other low-threat topics.

social distance – one of Hall's categories of personal space, it extends 4 to 12 feet from you and is the spatial zone usually reserved for professional or formal interpersonal encounters.

Social Information Processing Theory – a theory explaining how relationships develop online using the hyperpersonal perspective.

social media – forms of electronic communication (such as websites for social networking and microblogging) through which users create online communities to share information, ideas, personal messages, and other content (such as videos).

solution-oriented path – when a group begins to solve the problem at hand and devotes no time to discussing the parameters of the problem or analyzing it.

speech to inform – a type of speech with audience learning as its goal.

speech to persuade – a type of speech designed to making others (1) change the way they currently think about a subject, (2) consider your point(s) of view, and (3) adopt your suggestions/recommendations.

stagnating stage – a stage in relational development when two people extend circumscribing so far that they no longer talk much at all.

standpoints – positions that influence their perspectives and experiences.

stereotyping – the process of establishing a fixed mental image of a particular group of people and communicating with a single person as simply a member of that group.

strategic ambiguity – when we deliberately utilize a word that has multiple or vague meanings so we can avoid conflict.

style – deciding what language would be most effective in persuading the audience.

subordinate heading – the expansion of the main heading.

surveillance – the process of scanning the environment and deciding which events to focus on in reporting the news.

symbols – arbitrary labels or representations for phenomena.

synchronization – a process that involves listeners and other speakers unconsciously aligning themselves with what behavior precedes them.

synchronous – engaging with others through social media in real time while all are online at the same time.

synergy – when group members build on the ideas of others, usually creating a group decision that's of a higher quality than any individual's alone would be.

systematic desensitization – A process entailing an individual recognizing the various muscle groups that are tense and trying to relax those tensions.

tabula rasa – the belief that individuals are born with a blank slate.

talkaholism (egospeak) – a form of communication that prompts listeners to redirect the conversation to themselves.

technology – using the practical application of knowledge to accomplish a task, and converting that knowledge into some type of tool (like a telephone, a camera, and so forth).

terminating stage – a stage in relational development when two people end their relationship.

territorial markers – marking your territory in various ways, usually with items or objects.

territoriality – our sense of ownership of space.

thesis statement – a simple and brief declarative sentence that communicates to the audience the essence of your speech.

time-centered listeners – preoccupied with messages that are economically presented.

topical organizational pattern – an organizational structure that divides a speech topic into various divisions and subdivisions.

trait approach to leadership – an approach to understanding leadership by focusing on the important qualities a leader should possess, such as intelligence, self-confidence, determination, integrity, and sociability.

transactional – involving simultaneous messages between or among communicators.

transactional model of communication – a picture of communication characterized by the simultaneous providing and receiving of messages and the co-creation of meaning.

transformational approach – an approach to understanding leadership by focusing on the relationship between the leader and the follower; in transformational leadership they interact in such a way that both are changed by the relationship.

transphobic language – verbal symbols demeaning transgender individuals.

uncertainty avoidance – the extent to which individuals wish to avoid ambiguity and avoidance.

unitary sequence path – a rational approach to group decision making and problem solving, resembling Fisher's model.

unquestioned belief in the morality of the group – a symptom of groupthink occurring when group members share the belief that they're good and moral, and believe that the decisions they make are good and moral as well.

upward communication – messages sent from a subordinate to their superior.

utilitarianism – John Stuart Mill's idea that ethics are governed by what will bring the greatest good for the greatest number of people.

verbal codes – the words or vocabulary comprising a language.

verbal communication – when communicators exchange mutually understood verbal codes, following the rules of grammar governing the use of those codes.

verbal symbols – an element of Organizational Culture Theory, it includes things like stories, jokes, nicknames, and legends that members hear when they first join the organization and then they tell to others joining later.

visuospatial sketchpad – a component of Working Memory Theory; related to a pathway in the brain that stores the visual and spatial information.

volume – the use of one's voice to increase or decrease the speaking sounds to influence speaking effectiveness.

warranting – the perceived legitimacy and validity of information about another person that one may receive or observe online.

Working Memory Theory – the notion that our cognitive systems hold information temporarily in order to retrieve it.

xenophobia – fear, anxiety, or hatred of those from other lands.

References

Adams, J. Q. (1810). *Lectures on Rhetoric and Oratory: Delivered to the Classes of Senior and Junior Sophisters in Harvard University (Vol. 1)*. Boston: Hilliard and Metcalf.

Adesope, O. O., Lavin, T., Thompson, T., & Ungerleider, C. (2010). A systematic review and meta-analysis of the cognitive correlates of bilingualism. *Review of Educational Research*, *80*(2), 207–245.

Afifi, T., & Steuber, K. (2009). The revelation risk model (RRM): Factors that predict the revelation of secrets and the strategies used to reveal them. *Communication Monographs*, *76*(2), 144–176.

Agrawal, A. J. (2016). Five tips to give a top online sales presentation. *Forbes*, May 23; Media Insight Project.

Agrawal, A. J. (2017). *A new understanding: What makes people trust and rely on news*.

Andersen, J. (1996). *Communication theory: Epistemological foundations*. New York: Guilford Press.

Anderson, C. (2017). *TED Talks: The official TED guide to public speaking*. Chicago: Mariner Books.

Anderson, R., & Ross, V. (2002). *Questions of communication: A practical introduction to theory*, 2nd edn. New York: St. Martin's Press.

Antoniou, K., Grohmann, K. K., Kambanaros, M., & Katsos, N. (2016). The effect of childhood bilectalism and multilingualism on executive control. *Cognition*, *149*, 18–30.

Baddeley, A. (2007). *Working memory, thought, and action*. Oxford, UK: Oxford University Press.

Baddeley, A. (2014). *Essentials of human memory*. New York: Psychology Press.

Baddeley, A., Eysenck, M. W., & Anderson, M. C. (2014). *Memory*, 2nd edn. Abingdon: Psychology Press.

Bales, R. F. (1950). *Interaction process analysis: A method for the study of small groups*. Cambridge, MA: Addison-Wesley.

Barbaro, M., Parker, A., & Gabriel, T. (2016, March 12). *Donald Trump's heated words were destined to stir violence, opponents say. New York Times online*. Retrieved from https://www.nytimes.com/2016/03/13/us/politics/donald-trumps-heated-words-were-destined-to-stir-violence-opponents-say.html.

Barnlund, D. C. (1970). A transactional model of communication. In K. K. Sereno & C. D. Mortensen (eds.) *Foundations of communication theory*, pp. 83–102. New York: Harper.

Barsade, S. G. (2002). The ripple effect: Emotional contagion and its influence on group behavior. *Administrative Science Quarterly*, *47*(4), 644–675.

Bass, B. M. (1990). *Bass and Stodgill's handbook of leadership: Theory, research, and managerial applications*, 3rd edn. New York: Free Press.

Batanova, M. D., & Loukas, A. (2014). Maternal psychological control and peer victimization in early adolescence: An application of the family relational schema model. *The Journal of Early Adolescence*, *34*(2), 206–228.

Baxter, L. A. (1988). A dialectical perspective on communication strategies in relationship development. In S. Duck (ed.) *A handbook of personal relationships*, pp. 257–273. New York: Wiley.

Baxter, L. A. (2011). *Voicing relationships*. Thousand Oaks, CA: Sage.

Baxter, L. A., & Montgomery, B. M. (1996). *Relating: Dialogues and dialectics.* New York: Guilford.

Baxter, L. A., & Montgomery, B. M., & Norwood, K. M. (2015). Relational dialectics theory. *The International Encyclopedia of Interpersonal Communication*, 1–9.

Beavin-Bavelas, J. (1990). *Equivocal communication.* Newbury Park, CA: Sage.

Bechar-Israeli, H. (1996). *From < Bonehead > to < cLoNehEAd >: Nicknames, play and identity on the Internet. Relay Chat.* Retrieved from http://www.acuse.org.

Beck, D. (2017). Media representation: Sports. *The International Encyclopedia of Media Effects*, 1–9.

Beck, J. (2018, Jan. 11). How it became normal to ignore texts and emails. *The Atlantic.com.* Retrieved from https://www.theatlantic.com/technology/archive/2018/01/ignoring-each-other-in-the-age-of-instant-communication/550325/

Becker-Ho, A. (2015). *The essence of jargon: Argot and the dangerous classes.* New York: Autonomedia.

Behnke, R. R., Sawyer, C. R., & King, P. E. (1994). Contagion theory and the communication of public speaking state anxiety. *Communication Education*, *43*(3), 246–251.

Berg, H., Söderlund, M., & Lindström, A. (2015). Spreading joy: examining the effects of smiling models on consumer joy and attitudes. *Journal of Consumer Marketing*, *32*(6), 459–469.

Berg, J. H., & Archer, R. L. (1980). Disclosure or concern: A second look at liking for the norm-breaker. *Journal of Personality*, *48*, 245–257.

Blume, B. D., Baldwin, T. T., & Ryan, K. C. (2013). Communication apprehension: A barrier to students' leadership, adaptability, and multicultural appreciation. *Academy of Management Learning & Education*, *12*(2), 158–172.

Bodie, G. (2015). Listening. *The International Encyclopedia of Interpersonal Communication*, 1–7.

Bokore, N. (2016). Documenting refugee stories: Resettlement and integration challenges of East African refugees. *International Journal of Social Work*, *3*(1), 76.

Bond, B. J., & Compton, B. L. (2015). Gay on-screen: The relationship between exposure to gay characters on television and heterosexual audiences' endorsement of gay equality. *Journal of Broadcasting & Electronic Media*, *59*(4), 717–732.

Borisoff, D., & Merrill, L. (1991). Gender issues and listening. *Listening in everyday life: A personal and professional approach.* Lanham, MD: University Press of America.

Boromisza-Habashi, D., Hughes, J. M., & Malkowski, J. A. (2016). Public speaking as cultural ideal: Internationalizing the public speaking curriculum. *Journal of International and Intercultural Communication*, *9*(1), 20–34.

Bosmajian, H. (1974). *The language of oppression.* Washington, D.C.: Public Affairs Press.

Bostrom, R. N. (1990). *Listening behavior: Measurement and application.* Guilford Press.

Bowe, H., Martin, K., & Manns, H. (2014). *Communication across cultures: Mutual understanding in a global world.* Cambridge, UK: Cambridge University Press.

Bradley, A. (2010, January 7). *A new definition of social media. Gartner Blog Network.* Retrieved from https://blogs.gartner.com/anthony_bradley/ 192010/01/07/a-new-definition-of-social-media/

Brady, W. J., Wills, J. A., Jost, J. T., Tucker, J. A., & Van Bavel, J. J. (2017). Emotion shapes the diffusion of moralized content in social networks. *PNAS, 114* (28), 7313–7318.

Brands, R., Menges, J. I., & Kilduff, M. (2015). The leader-in-social-network schema: Perceptions of network structure affect gendered attributions of charisma. *Organizational Science*, *26*(4), 1210–1225.

Bronner, S. E. (2014). *The bigot: Why prejudice persists*. New Haven, CT: Yale University Press.

Brooks, D. (2017, July 7). *The golden age of bailing. New York Times*. Retrieved from https://www.nytimes.com/2017/07/07/opinion/the-golden-age-of-bailing.html

Brown, P., & Levinson, S. C. (1987). *Politeness: Some universals in language use*. Cambridge, UK: Cambridge University Press.

Brownell, J. (2002). *Listening*. New York: Routledge.

Brownell, J. (2013). *Listening: Attitudes, principles, skills*. Cambridge, UK: Routledge.

Bryman, A. (1996). Leadership in organizations. In S. Clegg, C. Hardy, & W. R. Nord (eds.) *Handbook of organization studies*, pp. 276–292. London: Sage.

Bullard, G. (2016). The world's newest world religion: No religion. Retrieved from https://news.nationalgeographic.com/2016/04/160422-atheism-agnostic-secular-nones-rising-religion/

Burgoon, J. K. (1978). A communication model of personal space violation: Explication and an initial test. *Human Communication Research*, *4*, 129–142.

Burgoon, J. K. (2009). Expectancy violations theory. In S. W. Littlejohn & K. Foss (eds.) *Encyclopedia of communication theory*, pp. 367–369. Thousand Oaks, CA: Sage.

Burgoon, J. K., & Dunbar, N. E. (2016). Accuracy of distinguishing truth from lie. In J. A. Hall, M. S. Mast, & T. V. West (eds.) *The social psychology of perceiving others accurately*, pp. 71–97. Cambridge, UK: Cambridge University Press.

Burley-Allen, M. (1997). *Listening: The forgotten skill*. New York: John Wiley & Sons.

Buzzanell, P. M., & Liu, M. (2005). Struggling with maternity leave policies and practices: A post-structuralist feminist analysis of gendered organizing. *Journal of Applied Communication Research*, *60*(3), 463–495.

Cacioppo, J., Cacioppo, S., Gonzaga, G. C., Ogburn, E. L., & VanderWeele, T. J. (2013). Marital satisfaction and break-ups differ across on-line and off-line meeting venues. *PNAS*, *110*(25), 10,135–10,140.

Campbell, E. (2014). *Getting it on online*. New York: Routledge.

Capaldi, N. (2004). *John Stuart Mill: A biography*. Cambridge, UK: Cambridge University Press.

Carbaugh, D. (1999). "Just listen":"Listening" and landscape among the Blackfeet. *Western Journal of Communication (includes Communication Reports)*, *63*(3), 250–270.

Carlin, D. B., & Winfrey, K. L. (2009). Have you come a long way, baby? Hillary Clinton, Sarah Palin, and sexism in 2008 campaign coverage. *Communication Studies*, *60*(4), 326–343.

Carmon, A. F. (2013). Is it necessary to be clear? An examination of strategic ambiguity in family business mission statements. *Qualitative Research Reports in Communication*, *14*(1), 87–96.

Carr, N. G. (2011). *The shallows*. New York: W.W. Norton & Company.

Catona, D., Greene, K., & Magsamen-Conrad, K. (2015). Perceived benefits and drawbacks of disclosure practices: An analysis of PLWHAs' strategies for disclosing HIV status. *Journal of Health Communication*, *20*(11), 1294–1301.

Chapman University Survey of American Fears (2017). *What do Americans fear most?* Orange, CA: Chapman University.

Chen, G. M. (2015). Losing *face* on social media: Threats to positive face lead to an indirect effect on retaliatory aggression through negative affect. *Communication Research*, *42*(6), 819–838.

Chotpitayasunondh, V., & Douglas, K. M. (2016). How "phubbing" becomes the norm: The antecedents and consequences of snubbing via smartphone. *Computers in Human Behavior*, *63*, 9–18.

Clawson, R., & Oxley, Z. (2017). *Public opinion: Democratic ideals, democratic practice*, 3rd edn. Thousand Oaks, CA: CQ Press.

Colby, S. L., & Ortman, J. N. (2015). *Projections of the size and composition of the U.S. population: 2014 to 2060*. Washington, D.C.: U.S. Census Bureau.

Cortazzi, H. (2006, April 27). Has Japan changed for the better? *Japan Times*, Retrieved from https://www.japantimes.co.jp/opinion/2006/04/27/commentary/has-japan-changed-for-better/#.WeOrMUzMznQ

Cowan, N. (2016). Working memory maturation: Can we get at the essence of cognitive growth? *Perspectives on Psychological Science*, *11*(2), 239–264.

Craig, C. S. (2013). Creating cultural products: Cities, context and technology. *City, Culture and Society*, *4*, 195–202.

Croucher, S. M. (2017). *Global perspectives on intercultural communication*. New York: Routledge.

Cupach, W. R., & Spitzberg, B. H. (2014). *The dark side of relationship pursuit: From attraction to obsession and stalking*. New York: Routledge.

Daimler, M. (2016). Listening is overlooked leadership tool. *Harvard Business Review*, May 25.

Dearing, J. W., & Rogers, E. M. (1996). *Agenda-setting*. Thousand Oaks, CA: Sage.

De Hoyos, B. (2017, February 23). How to use Instant Messaging to break up: When it's appropriate to end a relationship online. Retrieved from http://im.about.com/od/imetiquette/a/How-To-Use-Instant-Messaging-To-Break-Up.html.

Di Blasi, F. (2017). *From Aristotle to Thomas Aquinas*. South Bend, IN: St. Augustine's Press.

Doherty, R. W. (1997). The emotional contagion scale: A measure of individual differences. *Journal of Nonverbal Behavior*, *21*(2), 131–154.

Dorai, S., & Webster, C. (2015). The role of nonverbal communication in service encounters. In M. Hernández-López & L. Fernández Amaya (eds.) *A multidisciplinary approach to service encounters*, pp. 215–233. Leiden: Brill.

Drouin, M., & Landgraff, C. (2012). Texting, sexting, and attachment in college students' romantic relationships. *Computers in Human Behavior*, *28*(2), 444–449.

Duvall, D. L., & Jacob, M. (2011). *Secret history of the Cherokees*. Indian Territory Press: Cambridge, MA.

Earp, B. D. (2012). The extinction of masculine generics. *Journal for Communication and Culture*, *2*(1), 4–19.

Egan, T. (2016). The eight-second attention span. *The New York Times*, 22.

Eggermont, J. (2017). *Hearing loss*. London: Academic Press.

Ellingson, L. L. (2005). *Communicating in the clinic: Negotiating frontstage and backstage teamwork*. Cresskill, NJ: Hampton Press.

Englehardt, E. E. (2001). *Ethical issues in interpersonal communication*. Fort Worth, TX: Harcourt.

Esping-Andersen, G. (1999). *Social foundations of postindustrial economies*. Oxford, UK: Oxford University Press.

Farek, M., Jalki, D., Pathan, S., & Shah, P. (eds.) (2017). *Western foundations of the caste system*. London: Palgrave Macmillan.

Fasoli, R., Paladino, M. P., Carnaghi, A., et al. (2016). Not "just words": Exposure to homophobic epithets leads to dehumanizing and physical distancing from gay men. *European Journal of Social Psychology, 46,* 237–248.

Fay, S. (2012, June 18). *What's missing from Oprah's Book Club 2.0. The Atlantic.* Retrieved from www.theatlantic.com /entertainment/archive/2012/06/whats-missing-from-oprahs-book-club-20/ 258141/.

Ferrari, B. (2012). *Power listening: Mastering the most critical skill of all.* New York: Portfolio.

Fischer, C. S. (1992). *America calling: A social history of the telephone to 1940.* Berkeley, CA: University of California Press.

Fisher, B. A. (1970). Decision emergence: Phases in group decision making. *Speech Monographs, 37,* 53–66.

Floyd, K. (2002). Human affection exchange: V. Attributes of the highly affectionate. *Communication Quarterly, 50*(2), 135–152.

Folger, J. P., Poole, M. S., & Stutman, R. K. (2016). *Working through conflict: Strategies for relationships, groups, and organizations,* 7th edn. New York: Routledge.

Fox, J., Warber, K. M., & Makstaller, D. C. (2013). The role of Facebook in romantic relationship development: An exploration of Knapp's relational stage model. *Journal of Social and Personal Relationships, 30* (6), 771–794.

Franzoi, S. L., & Klaiber, J. R. (2007). Body use and reference group impact: With whom do we compare our bodies? *Sex Roles, 56* (3–4), 205–214.

Frey, L. R. (1994). The call of the field: Studying communication in natural groups. In L. R. Frey (ed.) *Group communication in context: Studies of natural group,* pp. ix–xiv. Hillsdale, NJ: Lawrence Erlbaum.

Gangestad, S. W., & Snyder, M. (2000). Self-monitoring: Appraisal and reappraisal. *Psychological Bulletin, 126,* 530–555.

Gardner, W. L. (2003). Perceptions of leader charisma, effectiveness, and integrity: Effects of exemplification, delivery, and ethical reputation. *Management Communication Quarterly, 16,* 502–527.

Garretson, J. J. (2015). Does change in minority and women's representation on television matter?: A 30-year study of television portrayals and social tolerance. *Politics, Groups, and Identities, 3*(4), 615–632.

Gehrke, P. J., & Keith, W. M. (eds.) (2015). *A century of communication studies: The unfinished conversation.* New York: Routledge.

Gibb, J. (1970). Sensitivity training as a medium for personal growth and improved interpersonal relationships. *Interpersonal Development, 1,* 6–31.

Gilchrist-Petty, E. S., & Long, S. D. (2016). *Contexts of the dark side of communication.* New York: Peter Lang.

Gilligan, C. (1982). *In a different voice.* Harvard University Press.

Gilligan, C. (2011). *Joining the resistance.* Cambridge, UK: Polity Press.

Goffman, E. (1959). *The presentation of self in everyday life.* New York: Anchor Books.

Golden, J. L., Berquist, G., Coleman, W. E., & Sproule, J. M. (2011). *The rhetoric of Western thought,* 10th edn. Dubuque, IA: Kendall-Hunt.

Gonzalez, P. (2014). *Race and ethnicity in video games: A reflection of social reality Racism, hate speech and prejudice: A manifestation of social stereotypes.* Unpublished paper.

Gonzalez, S. (2016, Nov. 3). There are more LGBTQ characters on broadcast TV than ever before, GLAAD study says. CNN Entertainment. Retrieved from http://

www.cnn.com/2016/11/03/entertain
ment/lgbtq-tv-glaad-study/index.html

Goren, C., & Neter, E. (2016). Stereotypical thinking as a mediating factor in the association
between exposure to terror and PTSD
symptoms among Israeli youth. *Anxiety,
stress, and coping, 29*(6), 644–659.

Goulston, M. (2015). *Just listen.* New York:
AMACOM.

Grande, S. (2015). *Red pedagogy: Native
American social and political thought.*
Lanham, MD: Rowman & Littlefield.

Graveline, D. (2013). How technology has changed public speaking. *Toastmaster,* 22–26.

Greenstein, S., & Devereux, M. (2017).
Wikipedia in the spotlight. *Kellogg School
of Management Cases,* 1–18.

Grice, H. P. (1975). Logic and conversation.
In P. Cole & J. L. Morgan (eds.) *Syntax
and semantics Vol. 3: Speech acts,* pp.
41–58. New York: Academic Press.

Guerrero, L. K., Andersen, P. A., & Afifi, W. A.
(2018). *Close encounters: Communication
in relationships,* 5th edn. Thousand Oaks,
CA: Sage.

Gunstad, J., Paul, R. H., Brickman, A. M., et al.
(2006). Patterns of cognitive performance
in middle-aged and older adults: A cluster
analytic examination. *Journal of Geriatric
Psychiatry and Neurology, 19*(2), 59–64.

Guo, J. (2016, January 8). *Sorry, grammar nerds.
The singular 'they' has been declared word
of the year. The Washington Post.* Retrieved
fromwww.washingtonpost.com/news/
wonk/wp/2016/01/08/donald-trump-
may-win-this-years-word-of-the-year/?
utm_term = .017396f016fc.

Guo, L., & Vargo, C. (2015). The power of message networks: A big-data analysis of the
network agenda setting model and issue
ownership. *Mass Communication and
Society 18*(5), 557–576.

Haiman, F. S. (1982). Nonverbal communication
and the First Amendment: The rhetoric of
the streets revisited. *Quarterly Journal of
Speech, 68*(4), 371–383.

Hall, E. T. (1959). *The silent language.*
New York: Doubleday.

Hall, E. T. (1966). *The hidden dimension.*
New York: Doubleday.

Hall, J. A., & Xing, C. (2015). The verbal and
nonverbal correlates of the five flirting
styles. *Journal of Nonverbal Behavior,
39*(1), 41–68.

Hata, M. (2014). Preschool girls and the media:
How magazines describe and depict gen-
der norms. *International Journal of Early
Childhood, 46*(3), 373–389.

Hatch, M. J. (2006). *Organizational theory:
Modern, symbolic, and postmodern per-
spective.* Oxford, UK: Oxford University
Press.

Hecht, M. L., Collier, M. J., & Ribeau, S. A.
(1993). *Language and language behaviors series, Vol. 2. African American
communication: Ethnic identity and cultural interpretation.* Thousand Oaks, CA:
Sage.

Heider, F. (1958). *The psychology of interpersonal relations.* New York: Wiley.

Herrick, J. (2017). *The history and theory of rhetoric: An introduction.* New York: Routledge.

Hinde, R. A. (1995). A suggested structure for
a science of relationships. *Personal
Relationships, 2,* 1–15.

Hofstede, G. (1980). Motivation, leadership, and
organization: do American theories apply
abroad? *Organizational Dynamics, 9*(1),
42–63.

Hofstede, G. (1984). *Culture's consequences:
International differences in work-related
values.* Thousand Oaks, CA: Sage.

Hofstede, G. (1991). *Cultures and organizations. Intercultural cooperation and its
importance for survival. Software of the
mind.* London: McGraw-Hill.

Hofstede, G. (2001). *Culture's consequences:
Comparing values, behaviors, institutions*

and organizations across nations, 2nd edn. Thousand Oaks, CA: Sage.

Hofstede, G. (2003). *Culture's consequences: Comparing values, behaviors, institutions and organizations across nations*, 3rd edn. Thousand Oaks, CA: Sage.

Hoijer, H. H. (1994). The Sapir–Whorf hypothesis. In L. A. Samovar & R. E. Porter (eds.) *Intercultural communication: A reader*. Belmont, CA: Wadsworth.

Holder, S. (2017, July 3). *How the psychology of cyberbullying explains Trump's tweets. Politico*. Retrieved from www.politico.com/magazine/story/2017/07/03/how-the-psychology-of-cyberbullying-explains-trumps-tweets-215333?cid = apn.

Horwitz, B. (2002). *Communication apprehension: Origins and management*. Boston: Cengage.

Imahori, T. T., & Cupach, W. R. (2005). Identity management theory. In W. B. Gudykunst (ed.) *Theorizing about intercultural communication*, pp. 195–210. Thousand Oaks, CA: Sage.

Imhof, M. (2003). The social construction of the listener: Listening behavior across situations, perceived social status, and cultures. *Communication Research Reports, 20*, 357–366.

Isaacs, E. E. (2016). Media representation of gender: Startup publications' coverage of 2016 presidential campaigns. University of Tennessee Honors Thesis Projects. Retrieved from http://trace.tennessee.edu/utk_chanhonoproj/1975

Ivy, D. K., Bullis-Moore, L., Norvell, K., Backlund, P., & Javidi, M. (1995). The lawyer, the babysitter and the student: Inclusive language usage and instruction. *Women and Language, 18*, 13–21.

Janis, I. L. (1972). *Victims of groupthink: A psychological study of foreign-policy decisions and fiascoes*. Boston, MA: Houghton Mifflin.

Jensen, J. V. (1997). *Ethical issues in the communication process*. Mahwah, NJ: Lawrence Erlbaum.

Jensen, K. B. (2012). Media reception: Qualitative traditions. In K. B. Jensen (ed.) *A handbook of media and communication research: Qualitative and quantitative methodologies*, pp. 171–185. New York, NY: Routledge.

Jhally, S., Kilbourne, J., & Rabinovitz, D., (2010). Media Education Foundation. *Killing Us Softly 4: Advertising's Image of Women*.

Johannesen, R. L. (2000). *Ethics in human communication*, 5th edn. Prospect Heights, IL: Waveland Press.

Johnston, M. K., Weaver III, J. B., Watson, K. W., & Barker, L. B. (2000). Listening styles: Biological or psychological differences? *International Journal of Listening, 14*(1), 32–46.

Kacirk, J. (2000). *The word museum: The most remarkable English words ever forgotten*. New York: Touchstone.

Kadoya, Y. (2016). What makes people anxious about life after the age of 65? Evidence from international survey research in Japan, the United States, China, and India. *Review of Economics of the Household, 14*(2), 443–461.

Kelley, H. H. (1967). Attribution theory in social psychology. *Nebraska Symposium on Motivation, 15*, 192–238.

Kendall, S., & Tannen, D. (2003). Discourse and gender. In D. Schiffrin, D. Tannen, & H. E. Hamilton (eds.), *The handbook of discourse analysis*, pp. 568–588. Malden, MA: Blackwell.

Kirby, E. L., & Buzzanell, P. M. (2014). Communicating work-life issues. In L. L. Putnam & D. K. Mumby (eds.) *The SAGE handbook of organizational communication: Advances in theory, research, and methods*, pp. 351–373. Thousand Oaks, CA: Sage.

Kirby, E. L., Wieland, S. M. B., & McBride, C. M. (2013). Work-life conflict. In J. G. Oetzel & S. Ting-Toomey (eds.) *The SAGE handbook of conflict communication: Integrating theory, research, and practice*, pp. 377–402. Thousand Oaks, CA: Sage.

Kluger, J. (2011). Slow down! Why some languages sound so fast. *Time*, September 8.

Knapp, M. L. (1978). *Social intercourse: From greeting to goodbye*. Boston, MA: Allyn & Bacon.

Knapp, M. L., Hall, J. A., & Horgan, T. (2013). *Nonverbal communication in human interaction*. Boston: Cengage.

Knapp, M. L., Hall, J. A., & Horgan, T. (2014). *Nonverbal communication in human interaction*. Boston, MA: Allyn & Bacon.

Knapp, M. L., Vangelisti, A. L., & Caughlin, J. P. (2014). *Interpersonal communication and human relationships*, 7th edn. Boston, MA: Pearson.

Knapp, S. (2016). *Crimes against India*. Bloomington, IN: iUniverse.

Krys, K., Vauclair, M., Capaldi, C. A., et al. (2016). Be careful where you smile: Culture shapes judgments of intelligence and honesty of smiling individuals. *Journal of Nonverbal Behavior*, 40(2), 101–116.

Kuehn, M. (2001). *Kant: A biography*. Cambridge, UK: Cambridge University Press.

Kuypers, J. A., & King, A. (eds.) (2001). *Twentieth-century roots of rhetorical studies*. Greenwood Publishing Group.

Lachover, E. (2017). Signs of change in media representation of women in Israeli politics: Leading and peripheral women contenders. *Journalism*, 18(4), 446–463.

LaFrance, M., & Vial, A. C. (2016). Gender and nonverbal behavior. In D. Matsumoto, H. C. Hwang, & M. G. Frank (eds.) *APA handbook of nonverbal communication*, pp. 139–161. Washington, D.C.: American Psychological Association.

Lakoff, R. (1975). *Language and women's place*. New York: Harper and Row.

Langan-Fox, J., Code, S., Gray, R., & Langfield-Smith, K. (2002). Supporting employee participation: Attitudes and perceptions in trainees, employees and teams. *Group Processes and Intergroup Relations*, 5(1), 53–82.

Lasswell, H. (1948). The structure and function of communication in society. In L. Bryson (ed.) *The communication of ideas*, pp. 32–51. New York: Harper & Row.

Levine, A. S. (2016, June 21). *New York today: Our disappearing languages*. Retrieved from www.nytimes.com/2016/06/21/nyregion/new-york-today-languages-disappearing-dialects.html.

Lewis, R. D. (2006). *When cultures collide: Leading across cultures*. Boston, MA: Nicholas Brealey Publishing.

Lin, R., & Utz, S. (2017). Self-disclosure on SNS: Do disclosure intimacy and narrativity influence interpersonal closeness and social attraction? *Computers in Human Behavior*, 70, 426–436.

Lippmann, W. (1946). *Public opinion*. New York: Transaction Publishers.

Lukacs, V., & Quan-Haase, A. (2015). Romantic breakups on Facebook: New scales for studying post-breakup behaviors, digital distress, and surveillance. *Information, Communication and Society*, 18(5), 492–508.

Malandro, L. A., & Barker, L. L. (1983). *Nonverbal communication*. New York: Addison-Wesley Longman.

Martin, P., & Papadelos, P. (2017). Who stands for the norm? The place of metonymy in androcentric language. *Social Semiotics*, 27(1), 39–58.

McCombs, M. E., & Shaw, D. L. (1972). The agenda-setting function of mass media. *Public Opinion Quarterly*, 36(2), 176–187.

McCombs, M. E., Shaw, D. L., & Weaver, D. H. (2014). New directions in agenda-setting theory and research. *Mass Communication and Society*, *17*(6), 781–802.

McCormick, M. (2018, January 6). *Newfound pride in Guaraní, a language long disdained in Paraguay. New York Times.* Retrieved from www.nytimes.com/2018/01/06/world/americas/paraguay-guarani language.html.

MacDonald, D. J., & Standing, L. G. (2002). Does the self-serving bias cancel the Barnum effect? *Social Behavior and Personality*, *30*(6), 625–630.

Mackenzie, C. (2013). *The Chinese art book*. London: Phaidon Press.

Marks, J., & Marks, S. C. (2005, February 10). *Let's legislate consensus building. The Christian Science Monitor.* Retrieved from https://www.csmonitor.com/2005/0210/p09s02-coop.html

Marsh, S. (2016). The gender-fluid generation: Young people on being male, female, or non-binary. *The Guardian*, March 23.

Martin, J. N., & Nakayama, T. K. (2018). *Intercultural communication in contexts*, 6th edn. New York: McGraw-Hill.

Martin, J. N., & Nakayama, T. K. (2017). *Intercultural communication in contexts*. New York: McGraw-Hill.

Martinez-Carter, K. (2013, July 23). *How the elderly are treated around the world.* Retrieved from http://theweek.com/articles/462230/how-elderly-are-treated-around-world.

Marwick, A. E. (2013). *Status update: Celebrity, publicity, and branding in the social media age*. New Haven, CT: Yale University Press.

McCroskey, J. C., & Richmond, V. P. (1995). Correlates of compulsive communication: Quantitative and qualitative characteristics. *Communication Quarterly*, *43*, 39–52.

McLuhan, M. (1964). *Understanding media*. New York: Mentor.

McQuail, D. (2010). *McQuail's mass communication theory*, 6th edn. Thousand Oaks: CA: Sage.

McQuail, D., & Windahl, S. (1993). *Communication models*, 2nd edn. London: Routledge.

Mencken, H. L. (1947). Names for Americans. *American Speech*, *22*(4), 241–256.

Mercado, M. (2017). 7 things you might not realize are cultural appropriation but really are. Retrieved from https://www.bustle.com/p/7-things-you-might-not-realize-are-cultural-appropriation-that-are-60679.

Merry, G. N. (1918). National defense and public speaking. *Quarterly Journal of Speech*, *4*(1), 53–60.

Miller, G. R., & Steinberg, M. (1975). *Between people: A new analysis of interpersonal communication*. Chicago, IL: Science Research Associates.

Miller, K., & Barbour, J. B. (2015). *Organizational communication: Approaches and Processes*, 7th edn. Boston, MA: Cengage.

Mipham, S. (2017). *The lost art of good conversation*. New York: Harmony Books.

Mishima, S. (2017). Tips on how to bow properly in Japan. *TripSavvy*. Retrieved from www.tripsavvy.com/how-to-bow-properly-in-japan-1550083.

Moeller, J., Trilling, D., Helberger, N., Irion, K., & DeVreese, C. (2016). Shrinking core? Exploring the differential agenda setting power of traditional and personalized news media. *info*, *18*(6), 26–41.

Morman, M. T., & Floyd, K. (1999). Affectionate communication between fathers and young adult sons: Individual- and relational-level correlates. *Communication Studies*, *50*(4), 294–309.

Morreale, S. P., & Vogl, M. W. (1998). *Pathways to careers in communication*. Washington, D. C.: National Communication Association.

Moss, D. (2016, November 27). Companies gain from giving back to their communities. Retrieved from www.shrm.org/hr-today/news/hr-magazine/1216/pages/companies-gain-from-giving-back-to-their-communities.aspx.

Mumby, D. K. (2013). *Organizational communication: A critical approach*. Thousand Oaks, CA: Sage.

Murray, D. (2017). People are calling Katy Perry out for cultural appropriation again because of her dance moves. Retrieved from www.elleuk.com/life-and-culture/news/a35952/people-are-calling-katy-perry-out-for-cultural-appropriation-again/.

Myers, S. A. (2015). Using Gold's typology of adult sibling relationships to explore sibling affectionate communication. *North American Journal of Psychology*, *17*(2), 301–310.

Nesi, J., Widman, L., Choukas-Bradley, S., & Prinstein, M. J. (2017).Technology-based communication and the development of interpersonal competencies within adolescent romantic relationships: A preliminary investigation. *Journal of Research on Adolescence*, *27*(2), 471–477.

Neuliep, J. W. (2017). *Intercultural communication: A contextual approach*. Sage.

Neville Miller, A. (2002). An exploration of Kenyan public speaking patterns with implications for the American introductory public speaking course. *Communication Education*, *51*(2), 168–182.

Nguyen, M., Bin, Y. S., & Campbell, A. (2012). Comparing online and offline self-disclosure: A systematic review. *Cyberpsychology, Behavior, and Social Networking*, *15*(2), 103–111.

Nichols, R. G. (1957). Listening is a 10-part skill. *Nation's Business*, *45*(7), 57.

Nolfi, J. (2017, Feb. 27). *Oscars make history with most black winners ever*. Entertainment Weekly. Retrieved from http://ew.com/awards/2017/02/26/oscars-2017-black-acting-winners/

Nuttin, J. M. (1975). *The illusion of attitude change: Towards a response contagion theory of persuasion*. Leuven, Belgium: Leuven University Press.

Ogden, C. K., & Richards, I. A. (1923). *The meaning of meaning*. London, UK: Kegan, Paul, Trench, Trubner.

O'Keefe, D. J. (2015). *Persuasion: Theory and research*. Thousand Oaks, CA: Sage.

Oliver, R. T. (1950). *Persuasive speaking: principles and methods*. Harlow, UK: Longmans Green.

Orbe, M. (1998). *Constructing co-cultural theory: An explication of culture, power, and communication*. Thousand Oaks, CA.: Sage.

Orbe, M. (2005). Continuing the legacy of theorizing from the margins: Conceptualizations of co-cultural theory. *Women & Language*, *28*(2), 65–66.

Orenstein, P. (2016). *Girls and sex*. New York: Harper Collins.

Pacanowsky, M. E., & O'Donnell-Trujillo, N. (1982). Communication and organizational cultures. *Western Journal of Speech Communication*, *46*, 115–130.

Pacanowsky, M. E., & O'Donnell-Trujillo, N. (1983). Organizational communication as cultural performance. *Communication Monographs*, *50*, 127–147.

Pacanowsky, M. E., & O'Donnell-Trujillo, N. (1990). Communication and organizational cultures. In S. R. Corman, S. P. Banks, C. R. Bantz, & M. E. Mayer (eds.) *Foundations of organizational communication: A reader*, pp. 142–153. New York: Longman.

Papademetriou, D. G., & Banulescu-Bogdan, N. (2016). *Understanding and addressing public anxiety about immigration*. Washington D.C.:, Transatlantic Council on Migration, Migration Policy Institute.

Park, G., Yaden, D. B., Schwartz, H., et al. (2016). Women are warmer but no less assertive than men: Gender and language on Facebook. *PLoS ONE, 11*(5): e0155885. https://doi.org/10.1371/journal.pone.0155885

Park, R. (1922). *The immigrant press and its control*. New York: Harper & Brothers.

Pearson, J. C., Child, J. T., & Kahl Jr., D. H. (2006). Preparation meeting opportunity: How do college students prepare for public speeches? *Communication Quarterly, 54*(3), 351–366.

Peck, E. (2016, June 1). Sheryl Sandberg's shoes perfectly illustrate the hypocrisy of tech's 'casual' dress code. *Huffington Post* Retrieved from www.huffingtonpost.com/entry/sheryl-sandberg-shoes_us_574f3845e4b0eb20fa0c988a.

Perloff, R.M. (2013). *The dynamics of political communication*. New York: Routledge.

Pew Research Center (2017, Jan. 12). *Mobile Fact Sheet*. Retrieved from http://www.pewinternet.org/fact-sheet/mobile/.

Pfeiffer, R. S., & Forsberg, R. L. (2005). *Ethics on the job: Cases and strategies*. Belmont, CA: Wadsworth.

Polonski, V. (2016, May 15). *Analysing the social media voices of the UK's EU referendum. Medium*. Retrieved from https://medium.com/@slavacm/social-media-voices-in-the-uks-eu-referendum-brexit-or-bremain-what-does-the-internet-say-about-ebbd7b27cf0f.

Poole, M. A., & Roth, J. (1989). Decision development in small groups IV: A typology of group decision paths. *Human Communication Research, 15*(3), 323–356.

Poole, M. A., Seibold, D. R., & McPhee, R. D. (1996). The structuration of group decisions. In R. Y. Hirokawa & M. S. Poole (eds.) *Communication and group decision making*, 2nd edn, pp. 114–146. Thousand Oaks, CA: Sage.

Poole, M. S., & DeSanctis, G. (1990). Understanding the use of group decision support systems: The theory of adaptive structuration. In J. Fulk & C. Steinfield (eds.) *Organizations and communication technology*, pp. 175–195. Thousand Oaks, CA: Sage.

Poole, M. S., & McPhee, R. D. (2005). Structuration theory. In S. May & D. K. Mumby (eds.) *Engaging organizational theory & research*, pp. 171–195. Norwood, NJ: Ablex.

Porter, E. (2016, February 23). *Nudges aren't enough for problems like retirement savings. New York Times online*. Retrieved from http://www.nytimes.com/2016/02/24/business/economy/nudges-arent-enough-to-solve-societys-problems.html.

Poteat, V., & Rivers, I. (2010). The use of homophobic language across bullying roles during adolescence. *Journal of Applied Developmental Psychology, 31*, 166–172.

Pransky, G. (2017). *The relationship handbook*. La Conner, WA: Pransky and Associates.

Putnam, L. L., & Nicotera, A. M. (eds.) (2008). *Building theories of organization: The constitutive role of communication*. Oxford, UK: Routledge.

Ramirez, A. & Wang, Z. (2008). When online meets offline: An expectancy violation theory perspective on modality switching. *Journal of Communication, 58*, 20–39.

Redding, W. C. (1988). Organizational communication. In E. Barnouw (ed.) *International encyclopedia of communications*, Vol. 3, pp. 236–239. New York: Oxford University Press.

Reddy, R. (2015). *The ultimate public speaking survival guide: 37 things you must know when you start public speaking*. Amazon Digital Services.

Rettberg, J. W. (2014). *Seeing ourselves through technology: How we use selfies, blogs and* wearable devices to see and shape ourselves. Basingstoke, UK: Palgrave Macmillan.

Richmond, V. P., Wrench, J. S., & McCroskey, J. C. (2012). *Communication apprehension, avoidance, and effectiveness.* New York: Pearson.

Ringwalt, R. (1898). Science and the society of friends. *Journal of the Franklin Institute, 145*(3), 229–231.

Rivers, I., Chesney, T., & Coyne, I. (2011). Cyberbullying. In C. P. Monks & I. Coyne (eds.) *Bullying in different contexts*, pp. 211–230. Cambridge, UK: Cambridge University Press.

Roberts, J. A., & David M. E. (2016). My life has become a major distraction from my cell phone: Partner phubbing and relationship satisfaction among romantic partners. *Computers in Human Behavior, 54,* 134–141.

Rogers, K. (2016, March 14). *Kim Kardashian, her selfie and what it means for young fans. New York Times.* Retrieved from https://www.nytimes.com/2016/03/15/style/kim-kardashian-selfie-fans.html?_r = 0.

Rogers, L. E., & Escudero, V. (eds.) (2014). *Relational communication: An interactional perspective to the study of process and form.* New York: Psychology Press.

Rosin, P., & Royzman, E. (2001). Negativity bias, negativity dominance, and cognition. *Personality & Social Psychology Review, 5,* 296–320.

Ross, L. R. (2016). *Interrogating motherhood.* Edmonton, AB: Athabasca University (AU) Press.

Sabee, C. M. (2015). Interpersonal communication skill/competence. *The International Encyclopedia of Interpersonal Communication,* 1–9.

Safire, W. (1999). *Spread the word.* New York: Crown.

Samp, J. A. (2015). Facework. *The International Encyclopedia of Interpersonal Communication,* 1–8.

Santilli, V., & Miller, A. N. (2011). The effects of gender and power distance on nonverbal immediacy in symmetrical and asymmetrical power conditions: A cross-cultural study of classrooms and friendships. *Journal of International and Intercultural Communication, 4*(1), 3–22.

Sargent, S. L., & Weaver, J. B. (2012). Listening styles: Sex differences in perceptions of self and others. *International Journal of Listening, 17,* 5–18.

Saylor, D., & Small, D. (2017). *Voice and delivery are key in the courtroom.* Retrieved from www.legalnews.com.

Schramm, W. L. (1954). *The process and effects of mass communication.* Urbana, IL: University of Illinois Press.

Schrodt, P. (2016). Relational frames as mediators of everyday talk and relational satisfaction in stepparent–stepchild relationships. *Journal of Social and Personal Relationships, 33*(2), 217–236.

Schrodt, P., Witt, P. L., & Shimkowski, J. R. (2014). A meta-analytical review of the demand/withdraw pattern of interaction and its associations with individual, relational, and communicative outcomes. *Communication Monographs, 81*(1), 28–58.

Schwartz, J., Collins, L., Stockton, H., Wagner, D., & Walsh, B. (2017). *The future of work: The augmented workforce.* Deloitte University Press. Retrieved from https://dupress.deloitte.com/dup-us-en/focus/human-capital-trends/2017/future-workforce-changing-nature-of-work.html.

Segrin, C. (2015). Pragmatics of human communication. *The international encyclopedia of interpersonal communication,* 1–9.

Shannon, C., & Weaver, W. (1949). *The mathematical theory of communication*. Urbana, IL: University of Illinois Press.

Sidelinger, R. J., & Bolen, D. M. (2016). Instructor credibility as a mediator of instructors' compulsive communication and student communication satisfaction in the college classroom. *Communication Research Reports*, *33*(1), 24–31.

Signorello, R., & Rhee, N. (2016). The voice acoustics of the 2016 presidential election candidates: A cross-gender study. *The Journal of the Acoustic Society of America*, *139*. Retrieved from http://asa.scitation.org/doi/abs/10.1121/1.4950321

Sile, E. (2016, September). Doing business in Dubai. *Departures*, 110–112.

Smith, A., & Duggan, M. (2013, October 21). *Online dating and relationships. Pew Research Center*. Retrieved from http://www.pewinternet.org/2013/10/21/online-dating-relationships/.

Snorton, R. (2004). *New poll shows at least 5% of America's high school students identify as gay or lesbian*. Retrieved from http://www.goldtalk.com/phpBB2/viewtopic.php?t = 5921&view = next&sid = 1fb3fd06f9c0f3c4497128d1afe0548d

Snyder, M. (1979). Self-monitoring processes. In L. Berkowitz (ed.) *Advances in experimental social psychology*, pp. 86–131. New York: Academic Press.

Solis, C., & Day, B. (2017, October 5). *SHRM's When Work Works project promotes flexibility*. Retrieved from https://www.shrm.org/resourcesandtools/hr-topics/behavioral-competencies/pages/shrms-when-works-project-promotes-flexibility.aspx.

Spitzberg, B. H., & Cupach, W. R. (2009). *The dark side of interpersonal communication*, 2nd edn. Mahwah, NJ: Lawrence Erlbaum.

Sumner, E. M., & Ramirez, A. (2017). Social information processing theory and hyperpersonal perspective. *The International Encyclopedia of Media Effects*, 1–11.

Sumner, W. G. (1906). *Folkways: A study of the sociological importance of usages*. Boston, MA: Ginn and Company.

Talbot, M. M. (2014). *Fictions at work: Language and social practice in fiction*. New York: Routledge.

Tannen, D. (2017). *You're the only one I can tell: Inside the language of women's friendships*. New York: Ballantine.

Tariq, M., & Syed, J. (2017). Intersectionality at work: South Asian Muslim women's experiences of employment and leadership in the United Kingdom. *Sex Roles*, *77* (7–8), 510–522.

't Hart, P. (1994). *Groupthink in government: A study of small groups and policy failure*. Baltimore, MD: The Johns Hopkins University Press.

Thibaut, J., & Kelley, H. (1959). *The social psychology of groups*. New York: Wiley.

Thoth, C. A., Tucker, C., Leahy, M., & Stewart, S. M. (2014). Self-disclosure of serostatus by youth who are HIV-positive: A review. *Journal of Behavioral Medicine*, *37*(2), 276–288.

Tine, M., & Gotlieb, R. (2013). Gender-, race-, and income-based stereotype threat: the effects of multiple stigmatized aspects of identity on math performance and working memory function. *Social Psychology of Education*, *16*(3), 353–376.

Ting-Toomey, S., & Chung, L.C. (2005). *Understanding intercultural communication*. New York: Oxford University Press.

Toma, C. L., & Choi, M. (2015). The couple who Facebooks together, stays together: Facebook self-presentation and relationship longevity among college-aged dating couples. *Cyberpsychology, Behavior, and Social Networking*, *18*(7), 367–372.

Tong, S. T., & Walther, J. B. (2015). The confirmation and disconfirmation of expectancies in computer-mediated communication. *Communication Research*, *42*(2), 186–212.

Towner, T., & Lego Munoz, C. (2016). Boomers versus millennials: Online media influence on media performance and candidate evaluations. *Social Sciences*, *5*(4), 56.

Townsley, N. C., & Broadfoot, K. J. (2008). Care, career, and academe: Heeding the calls of a new professoriate. *Women's Studies in Communication*, *31*, 133–142.

Turkle, S. (2011). *Alone together: Why we expect more from technology and less from each other*. New York: Basic Books.

Turkle, S. (2015). *Reclaiming conversation: The power of talk in a digital age*. New York: Penguin.

Turner, L. H., & West, R. (2018). *Perspectives on family communication*, 5th edn. New York: McGraw-Hill.

Twenge, J. W. (2017, September). *Have smartphones destroyed a generation? The Atlantic*. Retrieved from https://www.theatlantic.com/magazine/archive/ 192017/09/has-the-smartphone-destroyed-a-generation/534198/

Vandiver, D. M., & Dupalo, J. R. (2013). Factors that affect college students' perceptions of rape. *International Journal of Offender Therapy and Comparative Criminology*, *57*(5), 592–612.

Velten, J., & Arif, R. (2016). The influence of Snapchat on interpersonal relationship development and human communication. *The Journal of Social Media in Society 5*(2), 5–43 (thejsms.org).

Vennum, A., Lindstrom, R., Monk, J. K., & Adams, R. (2014). "It's complicated": The continuity and correlates of cycling in cohabiting and marital relationships. *Journal of Social and Personal Relationships*, *31*(3), 410–430.

Villaume, W. A., & Bodie, G. D. (2007). Discovering the listener within us: The impact of trait-like personality variables and communicator styles on preferences for listening style. *The International Journal of Listening*, *21*(2), 102–123.

Vivian, J. (2017). *The media of mass communication*, 12th edn. Boston, MA: Pearson.

Walther, J. B. (1996). Computer-mediated communication: Impersonal, interpersonal, and hyperpersonal interaction. *Communication Research*, *23*, 3–43.

Walther, J. B. (2010). Computer-mediated communication. In C. R. Berger, M. E. Roloff, & D. R. Roskos-Ewoldsen (eds.) *Handbook of communication science*, 2nd edn, pp. 489–505. Los Angeles, CA: Sage.

Walther, J. B.(2011). Theories of computer-mediated communication and interpersonal relations. In M. L. Knapp & J. A. Daly (eds.) *The handbook of interpersonal communication*, 3rd edn, pp. 443–479. Thousand Oaks, CA: Sage.

Walther, J. B., & Parks, M. R. (2002). Cues filtered out, cues filtered in: Computer-mediated communication and relationships. In M. L. Knapp & J. A. Daly (eds.) *The handbook of interpersonal communication*, 4th edn, pp. 529–563. Thousand Oaks, CA: Sage.

Watzlawick, P., Beavin, J. H., & Jackson, D. D. (1967). *Pragmatics of human communication*. New York: Norton.

Weathers, M. R., & Hopson, M. C. (2015). "I define what hurts me": A co-cultural theoretical analysis of communication factors related to digital dating abuse. *Howard Journal of Communications*, *26*(1), 95–113.

Webb, L. M. (2015). Research on technology and the family: From misconceptions to more accurate understandings. In C. J. Bruess (ed.) *Family communication in the age of digital and social media*, pp. 3–31. New York: Peter Lang.

Weber, N. L., & Pelfrey, W. V., Jr. (2014). *Cyberbullying: Causes, consequences, and coping strategies*. El Paso, TX: LFB Scholarly Publishing LLC.

Weigel. D. J. (2003). A communication approach to the construction of commitment in the early years of marriage: A qualitative study. *Journal of Family Communication*, *3*, 1–19.

West, R., & Turner, L. H. (2017). IPC3. Boston, MA: Cengage.

Whorf, B. (1956). *Language, thought, and reality*. Cambridge, MA: MIT Press.

Williams, B., Rosen, C., & Dvalidze, I. (2015, Aug. 28). *Why it should bother everyone that the Oscars are so white. Huffington Post*. Retrieved from www.huffingtonpost .com/2015/02/20/oscars-diversity-pro blem_n_6709334.html

Williams, J. (2016). *Listening, speaking, and critical thinking*. London: Global ELT.

Wilson, J. R., & Wilson, S. R. (2001). *Mass media mass culture*, 5th edn. New York: McGraw Hill.

Witt, P. L., Brown, K. C., Roberts, J. B., Weisel, J., Sawyer, C. R., & Behnke, R. R. (2006). Somatic anxiety patterns before, during, and after giving a public speech. *Southern Communication Journal*, *71*(1), 87–100.

Wolf, J. (2016, June 8). *The seven words I cannot say (around my children)*. Retrieved from

https://well.blogs.nytimes.com/2016/06/ 08/the-seven-words-i-cannot-say-around- my-children/?_r = 0.

Wolvin, A. D. (2010). *Listening theory. Listening and human communication: 21ˢᵗ century perspectives*. Oxford, England: Blackwell.

Wong, J. S., & Penner, A. M. (2016). Gender and the returns to attractiveness. *Research in Social Stratification and Mobility*, *44*, 113–123.

Wood, J. T., & Fixmer-Oraiz, N. (2017). *Gendered lives*, 12th edn. New York: Wadsworth.

Worthington, D., & Fitch-Hauser, M. (2017). *Listening: Processes, functions, and competency*. Boston: Allyn & Bacon.

Worthington, I. (ed.) (2010). *A companion to Greek rhetoric*. New York: John Wiley & Sons.

Yang, X., Chen, B.-C., Maity, M., & Ferrara, E. (2016). Social politics: Agenda setting and political communication on social media. Retrieved from http://arxiv.org/abs/1607 .06819v1.

Zangwill, I. (1908). *The melting pot* [play]. From the ghetto to the melting pot. In I. Zangwill (ed.) *Jewish plays*. Detroit, MI: Wayne State University Press.

Index